Bloom's Modern Critical Views

Bloom's Modern Critical Views

Bloom's Modern Critical Views

ARTHUR MILLER
New Edition

Edited and with an introduction by
Harold Bloom
Sterling Professor of the Humanities
Yale University

BLOOM'S
LITERARY CRITICISM
An imprint of Infobase Publishing

Cover photo: AP Images

Bloom's Modern Critical Views: Arthur Miller—New Edition

Copyright ©2007 by Infobase Publishing

Introduction ©2007 by Harold Bloom

Chelsea House
An imprint of Infobase Publishing
132 West 31st Street
New York NY 10001

Library of Congress Cataloging-in-Publication Data

Arthur Miller / edited with an introduction by Harold Bloom.
         p. cm. — (Bloom's modern criticial views)
   Includes bibliographical references and index.
   ISBN-13: 978-0-7910-9549-2 (hardcover : alk. paper)
   ISBN-10: 0-7910-9549-5 (hardcover : alk. paper)
   1. Miller, Arthur, 1915-2005—Criticism and interpretation.
   I. Bloom, Harold.
   PS3525.I5156Z5145 2007
   812'.52—dc22   2006102701

Cover design by Takeshi Takahashi/Joo Young An

Printed in the United States of America
Bang BCL 10 9 8 7 6 5 4 3 2 1

This book is printed on acid-free paper.

Contents

Editor's Note

My Introduction centers upon *Death of a Salesman*, and suggests that its truer title would be *Death of a Father*. I have seen perhaps half-a-dozen performances of the play, and the most moving was the Yiddish version by Joseph Buloff. Perhaps the truest title could be *Death of a Jewish Father*.

The immensely distinguished historian of Colonial America, Edmund S. Morgan, persuasively shows Miller's knowledge and understanding of Puritanism to be inadequate, with unhappy consequences for *The Crucible*.

David Savran meditates upon the irony of Miller's invocation of "authority," when in 1983 he himself denied permission to an experiential theater group to use fragments of *The Crucible* in a collage of their own.

"Authority" is the issue engaged by James A. Robinson in his interpretation of *All My Sons*, after which Valerie Lowe employs J. L. Austin's theory of "speech acts" to judge a crucial confession in *The Crucible*. *Death of a Salesman*, in John S. Shockley's view, was an accurate prophecy of the success of Ronald Reagan, while Miller's failed drama, *Broken Glass*, is praised by Susan C. W. Abbotson for its attempt to restore moral meaning to a Postmodern world.

Brenda Murphy discovers in Willy Loman the apotheosis of the Popular Sales Advice literature of the 1920's, after which Jeffrey Meyers sketches a portrait of Miller at the turn into the twenty-first century.

Some central myths of American Jewry are demonstrated to be relevant to *Death of a Salesman* by Julius Novick, while Jeffrey D. Mason examines the not un-Jewish ironies of Miller's 2002 play, *Resurrection Blues*.

The unhappy story of the now-vanished first film version of *Death of a Salesman*, which Miller angrily repudiated, is told by Kevin Kerrane, after which Laurence Goldstein gives us a summing-up of Miller's career.

Two further memorial tributes conclude this volume. Wendy Smith celebrates Miller's stand against merely commercial theater, while Steven R. Centola emphasizes the effect of the Holocaust upon Miller's "Art of the Possible."

HAROLD BLOOM

Introduction

ARTHUR MILLER (1915–2005)

I

"A man can get anywhere in this country on the basis of being liked." Arthur Miller's remark, made in an interview, has a peculiar force in the context of American political and social history. One reflects upon Ronald Reagan, a President impossible (for me) either to admire or to dislike. Miller, despite his palpable literary and dramatic limitations, has a shrewd understanding of our country. *Death of Salesman* is now half a century old, and retains its apparently perpetual relevance. The American ethos is sufficiently caught up by the play so that Miller's masterwork is clearly not just a period piece, unlike *All My Sons* and *The Crucible*, popular as the latter continues to be.

Arthur Miller is an Ibsenite dramatist, though his Ibsen is mostly a social realist, and not the visionary of the great plays: *Peer Gynt, Brand, Hedda Gabler*, and *When We Dead Awaken*. That Ibsen is himself something of a troll: obsessed and daemonic. Imaginative energy of that order is not present in Miller, though *Death of a Salesman* has an energy of pathos very much its own, the entropic catastrophe that Freud (with some irony) called "Family Romances."

Family romances almost invariably are melodramatic; to convert them to tragedy, you need to be the Shakespeare of *King Lear*, or at least of *Coriolanus*. Miller has a fondness for comparing *Death of a Salesman* to *King Lear*, a contrast that itself is catastrophic for Miller's play. Ibsen, at his strongest, can sustain some limited comparison to aspects of Shakespeare, but Miller cannot. Like Lear, Willy Loman needs and wants more familial love than anyone can receive, but there the likeness ends.

1

Does Miller, like Eugene O'Neill, write the plays of our moral climate, or have we deceived ourselves into overestimating both of these dramatists? American novelists and American poets have vastly surpassed American playwrights: there is no dramatic William Faulkner or Wallace Stevens to be acclaimed among us. It may be that day-to-day reality in the United States is so violent that stage drama scarcely can compete with the drama of common events and uncommon persons. A wilderness of pathos may be more fecund matter for storyteller and lyricists than it can be for those who would compose tragedies.

Perhaps that is why we value *Death of a Salesman* more highly than its actual achievement warrants. Even half a century back, an universal image of American fatherhood was very difficult to attain. Willy Loman moves us because he dies the death of a father, not of a salesman. Whether Miller's critique of the values of a capitalistic society is trenchant enough to be persuasive, I continue to doubt. But Loman's yearning for love remains poignant, if only because it destroys him. Miller's true gift is for rendering anguish, and his protagonist's anguish authentically touches upon the universal sorrow of failed fatherhood.

II

Forty years ago, in his introduction to his *Collected Plays*, Arthur Miller meditated upon *The Crucible*, staged four years before, in 1953. A year after that first production, Miller was refused a passport, and in 1956–57 he endured the active persecution of the American witch-hunt for suspected Communists. The terror created in some of his former friends and associates by the possibility of being branded as warlocks and witches "underlies every word in *The Crucible*," according to Miller. "Every word" necessarily is hyperbolical, since *The Crucible* attempts to be a personal tragedy as well as a social drama. Miller, Ibsen's disciple, nevertheless suffers an anxiety of influence in *The Crucible* not so much in regard to Ibsen's *An Enemy of the People* but in relation to George Bernard Shaw's *Saint Joan*. The frequent echoes of *Saint Joan* seem involuntary, and are distracting, and perhaps fatal to the aesthetic value of *The Crucible*. For all its moral earnestness, *Saint Joan* is enhanced by the Shawian ironic wit, a literary quality totally absent from Miller, here and elsewhere. Though a very well-made play, *The Crucible* rarely escapes a certain dreariness in performance, and does not gain by rereading.

This is not to deny the humane purpose nor the theatrical effectiveness of *The Crucible*, but only to indicate a general limitation, here and elsewhere, in Miller's dramatic art. Eric Bentley has argued shrewdly that "one never knows what a Miller play is about: politics or sex." Is *The Crucible* a personal tragedy, founded upon Proctor's sexual infidelity, or is it a play of social protest and warning? There is no reason it should not be both, except for Miller's inability to fuse the genres. Here he falls short of his master, Ibsen, who concealed Shakespearean tragic purposes within frameworks of social issues, yet invariably unified the two modes. Still, one can be grateful that Miller has not revised *The Crucible* on the basis of his own afterthoughts, which have emphasized the absolute evil of the Salem powers, Danforth and Hathorne. These worthies already are mere facades, opaque to Miller's understanding and our own. Whatever their religious sensibility may or may not have been, Miller has no imaginative understanding of it, and we therefore confront them only as puppets. Had Miller made them even more malevolent, our bafflement would have been even greater. I am aware that I tend to be an uncompromising aesthete, and I cannot dissent from the proven theatrical effectiveness of *The Crucible*. Its social benignity is also beyond my questioning; American society continues to benefit by this play. We would have to mature beyond our national tendency to moral and religious self-righteousness for *The Crucible* to dwindle into another period-piece, and that maturation is nowhere in sight.

III

Rather like Eugene O'Neill before him, Arthur Miller raises, at least for me, the difficult critical question as to whether there is not an element in drama that is other than literary, even contrary in value (supposed or real) to literary values, perhaps even to aesthetic values. O'Neill, a very nearly great dramatist, particularly in *The Iceman Cometh* and *Long Day's Journey into Night*, is not a good writer, except perhaps in his stage directions. Miller is by no means a bad writer, but he is scarcely an eloquent master of the language. I have just reread *All My Sons*, *Death of a Salesman*, and *The Crucible*, and am compelled to reflect how poorly they reread, though all of them, properly staged, are very effective dramas, and *Death of a Salesman* is considerably more than that. It ranks with *Iceman*, *Long Day's Journey*, Williams's *A Streetcar Named Desire*, Wilder's *The Skin of Our Teeth*, and Albee's *The Zoo Story* as one of the half-dozen crucial American plays. Yet its literary status seems to me somewhat questionable, which returns me to the issue of what there is in drama that can survive indifferent or even poor writing.

Defending *Death of a Salesman*, despite what he admits is a sentimental glibness in its prose, Kenneth Tynan memorably observed: "But the theater is an impure craft, and *Death of a Salesman* organizes its impurities with an emotional effect unrivalled in postwar drama." The observation still seems true, a quarter-century after Tynan made it, yet how unlikely a similar statement would seem if ventured about Ibsen, Miller's prime precursor. Do we speak of *Hedda Gabler* organizing its impurities with an unrivalled emotional effect? Why is the American drama, except for Thornton Wilder (its one great sport), addicted to an organization of impurities, a critical phrase perhaps applicable only to Theodore Dreiser, among the major American novelists? Why is it that we have brought forth *The Scarlet Letter, Moby-Dick, Adventures of Huckleberry Finn, The Portrait of a Lady, The Sun Also Rises, The Great Gatsby, As I Lay Dying, Miss Lonelyhearts, The Crying of Lot 49,* but no comparable dramas? A nation whose poets include Whitman, Dickinson, Frost, Stevens, Eliot, Hart Crane, Elizabeth Bishop, James Merrill and John Ashbery, among so many others of the highest aesthetic dignity—how can it offer us only O'Neill, Miller, and Williams as its strongest playwrights?

Drama at its most eminent tends not to appear either too early or too late in any national literature. The United States may be the great exception, since before O'Neill we had little better than Clyde Fitch, and our major dramas (it is to be hoped) have not yet manifested themselves. I have seen little speculation upon this matter, with the grand exception of Alvin B. Kernan, the magisterial scholarly critic of Shakespeare and of Elizabethan dramatic literature. Meditating upon American plays, in 1967, Kernan tuned his initially somber notes to hopeful ones:

> Thus with all our efforts, money, and good intentions, we have not yet achieved a theater; and we have not, I believe, because we do not see life in historic and dramatic terms. Even our greatest novelists and poets, sensitive and subtle though they are, do not think dramatically, and should not be asked to, for they express themselves and us in other forms more suited to their visions (and ours). But we have come very close at moments to having great plays, if not a great theatrical tradition. When the Tyrone family stands in its parlor looking at the mad mother holding her wedding dress and knowing that all the good will in the world cannot undo what the past has done to them; when Willy Loman, the salesman, plunges again and again into the past to search for the point where it all went irremediably wrong and cannot find any one fatal turning point; when the Antrobus family, to end on a more cheerful note, drafts stage hands from backstage to take the place of sick actors, gathers its feeble and ever-disappointed hopes, puts its miserable home together again after another in a series of unending disasters stretching from the ice age to the present; then we are very close to accepting our entanglement in the historical process and our status as actors, which may in time produce a true theater.

That time has not yet come, twenty years later, but I think that Kernan was more right even than he knew. Our greatest novelists and poets continue not to see life in historic and dramatic terms, precisely because our literary tradition remains incurably Emersonian, and Emerson shrewdly dismissed both history and drama as European rather than American. An overtly anti-Emersonian poet-novelist like Robert Penn Warren does see life in historic and dramatic terms, and yet has done his best work away from the stage, despite his effort to write *All the King's Men* as a play. Our foremost novelist, Henry James, failed as a dramatist, precisely because he was more Emersonian than he knew, and turned too far inward in nuanced vision for a play to be his proper mode of representation. One hardly sees Faulkner or Frost, Hemingway or Stevens as dramatists, though they all made their attempts. Nor would a comparison of *The Waste Land* and *The Family Reunion* be kind to Eliot's dramatic ambitions. The American literary mode, whether narrative or lyric, tends towards romance and rumination, or fantastic vision, rather than drama. Emerson, genius of the shores of America, directed us away from history, and distrusted drama as a revel. Nothing is got for nothing; Faulkner and Wallace Stevens, aesthetic light-years beyond O'Neill and Tennessee Williams, seem to mark the limits of the literary imagination in our American century It is unfair to *All My Sons* and *Death of a Salesman* to read them with the high expectations we rightly bring to *As I Lay Dying* and *Notes toward a Supreme Fiction*. Miller, a social dramatist, keenly aware of history, fills an authentic American need, certainly for his own time.

IV

The strength of *Death of a Salesman* may be puzzling, and yet is beyond dispute; the continued vitality of the play cannot be questioned. Whether it has the aesthetic dignity of tragedy is not clear, but no other American play is worthier of the term, so far. I myself resist the drama each time I reread it, because it seems that its language will not hold me, and then I see it played on stage, most recently by Dustin Hoffman, and I yield to it. Miller has caught an American kind of suffering that is also a universal mode of pain, quite possibly because his hidden paradigm for his American tragedy is an ancient Jewish one. Willy Loman is hardly a biblical figure, and he is not supposed to be Jewish, yet something crucial in him is Jewish, and the play does belong to that undefined entity we can call Jewish literature, just as Pinter's *The Caretaker* rather surprisingly does. The only meaning of Willy Loman is the pain he suffers, and the pain his fate causes us to suffer. His tragedy makes sense only in the Freudian world of repression, which happens also to be the world of normative Jewish memory. It is a world in which everything has already happened, in which there never can be anything new again, because there is total sense or meaningfulness in everything, which is to say, in which everything hurts.

That cosmos informed by Jewish memory is the secret strength or permanent coherence of *Death of a Salesman*, and accounts for its ability to withstand the shrewd critique of Eric Bentley, who found that the genres of tragedy and of social drama destroyed one another here. Miller's passionate insistence upon tragedy is partly justified by Willy's perpetual sense of being in exile. Commenting on his play, Miller wrote that: "The truly valueless man, a man without ideals, is always perfectly at home anywhere." But Willy, in his own small but valid way, has his own version of the Nietzschean "desire to be elsewhere, the desire to be different," and it does reduce to a Jewish version. Doubtless, as Mary McCarthy first noted, Willy "could not be Jewish because he had to be American." Nearly forty years later, that distinction is pragmatically blurred, and we can wonder if the play might be stronger if Willy were more overtly Jewish.

We first hear Willy say: "It's all right. I came back." His last utterance is the mere repetition of the desperately hushing syllable: "Shhh!" just before he rushes out to destroy himself. A survivor who no longer desires to survive is something other than a tragic figure. Willy, hardly a figure of capable imagination, nevertheless is a representation of terrible pathos. Can we define precisely what that pathos is?

Probably the most famous speech in *Death of a Salesman* is Linda's pre-elegy for her husband, of whom she is soon to remark: "A small man can be just as exhausted as a great man." The plangency of Linda's lament has a universal poignance, even if we wince at its naked design upon us:

> Willy Loman never made a lot of money. His name was never in the paper. He's not the finest character that ever lived. But he's a human being, and a terrible thing is happening to him. So attention must be paid. He's not to be allowed to fall into his grave like an old dog. Attention, attention must be finally paid to such a person.

Behind this is Miller's belated insistence "that everyone knew Willy Loman," which is a flawed emphasis on Miller's part, since he first thought of calling the play *The Inside of His Head*, and Willy already lives in a phantasmagoria when the drama opens. You cannot know a man half lost in the American dream, a man who is unable to tell past from present. Perhaps the play should have been called *The Dying of a Salesman*, because Willy is dying throughout. That is the pathos of Linda's passionate injunction that attention must be finally paid to such a person, a human being to whom a terrible thing is happening. Nothing finds Willy anymore; everything loses him. He is a man upon whom the sun has gone down, to appropriate a great phrase from Ezra Pound.But have we defined as yet what is particular about his pathos?

I think not. Miller, a passionate moralist, all but rabbinical in his ethical vision, insists upon giving us Willy's, and his sons', sexual infidelities as synecdoches of the failure of Willy's vision of reality. Presumably, Willy's sense of failure, his belief that he has no right to his wife, despite Linda's love for him, is what motivates Willy's deceptions, and those of his sons after him. Yet Willy is not destroyed by his sense of failure. Miller may be a better interpreter of Miller than he is a dramatist. I find it wholly persuasive that Willy is destroyed by love, by his sudden awareness that his son Biff truly loves him. Miller beautifully comments that Willy resolves to die when "he is given his existence ... his fatherhood, for which he has always striven and which until now he could not achieve." That evidently is the precise and terrible pathos of Willy's character and of his fate. He is a good man, who wants only to earn and to deserve the love of his wife and of his sons. He is self-slain, not by the salesman's dream of America, but by the universal desire to be loved by one's own, and to be loved beyond what one believes one deserves. Miller is not one of the masters of metaphor, but in *Death of a Salesman* he memorably achieves a pathos that none of us would be wise to dismiss.

V

All My Sons (1947), Miller's first success, retains the flavor of post–World War II America, though it is indubitably something beyond a period piece. Perhaps all of Miller's work could be titled *The Guilt of the Fathers*, which is a dark matter for a Jewish playwright, brought up to believe in the normative tradition, with its emphasis upon the virtues of the fathers. Though it is a truism to note that *All My Sons* is an Ibsenite play, the influence relation to Ibsen remains authentic, and is part of the play's meaning, in the sense that Ibsen too is one of the fathers, and shares in their guilt. Ibsen's peculiar guilt in *All My Sons* is to have appropriated most of Miller's available stock of dramatic language. The result is that this drama is admirably constructed yet not adequately expressed. It is not just that eloquence is lacking; sometimes the characters seem unable to say what they need to say if we are to be with them as we should.

Joe Keller ought to be the hero-villain of *All My Sons*, since pragmatically he certainly is a villain. But Miller is enormously fond of Joe, and so are we; he is not a good man, and yet he lives like one, in regard to family, friends, neighbors. I do not think that Miller ever is interested in Hannah Arendt's curious notion of the banality of evil. Joe is banal, and he is not evil though his business has led him into what must be called moral idiocy, in regard to his partner and to any world that transcends his own immediate family. Poor Joe is just not very intelligent, and it is Miller's curious gift that he can render such a man dramatically interesting. An ordinary man who wants to have a moderately good time, who wants his family never to suffer, and who lacks any imagination beyond the immediate: what is this except an authentic American Everyman? The wretched Joe simply is someone who does not know enough, indeed who scarcely knows anything at all. Nor can he learn anything. What I find least convincing in the play is Joe's moment of breaking through to a moral awareness, and a new kind of knowledge:

MOTHER: Why are you going? You'll sleep, why are you going?

KELLER: I can't sleep here. I'll feel better if I go.

MOTHER: You're so foolish. Larry was your son too, wasn't he? You know he'd never tell you to do this.

KELLER (*looking at letter in his hand*): Then what is this if it isn't telling me? Sure, he was my son. But I think to him they were all my sons. And I guess they were, I guess they were. I'll be right down.

(Exits into *house*.)

MOTHER (*to Chris, with determination*): You're not going to take him!

CHRIS: I'm taking him.

MOTHER: It's up to you, if you tell him to stay he'll stay. Go and tell him!

CHRIS: Nobody could stop him now.

MOTHER: You'll stop him! How long will he live in prison? Are you trying to kill him?

Nothing in Joe is spiritually capable of seeing and saying: "They were all my sons. And I guess they were, I guess they were." That does not reverberate any more persuasively than Chris crying out: "There's a universe of people outside and you're responsible to it." Drama fails Miller there, or perhaps he fails drama. Joe Keller was too remote from a felt sense of reality for Miller to represent the estrangement properly, except in regard to the blindness Joe manifested towards his two sons. Miller crossed over into his one permanent achievement when he swerved from Ibsen into the marginal world of *Death of a Salesman*, where the pain is the meaning, and the meaning has a repressed but vital relationship to the normative vision that informs Jewish memory.

EDMUND S. MORGAN

Arthur Miller's The Crucible *and the Salem Witch Trials: A Historian's View*

The historian who plays the critic runs the risk of being irrelevant as well as incompetent. A work of art must stand or fall by itself, and the author of *The Crucible* has warned off historians with the statement that his play is "not history in the sense in which the word is used by the academic historian." But when a play evokes a widely known historical event, art leans on history. No one who reads *The Crucible* can see it wholly fresh. The world into which it carries us is constructed from building blocks that are labeled Puritanism, Salem Village, witch-hunt, clergyman. Part of the verisimilitude of the play and part of its dramatic tension depend on our knowledge that men and women were hanged at Salem Village in 1692 for crimes they could not have committed.

Under these circumstances it may be permissible for a historian to examine the play's depiction of history and to ask how the author's assumptions about history have affected his understanding of his characters.

I do not expect an artist who deals with history to conform to every fact known to historians about the events he is concerned with. It does not bother me, for example, that Arthur Miller has simplified the legal transactions involved in the trials and assigned to some individuals judicial powers they did not have. Nor does it bother me that he has transformed Abigail

From *The Golden and Brazen World: Papers in Literature and History, 1650–1800.* © 1985 The Regents of the University of California, the University of California Press.

Williams from a child into a woman and given her a love affair with his principal character, John Proctor, a love affair that is nowhere suggested by the records. Miller's Abigail is not so much a transformation as a creation. So, for that matter, is his John Proctor. It might have been better not to have given either of them the name of an actual person who figures in the historical record. But the artist's relation to the historical record has to be different from the historian's.

If the artist binds himself too closely to known factual details, the result may be an aesthetic disaster. The artist must bring to his work a creative imagination that transcends historical detail in order to recreate living people and situations. He must persuade his audience that they have been transported back to the time and place in question, or at least persuade them to suspend their disbelief that they have taken such a voyage. And the historical record is almost never sufficiently full to equip the artist with the details he needs for persuading them, details of things said and seen and heard, without which his enterprise is doomed. Even where the record is especially full, aesthetic considerations may require violating or ignoring the details it furnishes and substituting imaginary ones in order to achieve, within the limits of the particular work, the development of characters and situations through which the artist makes his statement.

In order to make use of the building blocks that the audience will recognize, the artist must have his characters say things and do things that conform in a general way to known fact. But his characters inevitably assume a life of their own. They may say and do things that actual historical people are known to have said and done, but they do a lot of other things on their own, as it were, things dictated by the author's vision of them and what they were up to. That vision may be the product of careful study of the historical record or it may not, but it can never be as closely tied to the historical record as the historian's vision must always be. In other words, the artist's reconstruction of people and events must take place on a level that is denied to historians and that most historians would not have the imaginative power to reach anyhow.

Nevertheless, historians do engage, in their own less imaginative way, in the same sort of activity as novelists and playwrights and perhaps poets, namely, in the provision of vicarious experience. Granted, there are many pieces of historical writing that only faintly answer this description, the analytical and didactic and often unreadable monographs that historians direct at one another and which sometimes seem calculated to mystify outsiders. But it is surely at least one function, in my opinion the highest function, of the historian to recreate the past, however analytically and didactically, in order to release us from the temporal provincialism imposed on us by the time in which we happen to have been born, giving us experience of other times to expand our understanding of what it is to be a human being.

This function the historian shares with the novelist and playwright. The novelist and playwright, of course, are not confined to recreating experience out of the distant past. Indeed, they generally deal with experience available in their own time. And when they resort to history, they turn it into the present in a way that the historian does not pretend to do. But the artist and the historian do share some problems and responsibilities.

The artist by definition is governed by aesthetic considerations; the historian is less constrained by them but by no means exempt. He is not simply a compiler of annals or a transcriber of documents. He cannot attempt to tell everything that happened. He has to pick and choose. He has to leave things out. And though his choice of what to put in may depend on many considerations other than aesthetic, he has to construct something out of the details the record does furnish, something with a shape, a structure, a book or article that will have a theme and a beginning, middle, and end. Otherwise no one will read him, not even other historians.

In building a work around any theme, the historian and the artist who deals in history confront a problem that is particularly acute in *The Crucible*, as well as in the various historical treatments of the New England Puritans, the people whom Arthur Miller tries to bring to life for us. It is the problem of separating the universal from the unique, the timeless from the temporary. History does not repeat itself. No two persons are alike. Every event is in some way unique. And yet the only reason we are capable of vicarious experience is because history does in some sense repeat itself, because all persons are alike. In seeking to broaden our experience through art or through history we have to identify with people who think differently, talk differently, act differently; and we want to know precisely what was different about them. At the same time, we have to be able to recognize their humanity, we have to be able to put ourselves in their situation, identify with them, see in them some of the same weaknesses and strengths we find in ourselves. Otherwise they become too different to be believable and so can tell us nothing about ourselves.

It is easy to err in either direction, to exaggerate similarities to the past or to exaggerate differences. And it is all too tempting to do so in such a way as to flatter ourselves and avoid some of the hard lessons the past may have to teach us. If, on the one hand, we exaggerate differences, we may fall into the trap of viewing the past with condescension, bestowing a patronizing admiration on those quaint old folk who struggled along without benefit of the sophistication and superior knowledge we have arrived at. The past will then become a kind of Disneyland, an escape from the present, a never-never land of spinning wheels and thatched roofs and people dressed in funny old costumes. Or it may become simply a horror from which we can congratulate ourselves on having escaped, a land filled with superstition, poverty, and endless toil, a world of darkness from which we have emerged into the light.

If, on the other hand, we exaggerate the similarities of the past to the present, we may indulge in a comparable complacency, finding justification for everything we do or want to do in the fact that it has been done before: the founding fathers did it; what was good enough for them ought to be good enough for us, and so on. Or we may manufacture spurious arguments for some present policy or proposal on the grounds that it worked in the past, thus equating the past with the present, a very dangerous equation, as we know from those earnest military men who are always fighting the war preceding the one they are engaged in.

Historians and novelists and playwrights who take history seriously have to recognize both similarities to the past and differences. To overemphasize one or the other is not only to distort history but to diminish the impact of the experience it offers, indeed to escape that experience and nourish a temporal provincialism.

With regard to the Salem witchcraft of the 1690s, the temptation has always been to exaggerate the differences between that time and ours. The temptation was much more in evidence fifty or a hundred years ago than it is today. In the nineteenth century, when mankind, and especially Anglo-Saxon mankind, was progressing rapidly toward perfection, taking up the white man's burden, glorying in the survival of the fittest, and fulfilling manifest destiny, the Salem witch trials were obviously something long since left behind. Although it was a little embarrassing that the witch trials were not even farther behind, the embarrassment was compensated for by thinking how rapidly we had all progressed from that dreadful era of superstition and old night.

In the twentieth century, as perfection has eluded us and we have manufactured our own horrors to dwarf those at Salem, we have grown a little less smug. We even find something uncomfortably familiar in the Salem trials, with their phony confessions, inquisitorial procedures, and admission of inadmissible evidence. And yet there remains a temptation to flatter ourselves.

The temptation showed itself recently in the extraordinary publicity given to an article about the possibility of ergot poisoning as a cause of the symptoms displayed by the allegedly bewitched girls at Salem. Ergot poisoning comes from eating bread or flour made from diseased rye grain and produces seizures and sensations comparable to those that the Salem girls experienced or said they experienced. Although the evidence for ergot poisoning at Salem is extremely tenuous, and although if true it would in no way diminish the horror of what happened there, the article in a professional scientific journal was seized upon by the press as though modem science had now explained the whole episode. I can account for the attention given this article only by the flattering implication it seemed to carry (though probably not intended by the author) of the superiority of our own enlightened understanding of what happened in those benighted days. Yet what would be explained by ergot poisoning was only the odd behavior of a few teenage girls, not the hysteria of their elders, in which lay the shame of what happened at Salem.

Evidently the Salem trials are still something we feel uncomfortable about. We want to think that we would not behave the way people behaved then, we would behave better, we would not be fooled by a batch of bad bread. And that brings me back to *The Crucible*. Arthur Miller has probably done more than anyone else to remind us we are not so much better. *The Crucible*, as we all know, was written in the midst of the McCarthy era, and it was intended, I think, to suggest that we were behaving, or allowing our authorized representatives to behave, as badly as the authorities at Salem. There are no overt comparisons. The play is about Salem. But its success depends in part on the shock of recognition.

Let us look, then, at the design of *The Crucible*. How has the author dealt with the problem of similarity and difference? In spite of the apparent parallel with our own times, has he not flattered us a little, allowed us an escape from the hard lessons of Salem and thus denied us the full range of experience he might have given us?

The protagonist of *The Crucible* is John Proctor, a simple man in the best sense of the word, a strong man who does not suffer fools gladly. He has little of formal piety and even less of superstition. His wife is more devout but less attractive. She lacks his human warmth, or at any rate she has wrapped it in a shroud of piety and righteousness. Her husband has consequently found it the more difficult to resist the charms of an unscrupulously available serving girl, Abigail Williams. We cannot blame John Proctor. He is, after all, human, like you and me. But his wife does blame him, and he blames himself.

The antagonist of the play wears a mask, not literally but figuratively. And the mask is never fully stripped away because the author himself has never quite gotten behind it. The mask is Puritanism, and it is worn by many characters, to each of whom it imparts an inhuman and ugly zeal. Elizabeth Proctor wears it when she reproaches her husband for his weakness. Thomas and Ann Putnam wear it when they grasp at witchcraft as the source of their misfortunes. But mostly it is worn by the ministers, Samuel Parris and John Hale, and by the judges, Danforth and Hathorne. They are never explicitly labeled as Puritan; the author sees them so well as men that he has furnished them with adequate human motives for everything they do. Arthur Miller is too serious an artist to give us only a mask with no flesh and blood behind it. His object, indeed, is to show us human weakness. Nevertheless, the mask is there.

The men who kill John Proctor are easily recognized as Puritans. Miller has provided them with all the unlovely traits most of us associate with that name: they are bigoted, egotistical, bent on suppressing every joy that makes life agreeable. The worst of the lot, the most loathsome man in the play, is a Puritan clergyman. Samuel Parris, we are told, never conceived that "children were anything but thankful for being permitted to walk straight, eyes slightly lowered, arms at the sides, and mouths shut until bidden to speak." We are also told that in this horrid conception Parris was not unusual. He was "like the rest of Salem."

Puritanism sometimes seems more than a mask. Sometimes it becomes the evil force against which man must pit himself. Puritanism, repressing the natural, healthy impulses of children, breeds in the girls of Salem village an unnatural hysteria that proves the undoing of good men like John Proctor. Proctor seems the most un-Puritan man in the play, and Proctor triumphs in death, triumphs as a human being true to himself, triumphs over the hypocrisy and meanness that Puritanism has evoked.

The Crucible is a powerful play. Arthur Miller says he tried to convey in it "the essential nature of one of the strangest and most awful chapters in human history." He has succeeded—almost. The Salem episode was both strange and awful. If the author had known more abut the history of New England, however, it is possible that he might have found what happened at Salem less strange and more awful. To explain why, let me draw a picture of seventeenth-century Puritanism somewhat different from the one to be found in *The Crucible*. I speak not exactly as the devil's advocate but as what in this context may amount to the same thing, the Puritans' advocate.

Puritanism has been more often the object of invective than of investigation, and it is easier to say what it was not than what it was. It was not prudishness. The Puritans were much franker in discussing sex than most of us are outside the pages of the modem novel. The sober historical works of Governor Bradford and Governor Winthrop were expurgated when published in the present century. Puritanism was not prohibitionism. The Puritans did not condone excessive drinking, any more than we do, but they seldom drank water if they could avoid it. Puritanism was not drabness in clothing or furniture or houses. The Puritans painted things red and blue and wore brightly colored clothes, trimmed with lace when they could afford it. They forbade a number of things not forbidden today, such as the theater and card playing. They looked askance at mixed dancing and punished breaches of the sabbath. Otherwise their moral code was about the same as ours.

What distinguished the Puritans from us and, to a lesser degree, from their contemporaries was a profound vision of divine transcendence on the one hand and of human corruption on the other. The Puritan could never allow himself to forget God. Although he enjoyed the good things of life, he had always to do so with an awareness of the infinite perfection of the Being who created them. He had always to be comparing earthly pleasures with eternal ones in order to keep the earthly ones in proper perspective. This meant that he could never let himself go in sweet abandon; or rather, it meant that he must always blame himself afterwards when he did. To immerse oneself wholly, even for a short time, in the joys of the flesh was to put things above the Creator of things.

Other people have been overwhelmed with divinity in this way, but other people have found a refuge in asceticism: they have withdrawn from the world, turned their backs on the temptations that constantly invite man's attention away from God. For the Puritan, asceticism was no way out. God, he believed, had placed him in the world and created its good things for his use. He was meant to enjoy them. To turn his back on them was to insult their Maker. He had, therefore, to be in the world but not of it, to love God's creatures but not love them very much.

As he made his way through this too delightful world, the Puritan was inevitably a troubled person. His conduct might look exemplary to you and me, but not to him, because the errors he mourned lay more often in attitude than in act. A person might behave perfectly as far as the outward eye could detect—it was right to eat, to drink, and to be merry at it; it was right to love your wife or husband, play with your children, and work hard at your job. But it was wrong to forget God while you did so. And people were always forgetting, always enjoying food and wine and sex too much, and always condemning themselves for it. Sometimes the lapses were great and gross, sometimes trivial, but great or small they reminded Puritans constantly of their sinful nature. Every day of his life the Puritan reenacted the fall of Adam and felt the awful weight of God's condemnation for it.

The Puritan was as hard on his neighbors as he was on himself. When they visibly violated God's commands, he did not hesitate to condemn them. But his awareness of his own guilt and his conviction that all men are guilty made him somewhat less uncharitable than he may seem to us. He was a disenchanted judge who expected the worst of his fellow men and could not blame them more than he blamed himself. One of the first bands of Puritans to depart from England for the Massachusetts Bay Colony expressed the Puritan attitude well. In an address issued before their departure they implored their countrymen to consider them still as brethren, "standing in very great need of . . . helpe, . . . for wee are not," they said, "of those that dreame of perfection in this world."

The Puritan knew that God demanded perfection but knew also that no one could attain it. And because God could forgive the sinner who repented, the Puritan felt that he too must do so. Anyone who reads the records of New England churches and New England law courts will see how ready the Puritans were to forgive. A convicted drunkard who showed repentance after sobering up would generally receive the lightest of fines from the civil judge or perhaps no fine at all, but merely an admonition. The churches were even more charitable. According to Puritan practice only a small part of a congregation was admitted to church membership, only those who could demonstrate that they were probable saints headed for eternal glory. When a saint was found in open sin, say breaking the sabbath or drinking too much or becoming too friendly with another man's spouse, the church might by a formal vote admonish him or even excommunicate him. But if he repented and expressed sorrow for his conduct, they would almost invariably restore him to membership even if his repentance came years later. The churches exercised an almost foolish patience toward repeating offenders. A person might get drunk pretty regularly. Each time he would be admonished or excommunicated and each time, when he repented, restored.

This combination of severity and forgiveness affected the Puritans' upbringing of their children. The Puritans never supposed that children enjoyed more innocence than their elders. Men did not learn evil as they grew; it was in them from the beginning. A parent's job was to repress it in his children; just as a ruler's job was to repress it in his subjects. But the methods of repression need not be cruel or unbending. A wise parent was supposed to know his children as individuals and fit his discipline to the child's capacities and temperament. As Anne Bradstreet put it:

> Diverse children have their different natures; some are like flesh which nothing but salt will keep from putrefaction; some again like tender fruits that are best preserved with sugar: those parents are wise that can fit their nurture according to their Nature.

Although Puritan parents following this precept might still find the rod the most useful instrument in correcting some children, there is no evidence that they used it any more regularly than parents do today. Samuel Sewall, one of the judges who tried the witches, records in his diary an instance when he was driven to it. His son Joseph, future minister of the Old South Church, had thrown "a knop of Brass and hit his sister Betty on the forhead so as to make it bleed and swell; upon which," says Sewall, "and for his playing at Prayer-time, and eating when Return Thanks [saying grace], I whipd him pretty smartly." In practice Puritan children seem to have been as spoiled as children in other times and ages. Parents expected them to err and corrected them without expecting perfection.

The role of the Puritan clergyman in suppressing evil was a minor one. His function was educational rather than authoritative. It was proper for the authorities in the state to ask his advice when they were having difficulties in interpreting the will of God. But it was wrong for him to proffer advice unasked, and there was no obligation on the part of the authorities to accept it after they got it. Even within his own church he had no authority. Every action of the church in admonishing or excommunicating members was the result of a vote, and in most churches unanimity was required. The minister's job was to instruct his flock, to justify the ways of God to man, to help men detect the evil in their hearts, and also to help them detect the first stirrings of divine grace. He could only hope that through his preaching God might summon some of his listeners to eternal glory.

During the eighteenth century New England preaching became increasingly hortatory and relied more and more on moving appeals to the emotions. Particularly after the Great Awakening of 1741 had set the example, preachers found it advantageous to depict the torments of hellfire vividly to their listeners, in order to frighten them into awareness of their sins. But during the seventeenth century hellfire was conspicuously missing. Seventeenth-century sermons were more didactic than admonitory; the preacher devoted most of his time to the exposition of theological doctrine and applied the doctrine to his listeners only briefly at the end of his sermon.

By the same token the seventeenth-century preacher found little occasion for discussing the devil or his demons. The evil that Puritans feared and fought lay in their own hearts, not in the machinations of the devil. This is not to say that they denied the existence of supernatural evil. They would have been an extraordinary people indeed had they done so, because scarcely anyone in the seventeenth century did. But Puritan ideas on the subject were conventional, the same ideas that seventeenth-century Europeans and Englishmen held. And Puritans were rather less interested in supernatural evil than their contemporaries. Puritans were too preoccupied with natural evil to pay much attention to supernatural.

Why, then, the hysteria at Salem in 1692? If Puritans gave less attention than their contemporaries did to the devil, why did the devil give more attention to them? Why were there not much greater epidemics of witchcraft and witch-hunting in England and Europe than in Massachusetts? The answer is that there were. During the sixteenth and seventeenth centuries some thousands of witches were executed in the British Isles, an estimated 75,000 in France, 100,000 in Germany, and corresponding numbers in other European countries.

The European trials have mostly been forgotten and the Salem ones remembered because the European ones were too widespread and too common to attract special attention. The human imagination boggles at evil in the large. It can encompass the death of Anne Frank but not of several million anonymous Jews. It can comprehend twenty men and women of Salem

Village more readily than 75,000 in France. The Salem episode is the more horrible simply because we can take it in.

But even though we take it in, we can never quite understand it. In the effort to do so, we have tried to fasten the blame where it will not hurt any of us. Historians who should have known better once blamed it on the clergy. New ideas, we were told, had penetrated New England, ideas that were dissolving the enslavement of the people to Puritanism, ideas that threatened the dominant position of the clergy. In order to save their overweening influence, they blamed the devil and worked up the witch scare. All nonsense.

The witch scare was no heresy hunt; prosecutors and defendants alike were Puritans, and both believed in witchcraft. The role of the clergy was a deterring one. They recognized at an early stage that the trials were being conducted without regard to proper procedures. The court, on which of course no clergyman sat, was convicting on the basis of spectral evidence alone, evidence offered by a supposed victim of witchcraft to the effect that the devil tormenting him appeared in the shape of the accused. The assumption behind such testimony was that the devil could assume the shape only of a person who had confederated with him. The clergy knew that spectral evidence was considered acceptable in witch trials but that it was not generally considered sufficient in itself to warrant a conviction. The supposition that the devil could not assume the shape of an innocent person was questioned by many authorities, and courts generally demanded supporting evidence of a more objective nature. This might consist in the possession of dolls or wax images and the other paraphernalia of witchcraft. It might consist in the existence of so-called witch marks on a person's body. These were simply red or blue marks or excrescences, such as we would call birthmarks, at which the devil was supposed to suck, as on a teat. God help anyone who had both a birthmark and an old doll retained from childhood. And yet most previous trials of witches, where this kind of evidence was required, resulted in acquittals. The Salem court waived the necessity of such evidence and accepted the spectral evidence offered by a small group of hysterical teenage girls as sufficient in itself to justify conviction.

The clergy, knowing that this was dubious procedure, protested. They did not do so as soon or as loudly as they should have. And anyone occupying a position of influence and leadership who objected soon and loudly to the methods of the late Senator McCarthy is entitled to cast the first stone at the New England clergy of 1692. Some clergymen may have been caught up in the general hysteria; nevertheless, it was the belated protest of the clergy that finally brought the trials to a halt.

If the clergy did not promote the witchcraft scare, how did it happen? No one can give a complete answer. There was no leader who engineered it, no demagogue or dictator who profited from it or hoped to profit from it. It came when the times were out of joint, when the people of Massachusetts had suffered a cruel disillusionment.

Massachusetts had been founded as a city on a hill, to be an example to the world of how a community could be organized in subjection to God's commands. In the course of half a century the people of Massachusetts had seen the world ignore their example and go off after evil ways. Within Massachusetts itself, the piety of the founding fathers had waned in the second generation, or so at least the members of that generation told themselves. In 1685 the world moved in on Massachusetts. England revoked the charter that had heretofore enabled the colony to govern itself and installed a royal governor with absolute powers in place of the one elected by the people. New Englanders hardly knew at first whether to regard the change as a just punishment by God for past sins or as a challenge to a degenerate people to recover the piety and strength of their fathers. But in 1688, when England threw off its king, the people of Massachusetts gladly rose up and threw off the governor that he had imposed on them. There was great rejoicing throughout the colony, and everyone hoped and believed that God would restore the independence that might enable Massachusetts to serve him as only the Israelites had served him before. But the hope proved false. In 1691 the people of Massachusetts heard that they must serve England before God; the new king was sending a new royal governor.

A gloom settled over the colony far deeper than the depression that greeted the coming of the first royal governor. Men who had been rescued from despair only to be plunged back again were in a mood to suspect some hidden evil that might be responsible for their woes. They blamed themselves for not finding it; and when the girls of Salem Village produced visible and audible evidence of something vile and unsuspected, it was all too easy to believe them.

Although Puritanism was connected only indirectly with the witch scare, it did affect the conduct of the trials and the behavior of the defendants. Puritans believed that the state existed to enforce the will of God among men. If evil went unrebuked, they believed, God would punish the whole community for condoning it. It was the solemn duty of the government to search out every crime and demonstrate the community's disapproval of it by punishment or admonition. Once the witch trials began, the officers of government felt an obligation to follow every hint and accusation in order to ferret out the crimes that might be responsible for bringing the wrath of God on the colony. They were, of course, egged on by the people. Witch-hunts, whether in Massachusetts or Europe, generally proceeded from the bottom up, from popular demand. Even the Spanish Inquisition was much less assiduous in pursuit of suspected witches than were the people of the villages where the suspects lived. But popular pressure is not an adequate excuse for irregular judicial procedures. In their eagerness to stamp out witchcraft, the Massachusetts authorities forgot that they had a duty to protect the innocent as well as punish the guilty.

At the same time, they were trapped by their very insistence on mercy for the repentant. By releasing defendants who confessed and repented, they placed a terrible pressure on the accused to confess to crimes they had not committed. It is possible that some of the confessions at Salem were genuine. Some of the accused may actually have practiced witchcraft as they understood it. But undoubtedly a large percentage of the confessions were made simply to obtain mercy. Men and women who lied were thus released, whereas those whose bravery and honesty forbade them to lie were hanged. These brave men and women were Puritans too, better Puritans than those who confessed; their very Puritanism strengthened them in the refusal to purchase their lives at the cost of their souls.

Puritanism also affected the attitude of Massachusetts to the trials after they were over. No Puritan could do wrong and think lightly of it afterward. God was merciful to the repentant but not to those who failed to acknowledge their errors. And within five years of the witch trials, the people of Massachusetts knew that they had done wrong. They did not cease to believe in witchcraft, nor did they suppose that the devil had lost his powers or was less dangerous than before. But they did recognize that the trials had been unfair, that men and women had been convicted on insufficient evidence, that the devil had deluded the prosecutors more than the defendants. It was possible that Massachusetts had judicially murdered innocent men and women. The people therefore set aside a day, January 15, 1697, as a day of fasting, in which the whole colony might repent. On that day, Samuel Sewall, one of the judges, stood up in church while the minister, at his request, read his confession of guilt and his desire to take "the blame and shame" of the trials on himself. The jurors who had sat in the trials published their own confession. "We ourselves," they wrote, "were not capable to understand nor able to withstand the mysterious delusion of the power of darkness and prince of the air, whereby we fear we have been instrumental with others, though ignorantly and unwillingly, to bring upon ourselves the guilt of innocent blood."

These confessions brought no one back to life, but who will deny that it was good and right to make them? In 1927 the state of Massachusetts executed two men named Sacco and Vanzetti. They may have been guilty, just as some of the Salem witches may have been guilty, but experts agree that they did not receive a fair trial. A few years ago when the governor of Massachusetts acknowledged that fact officially, the people of Massachusetts, through their elected representatives, rebuked him. But today the people of Massachusetts are no longer Puritans and feel no need for contrition.

A knowledge of Puritanism can help us to penetrate behind the mask that disguises some of the characters in *The Crucible* and obscures the forces at work in the Salem tragedy. Arthur Miller knew his characters well enough as human beings so that they are never concealed from him by his faulty image of Puritanism. But he does not know them as Puritans. Too often their humanity is revealed as something at odds with Puritanism. We need to understand that their Puritanism was not really at issue in the tragedy. Insofar as it entered, it affected protagonist and antagonist alike. It conceals the issue to make Samuel Parris wear the mask of Puritanism and John Proctor stand like some nineteenth-century Yankee populist thrust back into Cotton Mather's court. Parris and Proctor were both Puritans and both men. We should not look on Proctor's refusal to confess as a triumph of man over Puritan. It was a triumph of man over man and of Puritan over Puritan. Elizabeth Proctor was a Puritan and a woman; we should not see her as a Puritan when she is cold to her husband and a woman when she is warm.

In other words, the profounder implications of the action in the play are darkened by a partial identification of the antagonist as Puritanism. The identification is never complete. If it were, the play would be merely a piece of flattery. But Miller has offered his audience an escape they do not deserve. He has allowed them a chance to think that John Proctor asserted the dignity of man against a benighted and outworn creed. Proctor did nothing of the kind. Proctor asserted the dignity of man against man. Man is the antagonist against which human dignity must always be defended; not against Puritanism, not against Nazism or communism, or McCarthyism, not against the Germans or the Russians or the Chinese, not against the Middle Ages or the Roman Empire. As long as we identify the evil in the world with some particular creed or with some other people remote in time or place, we flatter ourselves and cheapen the dignity and greatness of those who resist evil. The Germans, we say, or the Russians are inhuman beasts who trample humanity in the mud. We would never do such a thing. Belsen is in Germany. Salem Village is in the seventeenth century. It is a comforting and specious thought. It allows us to escape from the painful knowledge that has informed the great religions, knowledge incidentally that the Puritans always kept before them, the knowledge that all of us are capable of evil. The glory of human dignity is that any man may show it. The tragedy is that we are all equally capable of denying it.

DAVID SAVRAN

The Wooster Group, Arthur Miller *and* The Crucible

I consider Arthur Miller's play no different than his car. You wouldn't
drive off his car and say, "Oh, I'll bring it back later."
(David LeVine, president The Dramatists Guild,
as quoted in The New York Times)

Part I: Attempting to Secure Performance Rights

When the Wooster Group began working on Arthur Miller's play *The
Crucible* in November 1982, it immediately wrote to Dramatists Play Service
to secure performance rights. The reply that came from the Service's Leasing
Department, dated November 9, 1982, read: "I regret to inform you that *The
Crucible* is not available for production in New York City and so we cannot
grant you permission to perform. Sorry."

On January 15, 1983, Elizabeth LeCompte, artistic director of the
Wooster Group, wrote to Arthur Miller's agent, Luis Sanjurjo at ICM,
requesting "special permission to use excerpts from *The Crucible*" for a
new piece the Group was developing. Sanjurjo told her that before making
any decision he would have to see the piece with a lawyer. "When you have
something ready, call me," he told LeCompte. In February 1983, the Group

From *The Drama Review.* © 1985 New York University and the Massachusetts Institute of
Technology.

opened rehearsals to the public of the new work-in-progress entitled *L.S.D.*: a 45-minute version of *The Crucible*, using the final sections of each of its four scenes, prefaced by 20 minutes of excerpts from Timothy Leary's record album, *L.S.D.*

During the spring and summer of 1983, the Wooster Group was in Europe performing *Route 1 & 9* and developing a new piece, *North Atlantic*, written by Jim Strahs, which was to be used as Part II of *L.S.D.* When the Group returned to New York, it set to work rehearsing and adapting *North Atlantic* for an American cast and, in September, resumed performing open rehearsals of excerpts from *The Crucible*. In performance, the Wooster Group placed the play behind a long table, partially costumed it (combining 17th century dress with rehearsal clothes) and gave the men microphones. Miller's text was reduced to "just the high points," accompanied by music and dance. Invited to attend by the Group, Sanjurjo, in discussion after the performance, suggested that Arthur Miller himself see it.

During the following weeks, the Wooster Group tried in vain to contact Miller. One afternoon in late October, however, Peyton Smith, a member of the Group, was introduced to him at a reception at the Chelsea Hotel and persuaded him to attend a performance. He came to the show that night. Afterwards, he went upstairs to talk with the performers and compliment them on their work. According to LeCompte, he was polite and gracious and seemed "bemused." In conversation with her, Miller voiced three concerns. First, the audience might think LeCompte's interpretation a parody. Secondly, the audience might believe the piece was a performance of the entire play and not just excerpts. And thirdly, Miller feared that these performances might exclude a "first-class," i.e., Broadway, production. He left, saying he would have to think about it and he would be in touch with them again. A week later, he instructed ICM to write the Wooster Group, saying that he would not grant them permission to use excerpts from *The Crucible*. The letter, dated November 29, indicated that Miller believed the use would "among other things, tend to inhibit first-class productions" of the play.

Between November 30, 1983 and October 22, 1984, Elizabeth LeCompte sent three letters to Miller and/or his agent. She argued that the production of excerpts in a tiny Off-Off Broadway theatre would not affect the possibility of a "first-class" production. She also declared her serious regard for *The Crucible*, explaining that her work was not intended as parody, and elaborated the reasons for the incorporation of the play into *L.S.D.* Simultaneously, the Wooster Group continued the development of the piece. It retained the excerpts of *The Crucible* as Part II, reducing them to 25 minutes, and noted in the program that only a part of Miller's play was being used. The Group also excised *North Atlantic* (presenting it as a separate piece) and composed three new parts, all based on Leary material. In the spring, it added the subtitle (. . . *Just the High Points* . . .) and performed the first three parts in New York. The fourth was not yet ready for an audience. On the invitation of Peter Sellars, then artistic director of the Boston Shakespeare Company, the Group took *L.S.D.* (. . . *Just the High Points* . . .) to Boston, where it was opened to the critics, who reviewed it favorably. In the final days of the Boston run, the Group presented Part IV publicly for the first time.

In September, the Wooster Group began performing all four parts of *L.S.D.* in New York. LeCompte sent a letter to Sanjurjo informing him of the piece's development and explaining *The Crucible* excerpts had been conflated to a 25-minute sequence. In a collective decision, the Group opened *L.S.D.* to the press at the end of October. On October 31, Mel Gussow panned the piece in the *New York Times*, referring to Part II as a "send-up" of *The Crucible*. Ten days later, the Group received a "cease and desist" order from Miller's attorneys threatening to "recommend to Mr. Miller that he take any and all legal measures against you, including instituting court proceedings." LeCompte wrote Miller on November 15 to explain again her intentions. At the same time, in consultation with a copyright lawyer, she reworked Part II so that *The Crucible* would be performed in gibberish. The incident was reported two days later in the *New York Times* by Samuel G. Freedman and in the November 27 issue of the *Village Voice* by Don Shewey. According to Shewey, Miller denied receiving any of the letters—his agent refused to comment—and indicated that "The first thing they've gotta do is send me an apology." LeCompte did so in a letter dated November 26 in which she also announced that she had "with great sadness" stopped performances of *L.S.D.* the preceding night.

After the notice of cancellation, LeCompte received a telephone call from Miller in which, she reports, he apologized for the way the situation had developed. He explained that he had wanted to see the piece before it closed, but that he was very busy and that it was difficult for him to make it down to the City from his home in Connecticut. He would try, however, to make the last performance, a Sunday matinee. That morning LeCompte received another call from Miller in which he said he was unable to attend the show but would send a representative to take a look at it. "Later on we'll talk," he told her. When LeCompte had not heard from him or his representative by Thursday of the following week, she called him and asked him if his representative had seen the performance. Miller replied that he wasn't sure if she had made it or not. She then asked if she could send him the parts of the script, approximately two pages, she needed to keep the structure of the piece intact for a revised production. He said he was very busy and wouldn't be able to attend to it for another two weeks (he was to receive an award at the Kennedy Center and was working on the television version of *Death of a Salesman*). He told her to send them, however, which she did, and then she heard nothing.

In the meantime during the month of December, the Wooster Group reworked Part II of *L.S.D.*, substituting a text by Michael Kirby for most of Miller's. The new section followed the shape of *The Crucible*, but re-scored the original so that the few remaining fragments of Miller's script were obscured either by music or by the Kirby text. When a performer "accidentally" spoke a line of *The Crucible* or made a reference to one of Miller's characters, he or she was silenced by a buzzer. It was opened on January 4 for an eight performance run. On January 7, John A. Silberman, Miller's lawyer, wrote the members of the Wooster Group to inform them that one of the attorneys in his office had attended a performance on January 5. He told the Group that its current version "continues to constitute an infringement on Mr. Miller's copyright" and demanded that it "cease and desist." He said that "blatant and continuing violations of Mr. Miller's rights must not be allowed to continue." On January 8, the day it received the letter, the Wooster Group closed *L.S.D.*

◆ ◆ ◆

The issues raised by Arthur Miller's withholding of rights for *The Crucible* are numerous, touching highly emotional issues involving the certitudes of law and questions of interpretation as well as allegations of censorship and theft. Roughly, the aspects of the dispute can be divided into the legal and the extra-legal, the former dependent upon copyright laws and the latter upon more ambiguous and subjective notions of artistic freedom. The legal dimension has been widely reported in the press and, clearly, has been the decisive factor in the apparent resolution of the case. Indeed, Mr. Miller's rights are far reaching and absolute:

> No public or private performance—professional or amateur—
> may be given without the written permission of the producers
> and the payment of royalty. . . . Anyone disregarding the author's
> rights renders himself liable to prosecution.

This statement is printed on the verso of the title page of *The Crucible*. Since Arthur Miller retains the copyright to the play—that is, since he retains ownership of it—he has the right to withhold permission from the Wooster Group to perform the play. Its unauthorized production would therefore constitute a theft. Since, from February 1983 until November 1984, the Wooster Group chose to perform a substantial portion of the script without his approbation, it did so in clear violation of the law. In December 1984, however, the Group revised the piece under the guidance of a copyright lawyer, and it believes that the January 1985 version does not, in fact, violate Miller's copyright. It was forced to close, however, in recognition of the clear illegality of the earlier versions and the threat that Miller could institute court proceedings "based upon all past, present and future performances." Since the Group knows that legal action taken against it would cripple it financially, it was forced to halt performances of *L.S.D.*

The end of unauthorized performances, however, does not put to rest the ethical and interpretive questions. It only subordinates them to the exercise of juridical power. Arthur Miller is certainly acutely aware of the difference between his interpretation and that of the Wooster Group, since he has made the issue paramount in his interviews with the press. In an article in the *Village Voice* in December 1983, Robert Massa quotes Miller as saying, "The issue here is very simple. I don't want my play produced except in total agreement with the way I wrote it," that is, in accord with Miller's own interpretation. He objects to the Wooster Group's use because "It's a blatant parody." A year later, also in the *Voice*, Miller clarifies his position for Don Shewey, explaining that the insistence on a "first-class" production was a smokescreen: "I'm not interested in the money. The esthetics are involved. I don't want the play mangled that way. Period."

Elizabeth LeCompte's best defense against Miller's charges that she has "mangled" his play is probably her letter to him of November 30, 1983, in which she attempts to elucidate her strategy and explain what she is doing with *The Crucible* and why she is doing it:

> I want to use irony and distancing techniques to cut through to the intellectual and political heart of *The Crucible*, as well as its emotional heart. I want to put the audience in a position of examining their own relation to this material as "witnesses"—witnesses to the play itself, as well as witnesses to the "story" of the play. Our own experience has been that many, many of our audience have strong associations with the play, having either studied it in school, performed in it in a community theatre production, or seen it as a college play. And the associations with the play are important to my mise-en-scène. It is a theatrical experience which has cut across two generations, a literary and political icon.

LeCompte's analysis of her use of irony is evidently not acceptable to Miller since it contradicts his cited objection as well as the judgment of Mel Gussow, both of whom believe Part II of *L.S.D.* to be a parody of *The Crucible*. A look at the performance neither validates LeCompte's assertions nor provides an unequivocal evaluation of the effect of the liberties taken with Miller's script. She has fragmented it, distorted many of the spoken lines, and neglected to place it in the fictive historical setting prescribed by the stage directions. These choices, however, do not necessarily indicate that she is attempting a parody of the play. The contrary could be argued—that her modifications do indeed "cut through to the heart" and that, although they bespeak an ironic treatment, her approach is qualitatively different from parody. The dispute here, in regard to this central point, comes down to a disagreement over interpretation or personal taste (both highly subjective) and the fact that Miller's ownership of the play bestows legal force upon his interpretation.

Elizabeth LeCompte and the other members of the Wooster Group are disappointed that Arthur Miller is apparently not willing to accept their interpretation of his play. LeCompte understands, however, that Miller "was absolutely right to do what he did, considering his perspective and his interests." Norman Frisch, dramaturg for the Wooster Group, sees the situation in terms of differing ideologies that echo, in fact, one of the main antitheses implicit in *L.S.D.*:

> We begin with the knowledge that we're working in a different way from Arthur Miller. His theatre is predicated upon a certain set of assumptions central to which are the concepts that all theatrical activity builds on the work of the playwright and that the playwright owns the text as his personal property. The Wooster Group, on the other hand, is working from an opposing set of assumptions. Our hope, as the dialog with Miller opened up, was to engage him in the play of these two different ideas. Timothy Leary refers to his relationships with the authorities as a variation on the annual Harvard-Yale football game. Opposition is central to the relationship, but both teams recognize that they benefit from and enjoy the game. Unfortunately for us, Arthur Miller owns the ball. He's decided not to play and has taken the ball home with him.

The Wooster Group has presently set to work revising *L.S.D.*, substituting another text for *The Crucible* and excising all references to Arthur Miller's play. It plans to open the work at the Performing Garage in February with a new title since it will, perforce, be a different piece. In the aftermath of what has been a highly publicized dispute, LeCompte accepts the most recent turn of events as being "an inevitable outcome of our working process," that is, yet another strategic moment in the Group's ongoing confrontation with various authorities and institutions. She realizes that this process of questioning assumptions and beliefs sometimes necessitates trespassing upon cultural properties. "I always know we will be accused of stealing and cast as outlaws," she says. "But I see this as healthy. It's a necessary relationship to authority."

Part II: Before the Fall

The disagreement over *The Crucible* does not mark the first time that the Wooster Group has been engaged in controversy. In 1981 the Group had its funding cut by the New York State Council on the Arts (NYSCA) in its belief that *Route 1 & 9* was racist (the piece included a performance of a Pigmeat Markham comedy routine in blackface). The fact that neither dispute has been resolved in favor of the Wooster Group indicates, to my way of thinking, less a misinterpretation on the part of Arthur Miller and NYSCA than a failure or reluctance to credit the Group's intentions and strategies. The second part of this essay is an attempt to elaborate those intentions and strategies, to explain how the Wooster Group, in its working process, uses raw material and, in its performances, generates opportunities for meaning. We begin with LeCompte's notion of the work as a presentation of a scientific phenomenon.

> Most perceptive students . . . must see through the fundamental misrepresentation in the typical lecture-table "experiment," in which a subtle and beautiful phenomenon is distorted beyond all recognition in order that the ephemeral visual clues can be amplified for the benefit of people seated at a distance. They must be aware of the fact that demonstrations tend to wrench phenomena from their natural context in order to make a "main point" stand out clearly before the average student. And the most interested and intuitive students must be very uncomfortable when . . . the attention is displaced from the real effect to a substitute or analog, so that a gross model . . . becomes the means of discussing a basic phenomenon . . . without giving the class a glimpse of the actual case itself.

> (Gerald Holton, "Conveying Science by Visual Presentation" in
> *Education of Vision*, ed. Gyorgy Kepes)

Elizabeth LeCompte: *The initial design for* Rumstick Road *had the booth in the center, on top, almost naturally, because of the design picture I have here in* "Conveying Science by Visual Presentation." *I don't know whether I found this after or before, I can't remember. Everything is in here. I used to—every night, I'd go back and get into the bathtub. And I'd sit with this book, so it's all buckled. And I'd read it over and over again, to get back to it. Later, I had some idea, coming off this thing of lecture-demonstration, that we would do a science experiment in* Nayatt School, *but it never came to be. And it carries over through all the pieces.*

David Savran: *In* Nayatt *the huge jar of maraschino cherries looked like pickled lab specimens.*

Elizabeth LeCompte: *That's exactly it, it's all the leftover stuff from those ideas. But it's just the leftover, because originally I had all kinds of ideas about these wonderful science experiments that we'd do. Actual ones that are done in high schools and colleges, just to demonstrate different things.*

Ron Vawter: *The laws of physics. Simple demonstrations of the laws of physics.*

The lecture-demonstration never fully analyzes or explicates experiential reality, for it always transforms the phenomenon whose workings it attempts to explain. Either it isolates the phenomenon in an experimental or educational situation that bears little resemblance to its natural site, or else it replaces the phenomenon altogether by another one, of a completely different nature, on a completely different temporal and spatial scale. Thus, as an explanation of the movement of waves in the ocean, the water-wave tank may be a useful visualization, illuminating the *principles* of wave interaction, principles which may subsequently be used to understand the play of real ocean surf. But the demonstration itself will not, if only because of its scale, provide a realistic representation of the movement of the sea. Or yet again, in a demonstration of Brownian motion, the random movement of microscopic particles in a gas or liquid could be represented by a tray of mechanically agitated steel balls. The demonstration may allow the viewer to understand what Brownian motion is, although it operates according to principles that are entirely different from those governing the phenomenon in question. In both cases, it can be no more than a homology or metaphor for the original.

In each example, the phenomenon to be studied is removed from nature and the network of contingent events that comprise its context. It is analyzed either as a self-contained, discrete event, or else is represented analogically by a model that bears no more than a casual likeness to the original. In both cases, the naturally occurring event is nowhere to be seen: It takes place either outside the laboratory or classroom, or on a scale that renders it inaccessible to view. As a result, a replacement is used. Furthermore, this replacement is always manipulated to a certain pre-determined end. The demonstrator knows from the beginning the physical laws or principles that the presentation has been designed to prove. His energies are focused toward conveying information and knowledge to the curious onlookers—not by showing the richness and complexity of the phenomenon but by simplifying it, by reducing it to a straightforward, linear process that will lead the viewers to comprehend a set of abstract principles or mathematical formulas.

When Elizabeth LeCompte speaks of her activity as lecture-demonstration, she does so fully aware of the complexity of the phenomena she studies and the distortion requisite to all representation. As a result, her work is less a simple demonstration than a deconstruction of that same activity—a representation turned back upon itself and offered as a critique of itself and the assumptions, goals and methods that have allowed it to come into being. The demonstration itself becomes problematic; it is revealed to be an activity highly charged with ideology, dependent upon a certain mode of linear thinking and the belief that phenomena can be isolated and re-presented (re-enacted in a different context) and retain a uniform, stable function and meaning. The belief in the "neutrality" of the scientific method is challenged in order to reveal that the phenomena under investigation must be transformed in the process of presentation by a demonstrator whose credibility and employment are always on the line.

All of the Wooster Group pieces use certain characteristics of the lecture-demonstration but call them into question in the very act of appropriation. *L.S.D.* sets the performers behind a long table and gives them books to read: in Part I, works by Leary, Huxley, Ginsberg and other beat and counter-cultural heroes; in Part II, *The Crucible*; in Part III, fragments of all of the above; and in Part IV, excerpts from a Timothy Leary/G. Gordon Liddy debate. Most of the performers are given microphones and, throughout the piece, read the texts in front of them in a straightforward way, in order to provide the spectators with access to a collection of documents. The presentation is attuned to the simple statement of fact rather than the expression of the performers' subjective response to the material. It remains cool, despite the fact that the activity, particularly in Part II, alternates between the simple act of reading and a highly theatricalized mania. For even at the height of madness, in the courtroom scene in *The Crucible*, the performers' delivery never becomes heated. In Brechtian fashion, hysteria is held up as a phenomenon to be scrutinized, much as the lecturer in a scientific demonstration would hold up a psycho-social phenomenon for analysis.

LeCompte presents an assortment of disparate material from the '50s and '60s, not in an attempt to create a fictive synthesis but to encourage the spectator's contemplation of the material in all its complexity and heterogeneity. As a result, *L.S.D.* pens a kind of opaque writing in which texts by Leary, Miller and others are inscribed, less for their particular content than their iconic value. Ginsberg, Kerouac, Liddy, John Proctor and Abigail Williams become figures on a manuscript, pointers to ideology and attitude rather than "characters" around whom a narrative sequence is constructed.

So too, *The Crucible* is used not simply for the story that it dramatizes. If it were, lines would not be delivered in near-gibberish; the action would not be fragmented; the role of Deputy Governor Danforth would not be performed by a sixteen-year-old boy, nor that of Tituba by a white woman in blackface. All of these choices suggest that *The Crucible* is being used less for its intrinsic value (as a carrier of theme and message) than as an icon that gathers together a network of associations and experiences. As LeCompte suggests in her letter to Miller, the performance distances the spectator so that the play's attitudes are made visible. Miller's text takes its place in *L.S.D.* as a historical document of the early '50s, as a reminder of both a particular dramatic style and an approach to social and political issues. It becomes an index of ideology, a memento of a particular attitude toward dissent, and a highly equivocal portrait of the counter-cultural hero.

In its presentation of documentary material, *L.S.D.* is the very opposite of nostalgia. It indulges no melancholic yearning but instead keeps the icons of the '50s and '60s at a distance that allows us both to feel their seductive power and to be made uneasy by the attraction. Like all of the Wooster Group pieces, it presents cultural properties in such a way that their internal contradictions become evident; as LeCompte explains, "The performer doing the experiment or showing the material can't help but bring them out." In *L.S.D.* this process holds up *The Crucible* so that we are made aware that its attack on injustice and blindness brings with it a different set of inequities. It allows (but does not force) us to see the questionable practices that lie concealed beneath its idealism and good intentions, and to recognize in John Proctor a hero who oppresses others in the justification of his own moral crusade.

◆   ◆   ◆

Elizabeth LeCompte: *When I think of texts, / think of them in the way that Kurt Schwitters used to, in a collage. He found a certain amalgam of words that looked good, physically, and pasted it up flat, on a canvas, with the colors. You'd read the words, but you knew that he had just taken the paper off the floor.*

Elizabeth LeCompte: *The reason that I keep something . . . for instance, someone will say, "This doesn't work here. Ronnie getting up [in Part III of L.S.D.] and going over and touching the house doesn't work here because he's got to be over there, to tune his drums, or something." But by chance, in an improv, Ronnie has done that. And I take that chance occurrence and say, that is the* sine qua non, *that is the beginning, that is the text. I cannot stray from that text. As someone else would use the lines of a playwright, I use that action as the very baseline from which I am working. Therefore, I can't just erase it. He's made that text, by that action, and therefore, I must adjust around that. But it's a chance element, it's not thought out in the sense that a text is thought out. It's an action-text that's based on an improv that may have nothing to do with any thematic thing that we're working on. I call it chance work, like throwing a handful of beans up in the air. And when they come down on the floor, I must make a dance around that pattern. And I cannot alter that pattern until the last possible moment. I use that as one pole against which I work my dialectic. I cannot alter it unless, somehow, another structure, another bunch of beans, comes into conflict with the first. Then one bean must move, one way or the other. But only at that point.*

All of the Wooster Group pieces begin with a body of found "objects," much as the lecture-demonstration always begins with a phenomenon or case in point as its subject. The raw materials in *L.S.D.* are of five different orders: first, recordings of private interviews or public events, or excerpts from non-dramatic texts (the interview with Ann Rower, excerpts from the Leary/Liddy debate and the chronicles of John Bryan); secondly, dramatic texts (*The Crucible*); thirdly, music, film and video (the live band and Ken Kobland's video); fourthly, the performance space which is left from the last piece, containing various architectanic elements which will be used in the development of any new piece; and finally, improvised action-texts: gesture, dance and language discovered through improvisation and used either as an independent strand in the work or as an elaboration of other material.

Like a maker of collages, LeCompte takes up found material, gathered from the performer-collaborators or written texts that they bring in to the Performing Garage. An arbitrarily selected object will then form what LeCompte calls the *sine qua non*, a given against which other material is juxtaposed. The found object has come onto the scene without fixed meaning and will accrue function and significance only as it is placed or sited in the piece, in counterpoint against the other fragments. The process of composition pulls the object out of its original context, fragmenting or breaking it, in some way, and using it to form part of a new structure. The resultant interwoven network of objects is a "text" submitted to repetition and development, and given a permanent, if fluid, form. The arbitrary or spontaneous nature of the found object is preserved by virtue of its fragmentation and its location—or, more properly, its *dislocation* within the textual network. For even in combination with the other elements, it remains isolated from them, its casual nature now evident as a causal disjunction, a separation induced by a rupture of the laws of cause and effect.

The textual network of which every Wooster Group piece is composed is never simply an elaboration of a single pre-text, since none of the floating fragments, regardless of its size or prestige, ever becomes a foundation upon which a piece is built. Although *The Crucible* comprises the largest fragment in *L.S.D.*, it is not a centerpiece against which all else is measured or a fixture that is given a single interpretation by the rest of the piece. Rather, *The Crucible* becomes one locus among many others for an ever-changing set of associations and meanings. As the piece progresses, Miller's text is gradually broken down and reduced to fragments. It becomes truly an icon, a sacred relic to be torn apart and offered as a sacrifice (much like the witches of Salem) in a performance that litters the playing area with shards of countless other texts, wreckage from the '50s and '60s. In the end, *The Crucible* is reduced to a single line that, even in isolation, retains its plurality—a question, not an answer: "What is this dancing?"

◆   ◆   ◆

Elizabeth LeCompte: *And it's not to say the psychological content isn't important, it's just that it's definitely after the fact, and it's also one strain, one element in the work. It's not the central. It's not the core around which the piece is built. The core is dispersed in those pieces, always, the core structure is dispersed among many elements.*

Ron Vawter: *Bernard Berenson wrote a monograph on Piero della Francesca, it's called "The Ineloquent in Art." I read it when I was a student and was very, very impressed by it. And I remember thinking about it when I first saw* Sakonnet Point, *and I was very attracted to it. Berenson was saying that he found that the great works of art that meant anything to him were the ones which weren't trying to say something to him or convey a meaning but literally just were there. He was talking about Piero della Francesca, these figures that just sit there and don't seem to be trying to express anything. He also talked about the seated Buddhas . . . that those were the things that really allowed him to be engaged, when they weren't busy trying to speak to him.*

Elizabeth LeCompte: *Yes. That's also interesting that Piero della Francesca is often considered cold.*

Ron Vawter: *And only concerned with form . . .*

Elizabeth LeCompte: *Which is one of the attacks we got early on.*

Ron Vawter: *I remembered the essay when I first saw* Sakonnet. *I think one of the reasons why audiences do project onto it so heavily and why there's such massive interpretation of a lot of the things we make, is because you are discreet in that way . . .*

Elizabeth LeCompte: *I allow as many interpretations as possible to co-exist in the same time and same space.*

Ron Vawter: *You'll reject something that's too pointed.*

Elizabeth LeCompte: *It would make a meaning. Not that the meaning is wrong, I don't want one meaning. I want always at least two and, hopefully, many, many more meanings to coalesce at the same point.*

Ron Vawter: *Just recently you were saying, "We can't have Jeff Webster play Proctor and Leary, [in L.S.D.] because it's too much of a . . ."*

Elizabeth LeCompte: *It makes a meaning that I don't want.*

Ron Vawter: *An event which can be interpreted only one way inhibits and limits the possibility. It's not that we're deliberately trying to make pieces which are mute. Just the opposite. But it's difficult to make something which is an opportunity for more than . . . I often see a piece as an opportunity for a meaning, rather than an expression of a single meaning.*

In gathering together fragments of action, drama, film and video, the Wooster Group produces a kind of performance that is quite different from that of most scripted theatre. In building a piece, it does not begin with a theme or message to be communicated. (*L.S.D.* was never intended to be a "send-up" of *The Crucible*.) Ideas and themes that emerge from the pieces do so only in retrospect, as a residue of the textualizing process—much as, in a chemical reaction, solid flakes precipitate out of a solution. And for all the pieces, the most powerful reagent is the spectator, each of whom will see a different piece—much as each, in the laboratory, would see a different configuration of chemical flakes. Here, however, the work breaks with Newtonian physics, which assumes the uniformity of the phenomenon under scrutiny, regardless of vantage point. Instead, the Wooster Group initiates what could be described as an Einsteinian project that celebrates the multiplicity of perspectives and only one certainty: that the phenomenon will be perceived differently by each member of the audience.

As with any piece of theatre, each spectator will be assured a different chain of associations and way of making sense of the action. Unlike most literary theatre, however, the Wooster Group's work is carefully designed so that the different threads, the different texts, the different sets of data, can be articulated in many ways, rendering a single meaning impossible. Certainly, there are many factors that make for the open-ended and indeterminate structure of the work, including several that reach beyond the work itself to its social and esthetic context (and which remain operative in any act of interpretation). Leaving these aside, we can specify several reasons why the work authorizes multiple interpretations.

First, none of the Wooster Group's pieces rests upon a clear-cut narrative spine. In structure, *L.S.D.* could not be more unlike a play (such as *The Crucible*) that uses a highly delineated plotline and clearly drawn, idiosyncratic characters, whose development carries the emotional weight of the piece. In its place, *L.S.D.* offers a disjunctive juxtaposition of events (like L.S.D., the drug) that refuses linear developments—a collage in which several forms, drawn from different traditions, collide with each other. The characters are drawn in a two-dimensional, cartoon style, heavier with idea than with psychology. The performers' roles are transformed from one part of the piece to the next, not in imitation of some kind of psychological development but to allow a free-floating juxtaposition of ideas and images.

Secondly, the Wooster Group work is not bound by the laws of cause and effect. Thus, the disintegration of *The Crucible* in Part III is not the logical result of its relatively straightforward presentation in Part II. The connection between events in the piece, as in all the other Wooster Group pieces, is what Kenneth Burke calls an associative or qualitative one in which "the presence of one quality calls forth the demand for another" ("Antony in Behalf of the Play"). Thus, for example, the tightly choreographed structure and frenetic intensity of Part II evokes in the spectator the desire for some kind of relaxation. In Part III, the Millbrook section, this desire is fulfilled as *The Crucible* is broken down and inserted into the middle of a party that seems the antithesis of Miller's carefully structured play (it is, in fact, even more intricately choreographed). The clearly focused action and stylized, literary language give way in Part III to a diffused spectacle (there are always at least three things happening simultaneously) and a much freer use of language. Within itself, the sequence also bears witness to a process of disintegration as the party gradually winds down and the celebrants become progressively more sober and isolated from each other, lost in their own activities. Seeming the antithesis of *The Crucible*, Part III in fact provides an ironic counterpoint to Miller's play, the growing isolation of the tragic protagonist becoming, in the Wooster Group's transformation, the half-suicide, half-ecstasy of Kate Valk's "faint dance" or the solitary perusal of a newspaper by Ron Vawter.

Thirdly, none of the Wooster Group pieces, within itself, provides an unambiguous frame of reference or offers a clear signal of meaning. At no point in *L.S.D.* does the Wooster Group pass judgment on any of Miller's characters or indicate what attitude it wishes us to adopt toward them or toward the play. Similarly, it never dictates a response to Timothy Leary or his guests at Millbrook or to their attempts at instigating a psychedelic revolution. As in *Route 1 & 9*, there is no one outside of the performance except the spectators to pass judgement, no unchallenged voice of authority, no point of view that escapes the play of irony. Even Nancy Reilly, who reads the transcripts of the interview with Ann Rower (the only figure to provide a retrospective glance), is treated with considerable irony. Hers is not privileged, but only one voice among many.

All of the Wooster Group's pieces insist on a complexity of vision that deprives the spectator of the frame of reference he or she needs to separate the ironic from the non-ironic—or, in ethical terms, that which deserves disdain from that which is admirable. Instead, each piece mobilizes a free-floating irony, one whose drift constitutes the work's plurality or enunciates the various opportunities for meaning. In doing so, the Group questions both the self-containment of the work and the marginality of the spectator by urging the latter to make the kind of choices usually considered the province of the writer and/or performer. As a result, each piece can be no more than partially composed when it is presented to the public—not because it is unfinished but because it requires an audience to realize the multitude of possibilities on which it opens. As each spectator, according to his part, enters into a dialog with the work, the act of interpretation becomes a performance, an intervention in the piece.

The dispute between Arthur Miller and the Wooster Group bears witness to the status of interpretation as an act that cannot be separated from the work itself. Thus, from now on, *L.S.D.* will be in part "about" Miller's withholding of rights for *The Crucible*, in the same way that *Route 1 & 9* is now in part "about" NYSCA's funding cut. Looking at *L.S.D.* from this perspective, we note the ironic aspect of Miller's success—that one of the clearest aims of *The Crucible* is the questioning of arbitrary, inflexible and overzealous authority. Although Miller's rights in this case cannot be disputed, their exercise indeed appears to be all of the above. The irony of this situation would not have been lost on Miller's hero, John Proctor, who recognized how easily justice could be manipulated for self-interest: "I like not the smell of this 'authority.'"

JAMES A. ROBINSON

All My Sons *and* Paternal Authority

In a 1958 essay, "The Shadows of the Gods," Arthur Miller located the struggle between father and son "at the heart of all human development" because their conflict symbolizes larger issues of power and its renewal. The son's "struggle for mastery—for the freedom of manhood," the playwright asserted, "is the struggle not only to overthrow authority but to reconstitute it anew" (*Theatre Essays*, 185, 193). *All My Sons* (1946) and *Death of a Salesman* (1948), as well as the earlier, unproduced "They Too Arise" (1938), all concentrate in different ways on the battle between a father and two sons to reconstitute authority. This issue lies at the heart of *All My Sons* in particular, where the father-son relationship is linked to the play's central themes: the inseparability of past and present, and the connectedness of man to man. The past abuse of power by the father, Joe Keller, has not only killed innocent American fighter pilots, but brought about the death of his younger son Larry; the present discovery of that abuse outrages the surviving son Chris, whose accusations help precipitate his father's suicide. The play appears to repudiate the father's authority and reconstitute it in Chris, the idealistic proponent of brotherhood and social responsibility.

The repudiation and reconstitution, however, are riddled with ambivalence, as signaled both by the abruptness of the ending and by fundamental flaws In Chris's moral character. That ambivalence points to Miller's anxiety

From *Journal of American Drama and Theatre*. © 1990.

about the usurpation of authority, a disquietude produced partially by his own relationship with his father, but mostly by the conflict among Jewish, modernist and liberal elements within his own vision. The Jewish traditionalist yearns for the unimpeded passage of authority from generation to generation, seeing it as sanction for other human connections. The modernist suspects discontinuity and fragmentation are the ultimate reality, while the liberal strives to assert the value of brotherhood in the face of this chaos. The relationship between Joe and Chris Keller in *All My Sons* provides an intriguing early arena for this unresolved tension—one whose implications obviously go well beyond the vision of Arthur Miller.

The conflict between these impulses issues from Miller's identity as a contemporary Jewish American; and before turning to the text of the play, it may be helpful to explore its cultural sources at some length. Miller himself, it should be noted, has generally discouraged this approach, stressing Instead the universality of the father-son conflict. In a 1966 interview, the playwright typically claimed that the father-son relationship was "a very primitive thing in my plays. That is, the father was really a figure who incorporated both power and some kind of moral law which he had either broken or fallen prey to. He figures as an immense shadow. . . . The reason that I was able to write about the relationship, I think now, was because it had a mythical quality to me" (Roudane, 89–90).[1] A Jungian would argue that that "mythical quality" is universal, especially for men. But if so, Miller's upbringing in a patriarchal Jewish culture undeniably served to reinforce for him the mythic authority of male ancestors, and their connection to the moral law.

As the sacred text of a patriarchal religion, the Torah is rich in stories about fathers and sons (Abraham and Isaac, Isaac and Jacob, Jacob and Joseph, Solomon and David, David and Absalom—to name but a few). Moreover, modern Jewish literature often focuses on this relationship, with Miller's contemporaries Karl Shapiro, Delmore Schwartz, Bernard Malamud and Saul Bellow exhibiting a particular interest in the subject.[2] Since *All My Sons* is not an overtly ethnic play, however, little attention has been paid to how Miller's religious background may have determined his choice and treatment of this common Jewish subject.[3] Miller's recent volume of memoirs, *Timebends*, serves to correct this oversight. For in it, he recalls Orthodox services he attended as a child in which the gathering of male ancestors and descendants bodied forth a continuity of authority that had a powerful impact on his young, impressionable mind, preparing the way for the metaphoric use of fathers and sons in later plays.

In *The Jewish Family: Authority and Tradition in Modern Perspective*, the Jewish sociologist Norman Linzer notes that in Jewish tradition, parents symbolically represent God, tradition and history to their children. "As each reinforces the other," he asserts, "the child is exposed to a massive authority system that encompasses the entire Jewish past and is realized in the present" (71). It is precisely this "massive authority system," as embodied in male ancestors, that Miller describes in his account of childhood experiences in the 144th Street synagogue in Harlem. *Timebends* recollects Miller's awed feelings of "power and reassurance" as his great-grandfather

> would keep turning my face toward the prayer book and pointing at the letters, which themselves were magical, as I would later learn, and apart from their meaning were lines of an art first inscribed by men who had seen the light of God, letters that led to the center of the earth and outward to the high heavens. Though I knew nothing of all that, it was frightening at times and totally, movingly male.

> From where I sat, on my great-grandfather's lap, it was all a kind of waking dream; the standing up and then the sitting down and the rising and falling of voices passionately flinging an incomprehensible language into the air while with an occasional glance I watched my mother up in the balcony with her eyes on me and [Miller's brother] Kermit, on my great-grandfather and grandfather and father all in a row (36–37).

This "totally, movingly male" experience with his elders was grounded in the relationship of Jehovah, a transcendent paternal authority, to man: "the transaction called believing," he learned from these occasions, "comes down to the confrontation with overwhelming power and then the relief of knowing that one has been spared its worst" (37). That power is transmitted through the sacred books of the Torah as handed down by generations of holy men "who had seen the light of God," books read in Orthodox services where Miller's keenest memories are of his male forebears lined up "all in a row," with himself and his brother at the end of the line of transmission. This striking image has several implications for nearly all Miller's subsequent drama. It identifies the realm of power as an exclusively male domain. It invests enormous authority in male ancestors, linking them through a long, unbroken chain to an ultimate (male) authority. It indicates that meaning resides not simply in the ancestors, but in the connection to their living descendants: a major reason for Miller's obsessive interest in the relationship between past and present. It implies that brotherhood depends for its validation on this unbroken succession from a divine source. Finally (and most important), awareness of this succession produces "reassurance," a sense of belonging to both history and community.

Given the significance (and repetition) of this experience in Miller's early childhood, it is no wonder that Miller invests Joe Keller in *All My Sons*, Willy Loman in *Death of a Salesman*, and even the deceased father in the later *The Price* (1968) with such formidable—indeed, "mythical"—power over two sons. They all stand for the authority of God over man, collective over individual, past over present. Nor is it surprising that the transmission of authority from father to son via inheritances (emotional and/or economic) becomes a central concern in these plays. In *Sons*, this takes the secular form of a business legacy which Joe Keller wishes his son Chris to assume. This symbol of continuity is deeply corrupted by Joe's behavior, as we shall see. Yet the idea of continuity still appeals strongly to the traditionalist in Miller, as the play's obsession with the connection between past and present demonstrates.

But if Orthodox Jewish religion provided the young Miller with the father-son relationship as a mythic signifier of continuity and meaning, his experiences as a modern American Jew challenged that signification. American history can be read as a series of ruptures with authority—the Puritans, the Revolution, the Civil War. Miller himself remarks in *Time-bends* that American writers see themselves as "self-convinced and self-made, . . . as though they were fatherless men abandoned by a past that they in turn reject" (115). This is particularly true for children of immigrants—like Miller—children whose desire for integration with the mainstream culture encourages them to repudiate Old World customs and strictures, thus to symbolically rebel against authority.[4] The pressure to assimilate thus became an incentive toward discontinuity, a break from the connection to ancestors, from the past—and from the transcendent source of meaning that Miller's Judaism had promoted.

As Irving Malin has observed, "The archetypal Jew embraces the rule of the father; the archetypal American rebels against the father. Two mythic patterns clash: In this clash [Jewish] writers find tense, symbolic meaning," resulting in the depiction of "imperfect father-son relationships in which rebellion supplants acceptance; violence replaces tenderness; and fragmentation defeats wholeness" (pp. 35, 33). The description perfectly fits *All My Sons* (as well as *Death of a Salesman*), which describes the violent rebellion of two sons against their father. But Miller is torn in his sympathies. Beneath the overt condemnation of the fathers duplicity and destructiveness, the playwright longs for the continuity of authority—and the deep connection between past and present—represented by Joe's relationship with Chris; and the problem of the play's ending indicates his confusion over that connection's loss.

This longing for continuity was intensified, I would suggest, by the effect on Miller of the Holocaust—the epitome of catastrophic discontinuity, the full dimensions of which were revealed the year before Miller began work on *All My Sons* in 1946. Twenty years later, two years after *After the Fall* (1964) had employed the concentration camp as setting and symbol, Miller interpreted the camp as "the final expression of human separateness, and its ultimate consequence. It is organised abandonment": a radical symbol, in other words, of discontinuity and fragmentation, and thus "the logical conclusion of contemporary life" (*Theatre Essays*, 289). But fifteen years earlier—much closer in time of composition to Sons—Miller had also dealt with the Holocaust as an agent of discontinuity, and connected it more explicitly to a Jew's relationship with his ancestors. In the short story "Monte Sant'Angelo," Miller describes the alienation experienced by Bernstein, an American Jew visiting Italy, who has "no relatives that I know of in Europe. And if I had they'd have all been wiped out by now" (*I Don't Need You Anymore*, p. 56). Moreover, he takes "no pride" in the experience of his earlier European ancestors, symbolized for him by his father's vague memories of "a common barrel of water, a town idiot, a baron nearby." Rather, he feels only "a broken part of himself" that makes him wonder "if this was what a child felt on discovering that the parents who brought him up were not his own, and that he entered his house not from warmth but from the street, from a public and disordered place" (61). Bernstein has been thrice displaced: by the European Jew's historical marginalization, by immigration, and by the Holocaust, which has wiped out all traces of family in his ancestral homeland. Significantly for *All My Sons*, the sense of alienation bred by radical discontinuity, by the breaking of the chain of ancestral transmission, is figured by an analogy involving a child's discovery about the duplicity of his parents.

Ultimately, Bernstein has a mysterious encounter with an Italian Jew who has been so thoroughly assimilated into the surrounding Catholic culture that he has lost all consciousness of his Jewishness. The stranger's retention of traces of his ethnic heritage, however, moves the American toward a sense of connection, by means of this "proof as mute as stones that a past lived. A past for me, Bernstein thought" (69). The action of *All My Sons*, with the Holocaust fresh in Miller's memory, moves in the opposite direction, from a dramatization of the deep connection between father and son based on a shared personal history toward the modern sense of discontinuity and dispossession experienced by Bernstein early in the story. For Chris Keller, father and brother are likewise links to a deeply felt past that has, over the course of three years, been wiped out. He thereby encounters, in the void at play's end, a displaced version of the sense of discontinuity experienced by many American Jews following the war: a discontinuity that is also at the center of modernism. His desire to affirm his brotherhood with other American victims of the war assumes great poignancy when placed in the context of Miller's awareness of the slaughter of 6 million European Jews—inhabitants of the continent from which his own ancestors had emigrated earlier in the century, and thus symbolic fathers and brothers to him (as *After the Fall* makes clear). And that context explains, from a different angle, the centrality for Miller of the father-son relationship. It not only symbolizes for him the connection of past to present, a connection needed to fully understand and embrace one's cultural identity; its collapse also demonstrates the power of modern historical forces that shatter this identity, and threaten both continuity with the past and human brotherhood. While the traditional Jew in Miller longs to affirm this connection, the modern Jew cannot deny its weakness and vulnerability.

As so often in Miller, the Depression also played a profound role in his attitude toward the father-son relationship, complicating for him its traditional signification of authority and continuity. His recollected childhood impression of his father Isidore was one of awe: this successful immigrant clothing manufacturer maintained a self-assured "baronial attitude" that caused his young son to view him as an agent of "undefinable authority" and "moral force" (*Timebends*, 24). And this relationship affected his political attitudes. Before 1932, *Timebends* reveals, "life's structure was so fixed that it was not only Grandpa Barnett, a Republican, who was full of indignation at this Roosevelt even presuming to contest President Hoover's right to another term—I felt the same way. The truth, I suppose, was that we were really royalists to whom authority had an aura that was not quite of this world" (111). But the boy's reactionary attitude was overthrown by two events. One was gradual: his father's steady loss of income, causing a decline in both their standard of living and the father's morals. As *Timebends* reports,

> [By the fall of 1932] There was an aching absence in the house of any ruling idea or leadership, my father by now having fallen into the habit of endlessly napping in his time at home. . . . Never complaining or even talking about his business problems, my father simply went more deeply silent, and his naps grew longer, and his mouth seemed to dry up. I could not avoid awareness of my mother's anger at this waning of his powers; . . . I must have adopted my mother's early attitudes toward his failure, her impatience at the beginning of the calamity and her alarm as it got worse, and finally a certain sneering contempt for him that filtered through her voice. (109, 112: my ellipses)

Torn between love for his father's "warm and gentle nature," despair over "his illiterate mind," and anger and contempt for his failure, the 17-year-old Miller was vulnerable to his mother's criticisms of the father, which "divided us against ourselves" (113). No-one remained more divided than the young Miller, who observed the collapse of his primary domestic symbol of authority—contributing to the apparent confusion about the father's authority that is evident in the plot of *All My Sons.*

The other cause of Miller's new suspicion toward authority also planted the seed of his political liberalism. The teenaged Miller heard a college student outside a local drugstore one day, preaching on class differences in America and predicting a world-wide socialist revolution that would overthrow the capitalist system. As Miller remembers,

> This day's overturning of all I knew of the world revolutionized not only my ideas but also my most important relationship at the time, the one with my father. For deep down in the comradely world of the Marxist promise is parricide. For those who are psychically ready for the age-old adventure, the sublimation of violence that Marxism offers is nearly euphoric in its effects; while extolling the rational, it blows away the restraints in the Oedipal furies, clothing their violence with a humane ideal. . . . I had never raised my voice against my father, nor did he against me, then or ever. As I know perfectly well, it was not he who angered me, only his failure to cope with his fortune's collapse. Thus I had two fathers, the real and the metaphoric, and the latter I resented because he did not know how to win out over the general collapse. . . . [But] If Marxism was, on the metaphorical plans, a rationale for parricide, I think that to me it was at the same time a way of forgiving my father, for it showed him as a kind of digit in a nearly cosmic catastrophe that was beyond his powers to avoid (*Timebends*, 111–114: my ellipses).

Ambivalence riddles the passage. Respect for his father co-exists with both contempt and an Oedipal desire to murder him; he loved the "real" father, resented the "metaphoric" one; Marxism offered him a rationale for both parricide and forgiveness. Obviously, the economic dislocations wrought by the Depression transformed Miller, opening him up to the arguments of a Marxist ideology that viewed as reactionary the reassuring sense of continuity which his traditional view of the father-son relationship offered. Inevitably, this made its mark on *All My Sons*. In it, an idealistic son—indeed, two such sons, one dead, one alive—destroy a father who represents the capitalist business ethic. But, as I will argue below, the final scene undercuts this apparent affirmation of the son's new authority through the doubt it casts on his behavior. The liberal critique of the father's behavior is sincerely felt, and consistent with the play's assault on other sources of authority in American capitalist society. But the traditionalist—and the loyal son—in Miller remain uncomfortable with the void left by the father's death, and the ruptured relationship that provoked it.

At stake for Miller is an issue that goes to the heart of *All My Sons*, and much of his drama. If the father-son connection so central to the faith of his own fathers can be sustained, it offers a transcendently sanctioned model of relatedness that sanctions human brotherhood as well. Raymond Williams once remarked about Miller's early tragedies, "in both father and son there are the roots of guilt, and yet, ultimately they stand together as men—the father both a model and rejected ideal; the son both an idea and a relative failure. But the model, the rejection, the idea and the failure are all terms of growth, and the balance that can be struck is a very deep understanding of relatedness and brotherhood" (Weales, 319). The father-son relationship obsesses Miller as traditionalist, because its loss threatens his sense of connection with all other men. His anxiety about that loss—the anxiety of the Jewish modernist, who perceives discontinuity and fragmentation in the wake of the Holocaust—also subverts the explicit, liberal affirmations of brotherhood by Chris Keller in *All My Sons*. Its troubling, abrupt ending fails to resolve the problems the play has posed; and we are left with a survivor incapable of asserting the authority required to restore the symbolic connection with other men he has broken.

Perhaps his experiences in childhood and youth exerted their subconscious pressure as Miller wrote *The Man Who Had All the Luck* in the early 1940's. That play's subplot concerned a father's desire to make his son into a perfect baseball player, and Miller recalled in his Introduction to the 1957 *Collected Plays* that "in writing of the father-son relationship and of the son's search for his relatedness there was a fullness of feeling I had never known before; a crescendo was struck with a force I could almost touch. The crux of *All My Sons* was formed. . . ." (*Theatre Essays*, 126). The relation-ship of Joe and Chris Keller is inseparable from the latter's search for relatedness in *All My Sons*. The son's quest for a transcendent sense of connection—for brotherhood—is generated by a desire to give meaning to his wartime experience; but this conflicts with the major source of authority in his life, a relationship with his father that the idealistic son ultimately sacrifices to that desire for meaning. In seeking to substitute the authority of brotherhood for that of the father-son relationship, he tragically exposes himself—as well as Miller—to the modern sense of discontinuity that potentially explodes meaning altogether.

The force exerted by the father-son relationship is only the dominant one in a field of forces, for a summary of the plot reveals Miller's modernist subversion of various forms of authority operating in bourgeois American life. Frank Lubey, a minor character, represents the most easily satirized one, astrology. Lubey is a neighbor of Joe Keller, a Midwest manufacturer of aircraft engines whose younger son, Larry, was a World War II pilot reported missing in action nearly three years before the play begins. Joe's wife Kate refuses to accept her son's death; Lubey flatters her delusion by maintaining that Larry couldn't have died on the day he was reported missing because it was a favorable day in his horoscope. By play's end, the son's death—by suicide—is revealed in a letter produced by Ann, his former fiancee, who has arrived to become engaged to the surviving son, Chris. Larry's letter thus explodes the easy target, astrology; but it also exposes Kate's more conventional faith in a God who "does not let a son be killed by his father" (Plays, I, 114), since the letter reveals that Joe's conviction for supplying aircraft defective engines (resulting In the death of 21 American pilots) prompted the Larry's suicide. In this overtly secular play, divine authority is apparently dismissed by revealing the self-delusion of the only two characters who profess belief in it. But, as we shall see, Kate's assertion and subsequent loss of faith in the sanctity of the father-son relationship has deeper implications, since it represents the battle being fought within the playwright's own imagination.[5]

The revelation of the son's death leads to that of the father, who has resisted admission of his guilt partly because of his adherence to another, strictly secular source of authority: the business ethic. Despite his previous exoneration on appeal after shifting the blame to his business partner—Ann's father Steve—Joe now perceives his responsibility for the deaths and shoots himself. He has been forced to this recognition by the idealistic Chris, who has read Larry's letter to Joe to make him quit hiding behind his rationalizations of his crime as everyday business. Earlier, Joe had claimed after admitting the crime to Chris, "I'm in business, a man is in business; a hundred and twenty [engines] cracked, you're out of business; . . . You lay forty years into a business and they knock you out in five minutes, what could I do, let them take forty years, let them take my life away?" (115) Later, he claims a broader sanction for his deed in its typicality: "Did they ship a gun or a truck outa Detroit before they got their price? Is that clean? It's dollars and cents, nickels and dimes; war and peace, it's nickels and dimes, what's clean? Half the Goddam country is gotta go if I go!" (125) Keller's morally specious defenses of manslaughter are unacceptable to both sons, and (presumably) to Miller's audience. A problem play, *All My Sons* indicts war profiteering and the capitalist ethos that justifies it. Miller's embodiment of that callous capitalist code in a father whom two sons help destroy recalls Miller's interpretation of Marxism in *Timebends*, cited above: "deep down in the comradely world of the Marxist promise is parricide." On the socio-economic level, Miller thus asserts the necessity for disputing and ultimately overthrowing the paternal authority of a man corrupted by a capitalistic system that privileges the profit motive over human life. As he remarked in the 1957 "Introduction"—in rhetoric with unmistakable Marxist echoes—the play attacks "the concept of a man's becoming a function of production or distribution to the point where his personality becomes divorced from the actions it propels" (131). The ending thus reasserts Joe's connection to the consequences of his crimes by breaking his connection to his sons.[6]

Despite his negative associations with capitalism, however, Joe Keller's authoritative presence compels respect, especially in his surviving son. Their relationship points to the strong patriarchal model of Miller's Jewish tradition, inspiring the admiration in a son required to maintain that tradition. The Joe/Chris relationship is the most intense in the play. Described by the stage directions as a man "capable of immense affection and loyalty" (64), Chris directs it primarily toward his father, whose business he will carry on despite his lack of interest in it (and despite his repressed suspicions about his father's crime). Ann comments to Chris, "you're the only one I know who loves his parents" (83), after a scene in which Chris typically responds *"with admiration"* to his father's recollection of his brazen walk past his neighbors upon his release from jail, "Joe McGuts." Joe replies "with great force," "That's the only way to lick 'em is guts!" (80–81). The remark is typical of a character described as *"a heavy man of stolid mind and build . . . with the imprint of the machine-shop worker and boss still upon him . . . A man among men."* (58–59, my ellipses) Joe's deep belief in the paternal authority which his build and behavior symbolize is especially apparent in his Act II remark to Chris and Ann after Joe has offered to reinstate Ann's father upon his release from jail. Bewildered by Chris's refusal and Ann's resistance—"I don't understand why she has to crucify the man"—Joe utters *"a commanding outburst:* a father is a father!" (97) The "commanding" outburst blends manner with substance in the play's strongest assertion of the deference due patriarchal authority.

In the final act, we discover guilt over his betrayal of his partner Steve as a hidden motive for Joe's offer; but the deference to fathers he demands is nonetheless sincere, an article of faith for Joe. The reasons for this go beyond the immediate dramatic context. One, as suggested above, is connected to Miller's Judaism. In the first act Joe Is troubled by Chris's lack of enthusiasm for taking over the family business, "because what the hell did I work for? [The business is] only for you, Chris, the whole shootin' match is for you!" (69) When his crime is exposed, Joe again presents the transmission of a legacy as the profoundest motive for his crime. "Chris, Chris, I did it for you, it was a chance and I took it for you," Joe cries. "For you, a business for you!" (115) By expecting Chris specifically to take over the family business, Joe symbolically expresses a Jewish cultural imperative: to perpetuate a tradition or value by passing it on to one's son. As Linzer notes about the traditional Jewish community,

> Authority is the central concern because only through the force
> of authority can important values be transmitted to children. . . .
> The Jewish legal system sought to create a framework for norma-
> tive family living wherein filial obedience to parents regardless of
> their age is unquestioned. . . . thus, *the continuity of the tradition*
> *would be ensured by imbuing in children respect for, and obedience to*
> *authority.* (96; my emphasis)

In this light, Chris's reluctance to assume his father's business is a threat not
just to Joe's authority, but to the transgenerational continuity of traditional
values. And if, as Linzer concludes, "the major priorities of Jewish families
In the course of Jewish history" are "the preservation and transmission of the
tradition" (98), Joe's vehemence has a hidden ethnic foundation. Though
the Kellers are not presented as a Jewish family, the business legacy Joe
defends corresponds to a secularized, economic (albeit corrupted) version of
the Jewish traditions that were part of Miller's background. By means of the
father-son relationship, Miller may be examining his own mixed feelings as a
culturally assimilated Jew toward the spiritual legacy of his forefathers.

But for Miller, an even deeper motive exists, a motive that surfaces in
Joe's words when he fears his son will report him to the police. "I'm his father
and he's my son. . . . Nothin's bigger than that," Joe cries. "I'm his father and
he's my son, and if there's something bigger than that I'll put a bullet in my
head!" (120) For the father, the relationship—not the father nor the son
individually, but their connection—possesses a transcendent authority which
demands the son's forgiveness of the father's crime. As a modern liberal,
Miller castigates this narrow, socially irresponsible attitude, and subjects it to
tragic irony: the older son Larry has died as a result of Joe's confused priorities that place family above society. But Joe's remark also articulates Miller's
traditionalist view of the father-son relationship as the familial version of
the principle of continuity, the connection of past to present. That principle
exercises great power over Miller's imagination, as the play's very structure
suggests. As is all too apparent, *All My Sons* is an Ibsenesque well-made play
in which characters from the past (Ann, her brother George) return to the
neighborhood to set in motion a plot which eventually exposes the hidden
truth about Joe's past criminal act—a plot that climaxes after the production of a three-year-old letter reveals the most devastating consequence of the
crime. As Robert Brustein has pointed out disparagingly, the old-fashioned
plot mechanisms resemble those of Newtonian physics (22), but they are
inseparable from Miller's intention (emphasized in the 1957 Introduction)
to make the play "an experience which widens [an audience's] awareness of
connection—the filaments to the past and the future which lie concealed in
life" (*Theatre Essays*, 128). The primary explicit connection Miller intends

to demonstrate may be that between private and public realms, family and society: the dead pilots are indeed all Joe's sons. But the connection between father and son penetrates deeper, since it relates to the very principle of causality—and to the inescapability of the past of history—which constitutes the play's profoundest (and most universal) level of meaning.

That principle of causality is linked to both father-son relationships. First, the past actions of the father have not only killed 21 pilots, but have caused the suicide of his son Larry. Second, the force of Joe's personality, and the sacredness of their relationship, have had a strong impact on the surviving son Chris, blinding him to his father's crime despite his suspicion of him. As he tells Joe at the end, "I never saw you as a man, I saw you as my father. I can't look at you this way, I can't look at myself!" (125) Chris's outburst reveals not just his reverence for their relationship, but even implies an absorption into that relationship (a symbiosis anticipating that of Biff and Willy in Miller's next play). Chris's idealistic condemnations of his father are apparent attempts to escape from that symbiosis—hence, to escape from the past—by ultimately substituting for his reverence toward the father a sense of obligation toward the brother. One connection replaces another. He comments on his fellow soldiers, "they killed themselves for each other," and tells Ann

> I got an idea watching them go down. Everything was being destroyed, see, but it seemed to me that one new thing was made. A kind of . . . responsibility. Man for man. You understand me?– To show that, to bring that on to the earth again like some kind of a monument and everyone would feel it standing there, behind him, and it would make a difference to him. And then I came home and it was Incredible. I . . . there was no meaning in it here; the whole thing to them was a kind of a—bus accident. (85)

Intriguingly, Miller offers Chris's value of brotherhood as the product of particular historical circumstances, rooted in his experience in World War II. However noble, it is presented as a relative value, as its disregard by the civilians at home helps underscore. For Chris, it nonetheless assumes absolute status, and his final accusation (directed at both parents) is grounded in the proclamation of both actual and metaphorical brotherhood: "Once and for all you can know there's a universe of people outside and you're responsible to it, and unless you know that, you threw away your son [Larry] because that's why he died" (126–27). The gunshot of Joe's suicide melodramatically replies, signaling his recognition of the betrayal of that obligation. Finally for Joe, as well as Chris and Larry, the dead pilots were (in Joe's final words before exiting) "all my sons. And I guess they were, I guess they were" (126).

The curtain falls within seconds of these pronouncements, with Kate comforting Chris after Joe's suicide by advising him "Don't take it on yourself. Forget now. Live" (127).

The abruptness of the ending, however, indicates Miller's discomfort with it, stemming from the non-resolution of his own inner conflict. As a liberal moralist, Miller wants to drive home the message that social obligations transcend individual familial ones, and metaphorically substitute the connection of brother to brother for the connection of father to son. (Appropriately, two brothers, both veterans, collude in unintentionally driving the father to suicide). But the suddenness of the ending implicitly recognizes the problem of setting brotherhood in opposition to fatherhood, rather than seeing them as connected (as Miller the traditionalist wishes them to be). As noted above, the play explicitly presents the value of brotherhood as one developed in history. In contrast, the father-son connection, a metaphor for the inseparability of past from present—the play's central theme, according to the playwright—seems to be history, the historical principle of continuity as well as causality, the ground for all which transpires. As a modernist, Miller attempts to substitute a value he has dramatized as relative (brotherhood) for a repudiated absolute (fatherhood) that originates in his traditional religious background: it is one of countless modern variations on Nietzsche's "killing" of God.[7] But as traditionalist, Miller resists the attempt. The asserted connection between brothers remains on the level of rhetoric—especially since Chris's actual brother Larry is already dead—while the connection between father and son remains implicit in the plot structure and deepest level of the play. How, then, can the former be affirmed, the latter "killed?" The quickness of the curtain indicates Miller's confusion in the face of this question, which points to the underlying question that troubles him. How can an ideal of connection between brothers be confidently asserted when the prior, transcendent model of connection (father and son), absorbed from his Judaism, has been repudiated: on what larger basis does the fraternal connection then rest?

That uncertainty is deepened by the inability of the surviving son— the spokesman for brotherhood—to reconstitute the authority he has overthrown. The neighbor Sue Bayless accuses Chris of "phony idealism," since he holds others (among them Sue's husband Jim) to demanding ideals while resisting his own suspicions about his father's guilt. Chris's words about Joe ironically apply to him: he has a "talent for ignoring things" (68). This flaw would seem to pale in comparison to Joe's more egregious (and murderous) deceptions. But in an illuminating article on the play, Barry Gross perceives instead a decline from father to son. To Gross, Chris lacks the dedication of the father who takes enormous (even criminal) risks to preserve a legacy for his son: a legacy whose tainted nature the son has winked at. Moreover, in contrast to Joe's willingness to kill himself out of his devotion to the father-son relationship ("If there's something bigger than that I'll put a bullet through my head"), Chris is a narcissist who can only love Joe if Joe is innocent, who deceives himself about his father's guilt because his self-image is still so bound up with his image of his father. Idealizing Joe, he idealizes himself, and "cannot look at his father as no better than most because he cannot look at himself as no better than most" (Martine, 13–14). Hence, Gross concludes (alluding to Miller's comment in my opening paragraph), Chris "has achieved neither mystery nor manhood by play's end," and authority has not been "reconstituted" in him (18). I essentially concur—and would add that Chris's final, revealing gesture is to retreat to his mother's arms just before the curtain. His childishness and ultimate passivity are also apparent in his rationalizations of his refusal to perceive his father's guilt, and his subsequent reluctance to turn him in: "I was made yellow in this house because I suspected my father and did nothing about it" (123); "I could jail him, if I were human anymore. But I'm like everybody else now. I'm practical now. You made me practical" (123); "This is the land of the great big dogs, you don't love a man here, you eat him . . . The world's that way, how can I take it out on him?" (124; my emphases). Seeing himself purely as victim of family and society, Chris is unable to assume responsibility for his actions—in marked contrast to Joe, who ultimately does precisely that.

Chris's inability to take responsibility renders him incapable of restoring authority, leaving a void where the father's power existed before. It also casts doubt on Chris's reliability as a spokesman for brotherhood, and (hence) on the Ideal itself.[8] Again, the shattering of father-son continuity makes us question the connection Miller explicitly espouses between brother and brother. Despite his intentions, the traditionalist in him will not permit him to divorce the two. But Miller as modernist betrays the anxiety of their attempted separation. In place of fatherhood and brotherhood, we are left with a discontinuity and fragmentation which implicitly subvert all assertions of moral obligation—i.e., all authority—by absorbing them into relativism. Kate Keller's desperate belief, grimly satirized by Miller earlier, needs to be recalled: "God does not let a son be killed by his father," nor (we might add) permit a father to be killed by his son. But these primal crimes are permitted, leaving uncertainty and ambivalence where continuity, connectedness and belief used to be.

Miller's ambivalence regarding authority and brotherhood, as has been suggested, scarcely ends with All My Sons. Death of a Salesman, though it solves the problem of the abrupt suicidal ending by adding the "requiem" of Willy's funeral, betrays a similar anxiety about killing the patriarch. Biff explicitly repudiates Willy, while Happy affirms his connection with him at the end. And significantly, their father's death frees the brothers to go their separate ways—suggesting much more explicitly that the severance of the father-son bond dissolves the basis for brotherhood as well, though (again) the connection of past to present In the play's structure dramatizes the impossibility of such a severance. *After the Fall* and *The Price* offer a pairing similar to *Sons* and *Salesman*. The former affirms brotherhood—though it is a communion of sinners, now, and women are included—in the face of the void following the collapse of authority; the latter uses an occasion prompted by the father's death years before to imply brotherhood's impossibility. The mixture of Miller's traditional Jewish background with his modernist and liberal beliefs thus creates continual, intriguing tensions within and between individual works throughout his career. And that tension helps account for the continuing power of Miller's drama. The father-son relationship as depicted by Miller dramatizes the longings for authority and connection to the past that, as spiritual beings, we all fed, but its rupture is a symbolic expression of the pervasive sense of betrayal and discontinuity which, as modem western citizens, we all experience.

Sources Cited

Bigsby, C.W.E. *A Critical Introduction to Twentieth Century American Drama, Vol. II: Miller, Williams, Albee.* London: Cambridge University Press, 1984.

Brustein, Robert. "Drama in The Age of Einstein." *New York Times,* 7 August 1977, II, 1, 22.

Cohen, Sarah B., ed. From *Hester Street to Hollywood: The Jewish-American Stage and Screen.* Bloomington: Indiana University Press, 1983.

Fergusson, Francis. *The Idea of a Theatre.* Princeton: Princeton University Press, 1983.

Freedman, Morris. American Drama in Social Context. Carbondale: Southern Illinois University Press, 1971.

Gross, Barry. "*All My Sons* and the Larger Context." *Modem Drama* 18 (March 1975), 15–27; rpt. in Martine, James, ed. *Critical Essays on Arthur Miller.* Boston: G.K. Hall, 1979.

Handlin, Oscar. *The Uprooted.* Second edition. Boston: Little Brown and Co., 1973.

Linzer, Norman. *The Jewish Family: Authority and Tradition in Modern Perspective.* New York: Human Sciences Press, 1984.

Loughlin, Richard. "Tradition and Tragedy in *All My Sons.*" *English Record,* 14, 3 (1964), 23–27.

Malin, Irving. *Jews and Americans.* Carbondale: Southern Illinois University Press, 1955.

Miller, Arthur. *Collected Plays.* New York: Viking, 1957.

____. *Conversations with Arthur Miller,* ed. Matthew Roudane. Jackson: University Press of Mississippi, 1987.

____. *I Don't Need You Anymore.* London: Seeker and Warburg, 1967.

____. *Timebends.* New York: Grove Press, 1987.

____. *The Theatre Essays of Arthur Miller,* ed. Robert A. Martin. New York: Penguin, 1978.

Reno, Raymond. "Arthur Miller and the Death of God." *Texas Studies in Literature and Language*, 11 (1969), 1069–87.

Sollors, Werner. *Beyond Ethnicity: Consent and Descent in American Culture*. New York: Oxford University Press, 1986.

Weales, Gerald, ed. *Death of a Salesman: Texts and Criticism*. New York: Viking, 1967.

Notes

1. *Conversations with Arthur Miller*, 89–90. For Miller's other comments in interviews on fathers and sons, see pp. 50, 54, 91–92, 188–89, 197, 311–12, 327–28.

2. See Malin, *Jews and Americans*, chap. 3.

3. See Freedman, "The Jewishness of Arthur Miller," in *American Drama in Social Context*, 43–58, and Brater, "Ethics and Ethnicity In the Plays of Arthur Miller," in *From Hester Street to Hollywood*, 123–34. Freedman, who emphasizes the "ethnic anonymity" of Miller's drama, claims that only one moment in *All My Sons* (when Kate Keller fawns over George like a Jewish mother) suggests the playwrights' Jewish origins. Brater argues that Miller deliberately avoided the ethnic route traveled by Odets, and instead explored universal ethical conflicts "more Judaic than Jewish" in *All My Sons* and subsequent plays. Neither critic discusses the Jewish aspects of the father-son conflict in the play; nor does Richard Loughlin's cursory treatment of the play's Biblical parallels, in "Tradition and Tragedy in *All My Sons*," mention this possibility.

4. Miller reveals his youthful desire to assimilate in *Timebends*: "if ever any Jews should have melted into the proverbial melting pot, it was our family in the twenties; indeed, I would soon be dreaming of entering West Point, and in my most private reveries I was no sallow Talmud reader but Frank Merriwell or Tom Swift, heroic models of athletic verve and military courage" (p. 62). For analysis of the phenomena of assimilation and the forces promoting it, see Oscar Handlin, The Uprooted, and Werner Sollors, Beyond Ethnicity. Consent and Descent in American Culture.

5. It is interesting to note in this regard Miller's account of the play's composition process in the Introduction to the *Collected Plays*. "In [the play's] earlier versions the mother, Kate Keller, was in a dominating position; more precisely, her astrological beliefs were given great prominence. (The play's original title was *The Sign of the Archer*.) And this, because I sought in every sphere to give body and life to connection. But as the play progressed the conflict between Joe and his son Chris pressed astrology to the wall until its mysticism gave way to psychology" (132). I would argue that Miller never fully rid the play of these religious overtones, but instead displaced them onto the father-son relationship—a more comfortable site (given Miller's patriarchal religion) for the mystique attached to connection in the play.

6. As liberal social critic, Miller underscores how widely accepted Joe's inhumane values are by rooting them in the Kellers' neighborhood. "Everyone knows Joe pulled a fast one to get out of jail," Sue Bayless tells Ann, "but they give him credit for being smart" (94); within two years of his release from jail, everyone has accepted him back into the community.

7. For an intriguing discussion of this in Miller's work from *All My Sons* through The Price, see Raymond Reno, "Arthur Miller and the Death of God."

8. Unquestionably, as various critics have observed, the influence of Ibsen's *The Wild Duck* is pronounced here, with Gregers Werle serving as model for a self-righteous, (unconsciously) hypocritical young idealist who makes life difficult for others. (For the most stimulating recent discussion of this, see Bigsby, 168–171.) But Ibsen's impact

reaches deeper than this. Not only does the abrupt, violent ending recall *Hedda Gabler* and *Ghosts*, but the implications of the latter's ending are similar to those of *All My Sons*. *Ghosts* ends with Mrs. Alving screaming as she is faced with the dilemma of whether to kill her own syphilitic son (the victim of her hypocrisy in remaining with her husband). As Francis Fergusson observes, Mrs. Alving thereby fails to attain a final tragic epiphany. Hence, the play's action is "neither completed nor placed in the wider context of meanings" that is found in classical tragedy, partly because Ibsen's romantic imagination did not fit comfortably into the form of the realistic problem play—where his desire to epater le bourgeois resulted in a shocking, unresolved conclusion that truncated the development of his protagonist (156–57). Miller's dilemma also consists in striving to place a wider (even absolutist) vision, the product of his Judaism, into the form of the realistic problem play. His desire to attack his society's inhumane business ethics similarly concludes in an abrupt, shocking finale which neither resolves the play's deeper conflicts, nor allows his protagonist, Chris, to develop.

VALERIE LOWE

'Unsafe convictions': 'unhappy' confessions in The Crucible

1 Introduction

Austin (1962: 6) argues that 'the issuing of the utterance is the perform-
ing of an action—it is not normally thought of as just saying something.'
In Arthur Miller's play, *The Crucible*, the characters are not 'just saying
something', their utterances perform actions which affect their whole lives.[1]
The tragedy of *The Crucible* exemplifies the problems which can arise when
Austin's rules for 'happy performatives' are not strictly adhered to.[2]

The play is set during the Salem witchcraft trials of the seventeenth
century, and characters in the unenviable position of being accused of witchcraft are faced with the choice of (i) 'confessing' to the charge (regardless of
whether or not the accusation is true) or (ii) denying it, in which case they will
be hanged. The 'evidence' of witchcraft is based on the 'confession' of a black
female slave, Tituba, but on close examination of her utterances it appears
that Tituba initially does not actually 'confess' to anything. She merely allows
herself to be implicated in witchcraft. She is a victim of the unequal power
relationships at work in Salem which render her unable to deny her guilt.
The white people who are accused can choose to deny the charge of witchcraft and at least keep their 'good names'. Rebecca Nurse, and (eventually)
John Proctor, for example, are characters who prefer to die rather than provide false confessions. Tituba's powerless position, however, means that she is

From *Languages and Literature*. © 1994 Lancaster University, UK.

unable to deny her guilt, since her denials are ignored and she is treated as if she had indeed confessed. I will attempt to explain the reasons why individual speech acts are perceived differently in the play according to who is speaking. I will argue that Tituba's 'confession' is void according to Austin's rules for 'happy performatives', and that the asymmetrical power relationships which exist in Salem am directly responsible for the (mis)interpretation of her utterances by her accusers.

2   Context of Tituba's 'confession'

Four young white girls, Abigail, Betty, Mercy and Mary have been caught dancing naked in the woods at night by Abigail's Uncle and Tituba's master, the Reverend Parris. Dancing or any form of entertainment is banned in Salem and is punished by whipping. However, the girls have also asked Tituba to 'conjure spirits', for which they can be accused of witchcraft. On being discovered, Betty takes fright and falls into an apparent coma from which she cannot be woken. Afraid that they will be condemned as 'witches', Abigail accuses Tituba claiming that she 'made them do it' (Act I, p. 45). However, the reader/audience has previously witnessed a conversation between Abigail, Mercy and Mary in which it is apparent that it is Abigail who instigates the 'witchcraft', asking Tituba for 'a charm to kill Goody Proctor', (Act I, p. 26) the wife of John Proctor with whom Abigail has had an affair. The Reverend Parris summons the Reverend Hale, an expert in 'witchcraft', who questions Abigail and Tituba, and elicits Tituba's 'confession'.

3   Text of the confession: Act I, pp. 45–8
(turns are numbered for ease of reference)

[*Mrs Putnam enters with Tituba, and instantly Abigail points at Tituba*]

1	Abigail	She made me do it! She made Betty do it!
2	Tituba	[*shocked and angry*] Abby!
3	Abigail	She makes me drink blood!
4	Parris	Blood!!
5	Mrs. Putnam	My baby's blood?
6	Tituba	No, no, chicken blood. I give she chicken blood!
7	Hale	Woman, have you enlisted these children for the Devil?
8	Tituba	No, no sir, I don't truck with no Devil!
9	Hale	Why can she not wake? Are you silencing this child?
10	Tituba	I love me Betty!
11	Hale	You have sent your spirit out upon this child, have you not? Are you gathering souls for the Devil?
12	Abigail	She sends her spirit on me in church; she makes me laugh at prayer!
13	Parris	She have often laughed at prayer!

14	*Abigail*	She comes to me every night to go and drink blood!
15	*Tituba*	You beg *me* to conjure! She beg *me* make charm –
16	*Abigail*	Don't lie! [*To Hale*] She comes to me while I sleep; she's always making me dream corruptions!
17	*Tituba*	Why you say that, Abby?
18	*Abigail*	Sometimes I wake and find myself standing in the open doorway and not a stitch on my body! I always hear her laughing in my steep. I hear her singing her Barbados songs and tempting me with –
19	*Tituba*	Mister Reverend, I never –
20	*Hale*	[*resolved now*] Tituba, I want you to wake this child.
21	*Tituba*	I have no power on this child, sir.
22	*Hale*	You most certainly do, and you will free her from it now! When did you compact with the Devil?
23	*Tituba*	I don't compact with no Devil!
24	*Parris*	You will confess yourself or I will take you out and whip you to your death, Tituba!
25	*Putnam*	This woman must be hanged! She must be taken out and hanged!
26	*Tituba*	[*terrified, falls to her knees*] No, no, don't hang Tituba! I tell him I don't desire to work for him, sir.
27	*Parris*	The Devil?
28	*Hale*	Then you saw him! [*Tituba weeps*] Now Tituba, I know that when we bind ourselves to Hell it is very hard to break with it. We are going to help you tear yourself free –
29	*Tituba*	[*frightened by the coming process*] Mister Reverend, I do believe somebody else be witchin' these children.
30	*Hale*	Who?
31	*Tituba*	I don't know, sir, but the Devil got him numerous witches.
32	*Hale*	Does he! [*It is a clue.*] Tituba, took into my eyes. Come, look into me. [*She raises her eyes to his fearfully*] You would be a good Christian woman, would you not, Tituba?
33	*Tituba*	Aye, sir, a good Christian woman.
34	*Hale*	And you love these little children?
35	*Tituba*	Oh, yes, sir, I don't desire to hurt little children.
36	*Hale*	And you love God, Tituba?
37	*Tituba*	I love God with all my bein'.
38	*Hale*	Now in God's holy name –

39	*Tituba*	Bless him. Bless Him. [*She is rocking on her knees, sobbing in terror*]
40	*Hale*	And to His glory –
41	*Tituba*	Eternal glory. Bless Him – bless God . . .
42	*Hale*	Open yourself, Tituba – open yourself and let God's holy light shine on you.
43	*Tituba*	Oh, bless the Lord.
44	*Hale*	When the Devil comes to you does he ever come – with another person? [*She stares up into his face*] Perhaps another person in the village? Someone you know.
45	*Parris*	Who came with him?
46	*Putnam*	Sarah Good? Did you ever see Sarah Good with him? Or Osburn?
47	*Parris*	Was it man or woman came with him?
48	*Tituba*	Man or woman. Was – was woman.
49	*Parris*	What woman? A woman, you said. What woman?
50	*Tituba*	It was black dark, and I –
51	*Parris*	You could see him, why could you not see her?
52	*Tituba*	Well they was always talking; they was always runnin' round and carryin' on –
53	*Parris*	You mean out of Salem? Salem witches?
54	*Tituba*	I believe so, yes, sir. [*Now Hale takes her hand. She is surprised*]
55	*Hale*	Tituba. You must have no fear to tell us who they are, do you understand? We will protect you. The Devil can never overcome a minister. You know that, do you not?
56	*Tituba*	[*kisses Hale's hand*] Aye, Sir, Oh, I do.
57	*Hale*	You have confessed yourself to witchcraft and that speaks a wish to come to Heaven's side. And we will bless you, Tituba.
58	*Tituba*	[*deeply relieved*] Oh, God bless you, Mr Hale.

4   Speech act theory

4.1   Illocutionary force and perlocutionary effects

Speech act theory can help to explain the feeling of unease which the reader/audience experiences at Hale's declaration 'You have confessed yourself to witchcraft . . .' (turn 57). The strength of speech act theory lies in its ability to explain the way people can 'do things with words', to generate meanings which may not be literally contained in the words produced. Yet one of the problems associated with the theory is the unpredictability of the effects of utterances on interlocutors. What a person intends to 'do with words' may not be what the words actually 'do'. Austin distinguishes among:

LOCUTIONARY act   =   meaning
ILLOCUTIONARY act   =   force
PERLOCUTIONARY act =   achievement of certain effects
                                              (Austin, 1962: 120)

Speech acts can achieve results quite different from those intended, a feature which is explored by Austin in his discussion of illocutionary force and per-locutionary effects. In this respect, Austin's position differs in emphasis from that of Searle, since Austin argues that the illocutionary force of an utterance is produced by the speaker, whereas Searle suggests that it is a product of the listener. This is a problem for conversationalists, since there is always a potential gap between the speaker's intended meaning, and the interpretation of the utterance by the hearer. Both aspects are important in an analysis of *The Crucible*, since in Salem those speakers whose 'intention' is to deny their guilt have their denial 'interpreted' by their accusers as evidence of their guilt. Rebecca Nurse is one such character whose refusal to 'damn' herself is seen as evidence of her part in 'the conspiracy' (Act IV, p. 121).

In Tituba's case the situation is further complicated since her presumed intention, to deny her guilt, is unrecognised, due to her accusers' interpreta-tion of her utterance as a 'confession'. There is therefore differential treat-ment of denials according to social status. The white characters' denials are accepted, and taken as evidence of their involvement in witchcraft. Tituba's denials are not even recognised as such, but are interpreted by her accusers as a 'confession'. The white characters realise their conversational intentions in a way in which Tituba is unable to do.

The play can be seen therefore as exemplifying the potential gap between the effective realisation of a speaker's intention and the actual consequences of his/her speech acts, and shows the multiplicity and uncontrollability of perlocutionary effects associated with utterances. For example, Tituba's 'con-fession' leads to a promise of salvation for Tituba, as Hale promises that she will be 'blessed' for having confessed (turn 57). This has the perlocutionary effect of encouraging Abigail and Betty to 'confess' in order to receive similar treatment (Act I, p. 49). In addition, the white people of Salem find that a confession has the illocutionary force of an admission of guilt, and several perlocutionary effects. In addition to being imprisoned and losing their 'good name', characters have land confiscated for being 'unchristian', which has the perlocutionary effect of encouraging unscrupulous characters to accuse their neighbours of witchcraft in order to obtain their land. This has a further consequence in that some characters refuse to answer the charge so that their land may not be taken away. Giles Corey is one character who may have confessed but for this perlocutionary complication, since his main reason for *not* confessing is in order to retain his land for his sons (Act IV, p. 118).

In Austin's terms, those characters who lie produce confessions that are 'void', since they fail to fulfil the conditions for 'happy performatives'. One of these conditions is that 'a person participating in and so invoking the procedure must in fact have those thoughts and feelings . . .' (Austin 1962: 15). Characters in *The Crucible* who go through the procedure of 'confessing' without having the requisite thoughts and feelings (i.e. believing that they are guilty) produce insincere 'confessions' which constitute an 'abuse of the procedure'. Austin excludes those performatives which are 'done under duress . . .', claiming that these are 'unhappy' and 'come under the heading of "extenuating circumstances" or of "factors reducing the agent's responsibility" . . .' (1962: 21). It is exactly those performatives which Austin excludes which are so important for the plot of Miller's play: it is the 'unhappiness' of the confessions elicited under 'duress' which provides the basis for the tragedy of Salem.

4.2   *Perlocutionary objects and sequels*

The notion of locutionary, illocutionary and perlocutionary acts is therefore particularly effective in describing the plot of *The Crucible*. An accusation has an intended perlocutionary force of 'persuading' a guilty person to 'confess', but also has other unforeseen perlocutionary consequences. Austin argues that a 'perlocutionary act may be either the achievement of a perlocutionary object . . . or the production of a perlocutionary sequel' (1962: 118). The 'object' is that which is intended by the speaker, whereas the 'sequel' is an unforeseen or unintentional result arising, for example, from the hearer's (mis)interpretation of the speaker's meaning. In Miller's play, the perlocutionary object is achieved if characters confess while believing themselves to be guilty. However the persuasion of characters to 'confess' who believe themselves to be innocent is an unintended perlocutionary sequel. The accusations do not always 'happily' realise an admission of guilt since at least some of the confessions are based on a lie. The 'confessions' of Abigail and Betty (Act I, p. 49) may be seen as falling into this category, as they are based on the 'evidence' that they are able to name those that they have seen 'with the Devil', something which Betty later admits is not true (Act III, p. 92).

The illocutionary act of 'accusing' therefore also carries the perlocutionary force of a 'threat', namely that those who deny the accusation will hang. This is due to the characters' background knowledge of what happens to those who do not confess, which forms the precondition for some of the false confessions. They know that 'Goody Osburn – will hang . . . but not Sarah Good. For Sarah Good confessed' (Act II, p. 56). Since the only possible 'happy' outcome of an accusation as far as the accusers are concerned is a confession, there arises a paradox whereby the characters who 'confess' are those who lie, and those who tell the truth are hanged. The speakers' (i.e. accusers') intention is to elicit the truth, yet the actual consequence is to receive a lie. The speech acts and their intended/unintended effects may be shown as follows (see Table 1).

An accusation is intended to elicit a true confession from the accused, the production of which is seen in this play as evidence that the woman concerned has renounced witchcraft. As a consequence, her life is spared and the character can be deemed to have been *persuaded* to confess. In this instance, the accuser has achieved his perlocutionary object. However, the fact of an accusation, combined with the characters' background knowledge that others have been

TABLE 1: INTENDED OBJECTS AND UNINTENDED SEQUELS

Illocution	Perlocution	Intended object	Unintended sequel	Result
Accusation	Persuasion	(True) Confession		Life
Accusation	Threat		(False) Confession	Life
Accusation	Threat		Denial	Death

hanged for denying similar charges, carries the force of a *threat*, and may give rise to a false 'confession', an unintended perlocutionary sequel. In both cases, the 'confessor' is saved, since the accusers have no way of knowing whether a 'confession' is false or true. Unfortunately this is also true in the case of a denial, since the accusers cannot assume that someone who denies the charge is telling the truth. A denial is therefore an unintended perlocutionary sequel providing 'evidence' of witchcraft and resulting in death for the accused.

The speech acts of 'confession' or 'denial' in the extract are chosen according to which a character accused of witchcraft values most; her life or her 'good name', and in this way, characters are judged according to whether they choose to lie in order to save their lives, or prefer to die rather than have their name associated with witchcraft. This separation into 'good' and 'bad' characters may usefully be discussed in relation to Grice's conversational maxims and the notion of conversational implicature.

5   The Co-operative principle and conversational implicature

Grice's Co-operative Principle and its maxims of Quality, Quantity, Relation and Manner are probably too familiar to need much discussion here. However, the Maxim of Quality is a particularly useful way of distinguishing the 'good' from the 'bad' characters in *The Crucible*. Grice argues that in most 'normal' conversations participants co-operate by refraining from saying that which is 'false' or for which they 'lack adequate evidence' (Grice 1975: 46).

The reader/audience is able to judge the characters in the play according to their orientation to this maxim. The intention behind the accusations is to elicit confessions of guilt and thereby rid the community of 'witchcraft', but the actual consequence of the accusations is to rid the community of the 'good' characters, such as Rebecca Nurse, for whom death is preferable to the 'damnation' which is seen as the consequence of lying (Act IV, p. 121).

The kinds of speech acts employed by the characters are therefore indications of their personalities. However, the reader/audience's judgement of the characters as 'good' or 'bad' is different from that of the characters themselves. Short's discussion of the different levels of discourse can help to explain the way in which the conversational implicatures which pass between the characters are different from those which pass from playwright to reader/audience. Short argues that 'character speaks to character, and this discourse is part of what the playwright 'tells' the audience' (Short 1989: 149). The play is an act of communication between playwright and the reader/audience on one level, within which is embedded the level of discourse between the characters. By allowing access to the conversation between Abigail, Mercy and Mary in which the girls discuss what really happened in the woods, Miller places the reader/audience in the privileged position of knowing that Abigail is lying to her accusers, and that therefore she should be judged negatively as one of the 'bad' characters. The reader/audience has 'overheard' the previous conversation in which Betty states 'You drank blood, Abby . . . You drank a charm to kill John Proctor's wife . . .' (Act I, p. 26) and has access to information that is denied to the other characters. Therefore when Abigail claims that Tituba 'makes' her 'drink blood' (turn 3), Miller is telling us something about Abigail's personality, since we know that she is not telling the truth. In Gricean terms, Miller aims at a 'maximally effective exchange of information' between himself and his reader/audience. Abigail's accusers, by contrast, have no reason to believe that she is not telling the truth and their judgement of her is the reverse. The reader/audience's superior knowledge of the truth of events lends poignancy to the accusers' apparent inability to distinguish the good characters from the bad. One such example is Elizabeth Proctor who 'in her life' has 'never lied' (Act III, p. 99), but finds herself forced into breaking the maxim of Quality in an attempt to defend her husband of the charge of lechery (Act III, p. 100). Finding that truthfulness does not bring its own reward in Salem, the good characters must decide whether or not to remain truthful, or to try to save themselves by lying. In this way, the final judgement of John Proctor as 'good' or 'bad' is delayed, as the reader/audience has witnessed his discussion with Elizabeth and knows that he does not believe himself to be guilty of witchcraft, (Act IV, p. 118) but must wait until the end of the play to see whether he will choose to lie or be hanged.

The implicatures generated by the characters' utterances are therefore different for the reader/audience than for the other characters, due to the former's knowledge of the truth or falsity of their utterances. The accusers can never know for certain whether or not a character is telling the truth, leading to a situation where a denial of guilt is interpreted by them as evidence of being 'bewitched' and a confession of guilt is seen as a desire to be saved. This forms the basis of the tragedy in Salem. John Proctor's ultimate decision to refuse to 'confess' places him at last on the side of the good characters but results in his death. The unintentional perlocutionary effect of the accusations is to rid Salem of the good characters and leave the liars behind.

6   Power relationships

6.1   Duress

In Tituba's case, her denials of witchcraft are overruled by her accusers' interpretation of her utterances as constituting a 'confession'. Further, her 'confession' provides the catalyst for all the others even though it does not, in fact, constitute a confession at all. Even had Tituba actually admitted her guilt in words and said 'I confess' (which she does not) the 'extenuating circumstances' would have rendered her 'confession' 'void' according to Austin's criteria, since it is extorted under duress. Her 'confession' fails to comply with the constitutive rules which are later strictly adhered to, for example, in the case of John Proctor (Act IV, p. 123).

In order to fully appreciate the amount of duress to which Tituba is subjected it is useful to interpret the characters' speech acts together with the additional information supplied by the stage directions, the background information supplied by the playwright, The stage directions provide the context against which the reader/audience can decide whether or not the characters' utterances can be taken at face value. Although it is through the dialogue that the characters condemn or redeem themselves, account must also be taken of the factors which reinforce the 'duress' which constitutes the 'infelicitous' conditions for the speech acts. Austin argues that in order to show how speech acts can 'go wrong', 'we must consider the total situation in which the utterance is issued – the total speech act . . .' (1962: 52). The speech acts in *The Crucible* do in fact 'go wrong', and this is a result of the 'total speech situation'. Although the reader/audience can recognise the 'confessions' as 'void', the accusers accept the speech acts as valid and act on them accordingly. Although all of the 'confessors' are subject to duress, the pressure on Tituba to confess is reinforced as a result of Salem's unequal social relationships.

Since the reader/audience has no access to the characters' thoughts, these must be inferred from a combination of their speech acts and the paralinguistic and contextual information provided by the playwright *via* stage directions. Writing about the gestures and movements of actors during the performance of a play, Elam suggests that 'one of the characteristics of the parakinesic signal is that it cross references . . . the linguistic message emitted or received' (1980: 72). The same may be said of the implied parakinesic signals provided by the stage directions which the reader reproduces mentally. Elam argues that 'such features supply essential information regarding the speaker's state, intentions and attitudes, serving . . . to disambiguate the speech act . . .' (1980: 79). The stage directions provide information about physical posture, gestures, spatial orientation etc. which allows the reader/audience to judge the amount of duress to which Tituba is subjected. From her first introduction it is apparent that Tituba is physically intimidated by Parris, her white 'master'. She enters to enquire after the health of Betty, but is 'already taking a step backwards' and 'backing to the door' as Parris ushers her out of the room in a fury and 'She is gone' (Act I, p. 17). From the very beginning, then, Tituba is shown as an intruder into the space of the white people, and Parris has the power to exclude her from Betty's presence. This, combined with our knowledge of her skin colour and the portrayal of her speech as non-standard, is information which helps us to 'disambiguate' her speech acts and assess their (mis)interpretation by those of 'superior' status. Miller makes Tituba's subordination explicit for the reader, telling us that she is 'very frightened because . . . trouble in this house eventually lands on her back' (Act I, p. 17). The stage directions support the preferred reading of the characters' speech acts, allowing the reader/audience to draw conclusions about the conditions for the act of confession.

In addition, the beliefs of the characters and those of the reader/audience may be the reverse of one another. Unlike the reader/audience, who knows that Abigail is lying, the characters are predisposed to believe Abigail, given the fact that she is white and the minister's niece. Similarly, Tituba's denials are treated with suspicion, since she is a black female slave and therefore 'inferior' in their eyes. The unequal distribution of power in Salem is reinforced by the ability of the white people to impose their beliefs on Tituba. Partly this may be explained by the presuppositions held by the characters, and the way in which Tituba's beliefs and those of the white people are similar in some ways but different in others.

6.2   Presupposition

Short argues that 'presuppositions often form part of the preconditions for the felicitous production of speech acts' (Short 1989: 145). In his discussion, Short describes the way that presuppositions can be separated into three types, existential', 'linguistic' and 'pragmatic'. 'Existential presuppositions' concern the 'truth' value of a statement. 'A statement such as 'The King of France is wise' is based on the presupposition that the King of France exists (Levinson, 1983: 170). Historically, the debate centred around the issue of whether the statement is false because it fails to refer (Frege) or because it is based on a false presupposition (Strawson). 'Linguistic presupposition' refers to the 'clauses or phrases embedded inside sentences . . .' (Short 1989: 147). For example, the assertion, 'the man that I met yesterday is ill', contains the linguistic presupposition 'I met a man yesterday'. 'Pragmatic presupposition' 'relates to the immediate context and immediate social relations'. For example, the master/servant relationship between Tituba and Parris is established immediately at the beginning of Miller's play, as Parris is able to order Tituba 'Out of here . . . Out of my sight!' (Act I, p. 17). This presupposes his ability to command her, a presupposition which is confirmed as Tituba leaves the stage.

Belief in the fictional world of Salem relies on the reader/audience's acceptance of the presuppositions held by the characters, even though they are not necessarily shared by us. The use of 'linguistic presuppositions' helps to establish that world. For example, when Tituba states 'the Devil got him numerous witches' (Act I, p. 47), we can distinguish between what the sentence asserts, 'The Devil has numerous witches working for him' and what it presupposes, i.e the *existence* of the devil and witches. The presuppositions help to establish Salem as a place where witchcraft and the devil are accepted as inevitable facts of life. For most people today this presupposition is false, but not for the characters in *The Crucible*, who may choose to reject or embrace witchcraft, but not to doubt its existence.

Although Tituba and the white characters share a belief in the existence of witchcraft, their beliefs differ in other respects. The unequal social relationships in Salem mean that Tituba is powerless to deny that she has power. The paradox whereby the most powerless person in the play is seen to be the most powerful is achieved through a (partial) 'clash of presuppositions' (Short, 1989: 147) on two levels: (i) between what the people of Salem apparently believe and what a contemporary reader/viewer is likely to believe, and (ii) between what the people of Salem perceive as appropriate behaviour and Tituba's different perceptions. There is a clash of beliefs between the reader/audience interpretation of Tituba's and Abigail's utterances which is the reverse of those of the characters. The reader/audience believes that Tituba is telling the truth and that it is Abigail who is the most powerful person in the play. The characters believe that Tituba is the most powerful, due to her association with the devil. In addition, Tituba herself appears to have internalised the beliefs of her white 'superiors' which explains why the clash is only partial. Her love of singing and dancing is seen as evidence of her wickedness, according to Salem's beliefs, and her minority status forces her to accept their judgement. (In fact, Tituba's belief in the 'goodness' of white people has faltered by the end of the play. Not surprisingly, she comes to believe that it is preferable to belong to the devil

(Act IV, p. 108). However, Tituba's possible confusion over whether or not she is 'guilty', (depending on whose beliefs she adheres to) is probably irrelevant to the discussion of whether or not she 'confesses'. Tituba's love of singing and dancing is incompatible with Salem's perception of 'goodness', which predisposes them to believe her to be in association with the devil. In addition, their perception of their own 'moral superiority' leads them to believe Abigail's accusations rather than Tituba's denials (see Table 2 below).

The clash between Tituba's and Salem's beliefs about the status of singing and dancing means that Tituba cannot believe that she is 'good' while she indulges in these forms of entertainment. The perception of Tituba as 'wicked' therefore arises partly due to her participation in activities which Salem believes to be 'bad', and which she uses to 'tempt' Abigail (Act I, p. 46). Abigail's 'goodness' as a white person is taken for granted, and any misbehaviour is attributed to Tituba's power over her. Given Tituba's internalisation of the belief in white people as 'good', Tituba is forced to re-align herself on the side of the devil and 'badness' (see Table 3 below).

TABLE 2: CLASH OF BELIEFS (PRE-'CONFESSION')

Tituba's Beliefs	Clashes	Salem's beliefs
Good		*Bad*
Singing	clash	Singing
Dancing	clash	Dancing
Tituba	clash	Tituba
God		The Devil
White People		Witches
Bad		*Good*
The Devil		God
Witches		White People

TABLE 3: BELIEFS POST-'CONFESSION'

Tituba's Beliefs	Salem's Beliefs
Good	*Good*
God	God
White People	White People
Bad	*Bad*
Singing	Singing
Dancing	Dancing
Tituba	Tituba
The Devil	The Devil
Witches	Witches

Since white people and God are on the same side, Tituba must accept the white perception of herself as 'wicked', due to the incompatibility of her beliefs with Salem's. Tituba's inability to realise her conversational intentions is therefore part of a larger problem, namely that she is seen by the people of Salem as 'inferior' and potentially wicked. It is this erroneous belief in the morality and truthfulness of white people in general, and Abigail in particular, which forms the preconditions for Tituba's confession. In particular, the perception of their own superiority gives the white people an advantage in conversational terms which renders Tituba powerless to deny the charges. Her white accusers' certainty that she is wicked leads them to believe that her 'real' intention must be to confess. In the face of this certainty, Tituba's presumed intention to deny the charge is irrelevant.

7   Analysis

A detailed analysis of the text (see section 3) can show how all the factors discussed so far produce the conditions for Tituba's 'confession'. At the beginning of the text, stage directions tell us that 'Mrs Putnam enters with Tituba, and instantly Abigail points at Tituba'. The pointing finger would probably be accompanied by an emphasis on 'made' and 'Betty' in Abigail's accusation; 'She made me do it! She made Betty do it!' (turn 1). The emphasis on these words is an attempt by Abigail to indicate her powerlessness and therefore her lack of responsibility for her actions. The exclamation marks provide paralinguistic information indicating emotion, suggesting a widened pitch span (Brown 1977: 133) and suggests that Abigail intends to convey an impression that the accusation is forced out of her. She is already under suspicion and her best option seems to be to confess her guilt, while simultaneously denying responsibility for her actions. Abigail is able to instill the belief in her accusers that she is powerless under Tituba's control, and the questioning of Tituba which follows accepts this situation as a fact, showing that Abigail has successfully manipulated her accusers into a belief that Tituba is to blame for Abigail's actions. In this situation, both Tituba and Abigail are powerless in relation to their accusers, but Abigail is more powerful than Tituba. The asymmetrical power relationship between them is reinforced by the belief of the people of Salem that a white woman is more likely to tell the truth than a black woman. In addition, the white male accusers' perception of the differences between white and black women aid Abigail in her attempt to convince them that she is a victim of Tituba's power, since Abigail and her friends are consistently referred to as 'children' (turns 7, 9, 11, 20, 34) whereas Tituba is seen as a 'woman' (turns 7, 25, 32). This is probably a factor which helps Abigail in her defence since 'childishness' and innocence are assumed to be related.

Tituba's reaction to Abigail's accusation is disbelief, as indicated by the stage directions; she is 'shocked and angry' (turn 2) and her vocative 'Abby!' followed by the exclamation mark indicates this emotion. The diminutive 'Abby' as opposed to 'Abigail' suggests that Tituba assumes a fairly intimate relationship between herself and Abigail (Betty addresses Abigail in the same way). It would be expected that a black female slave would use a more polite term to refer to someone who is her 'superior' although it could be interpreted by the characters as evidence of her power over Abigail. The inference to the reader/audience is that Tituba sees Abigail as a 'friend' and part of her anger and shock arises because she feels herself betrayed by Abigail's accusation. Abigail's pointing finger and the 'she' with which she addresses Tituba reinforce the impression that she is prepared to sacrifice Tituba to save herself, and the effect is to suggest distance between them. Referring to her as 'Tituba' without pointing would have had a much less forceful effect.

Abigail's accusation 'She makes me drink blood!' (turn 3) seems to be an attempt to shock her accusers into a belief in Tituba's power over her. The implication is that since drinking blood is not a normal, nor presumably a pleasant, activity, then Abigail would not do this willingly. The word 'blood' is repeated by Parris (turn 4) possibly because Abigail's accusation is too horrific for Parris to believe. The impression given is that he believes Abigail's accusation, as his horror, indicated by the exclamation marks, can be seen to stem from this very belief.

For Mrs Putnam, Abigail's accusation is proof of Tituba's involvement in witchcraft. Her question 'My baby's blood?' (turn 5) indicates her preoccupation with the untimely death of her children, and her belief that the cause is witchcraft. It also suggests that Mrs Putnam believes Abigail's accusation: the implication is that Tituba is in some way responsible for the death of her children, as Mrs Putnam apparently feels it quite possible for Tituba to be able to obtain her baby's blood. Presumably her question is directed at Abigail, but it is Tituba who responds (turn 6). It could be speculated that Abigail purposely does not answer in order to give the impression that she does not want to say 'that which is false'. If she wishes to appear to be an innocent victim of Tituba's power, she must implicate an inability to specify where Tituba obtained the blood.

Tituba attempts to avoid being further implicated in witchcraft by 'self-selecting' but she unwittingly supplies further 'ammunition' for the Reverend Hale. Coulthard (1977: 60–1) quotes the work done by Sacks, Schegloff and Jefferson on speaker 'turns' in conversation, and the way that self-selection occurs when a speaker decides to 'continue the conversation by selecting himself'. Tituba's use of self-selection is an attempt to defend herself. When used by Abigail, self-selection appears to be used deliberately in order to deny Tituba the opportunity of protesting her innocence, and Tituba is denied many turns to speak in this way. Tituba's admission that she gives Abigail chicken blood to drink may be intended as a denial of involvement in witchcraft, yet the unintended perlocutionary sequel of her utterance is to strengthen the evidence against her. Her utterance 'I give she chicken blood' (turn 6) need not entail her having power over Abigail, since she may give Abigail blood at Abigail's request, or as the result of an order from Abigail. In fact the reader/audience knows that Abigail asks Tituba for the blood ('a charm to kill Goody Proctor') but Tituba's utterance is 'underinformative' for the accusers. The effect of her denial has perlocutionary repercussions, since she fails to provide the reason for her actions. This is presupposed by Hale in his next question, 'Have you enlisted these children for the Devil?' (turn 7).

Hale refers to Tituba as 'Woman' (turn 7) indicating that he does not feel obliged to show her any respect. This may be partly due to her 'inferior' status, (the asymmetrical relationships are marked by the forms of address used by the characters) but it could be predicted that he would refer to any woman he suspected of witchcraft in a similar way. His question 'Have you enlisted these children for the Devil?' suggests that he has already found her guilty. This is partly conveyed by the word 'enlisted', since this presupposes that only someone who is already part of the devil's 'army' could recruit new members. The question from Hale (turn 7) is followed by two others which presuppose Tituba's power over Betty (turn 9), a fact which Tituba denies. Tituba's response 'I love me Betty' (turn 10) is 'relevant', implicating that she would not hurt anyone she loves. However Hale appears to interpret this as avoiding the question, since Tituba's most appropriate response would again be to deny the charge. Since people co-operate by giving the optimum amount of available information, Tituba could be assumed to be responding evasively, and this would implicate that she is unable to deny her guilt.

Hale changes tactics by using an assertion; 'You have sent your spirit out upon this child' followed by a tag question 'have you not?' (turn 11). Fowler (1986: 115) argues that the tag questions can be '. . . very demanding, pointedly requesting confirmation of an assertion made in the main part of the utterance'. In this instance the tag serves the purpose of reinforcing the truth of Hale's assertion, i.e. it challenges Tituba to deny it. Without giving her the chance to respond he produces another question: 'Are you gathering souls for the Devil?' (turn 11). Tituba is unable to answer as Abigail self-selects, denying Tituba a turn to speak (turn 12). Abigail picks up on Hale's first assertion and uses it as an excuse for her own 'bad' behaviour, thereby reinforcing the impression of Tituba's power over her and strengthening the case against her. Abigail supports Hale's accusation by providing further evidence of Tituba's power, 'She sends her spirit on me in church: she makes me laugh at prayer' (turn 12). This 'supporting move' is itself followed by a supporting move by Parris (turn 13) 'She have often laughed at prayer'. The function of 'supporting moves' as defined by Burton (1980: 150) is '. . . to facilitate the topic presented in a previous utterance, or to facilitate the contribution of a topic implied in a previous utterance.' The white characters frequently support one another's conversational contributions through the use of supporting moves. In itself Parris's statement 'She have often laughed at prayer' could be used against Abigail as confirmation of her own 'witchcraft'. However, following on as it does Abigail's accusation against Tituba, Parris' statement supports Abigail's 'evidence' and is seen as confirmation of Tituba's power over her.

Abigail's accusation 'She comes to me every night to go and drink blood' (turn 14) is a lie, since the reader/audience knows from her previous conversation with her friends that it is Abigail who has asked Tituba to make a 'charm to kill Goody Proctor'. This is, in Labov's terms, an 'AB event' known to both Abigail and Tituba, (and to the reader/audience) but not to the other characters present. In his discussion to Labov's work Coulthard claims that 'one can distinguish "A events", things that A alone knows about, "B events", things that B alone knows about, and "AB events", things that are known to both' (1977: 61). Both Abigail and Tituba know the truth about what happened in the woods and this is therefore an 'AB event'. When questioned about the events, Abigail lies, and it is her word against Tituba's. However the truth is known also to Betty and to the reader/audience. One could almost name this an 'AB, (CD) event', reflecting the secondary layer represented by these unacknowledged participants.

Tituba first addresses Abigail, disputing the truth of her accusation, 'You beg *me* to conjure!' (turn 15) before presumably turning to face Hale and addressing him, 'She beg me make charm'. It is evident from the repetition of the statement that Abigail will not accept Tituba's denial and that therefore Tituba must try to make Hale believe her. Although the stage directions do not give any information on this point, the reader infers that Abigail must provide some sort of non-verbal information which allows Tituba to realise that appeals to her are useless. The use of italics indicates that the stress is on the word 'me', suggesting that Tituba wishes to emphasise that it is Abigail who has power over Tituba, not the reverse. It appears from the use of the dash which 'ends' Tituba's denial that she is interrupted by Abigail's accusation, 'Don't lie!' (turn 16). This suggests to the other characters that Abigail knows that Tttuba's utterances are false, as the co-operative principle suggests that you cannot accuse someone of lying if you know that their utterances are true, which presumably persuades the others to believe Abigail. The reader/audience however knows that it is Abigail who is lying, but it is her audacity in violating the co-operative principle which confirms her power. Tituba, by contrast, merely implicates that Abigail is lying though her denials. By accusing Tituba of lying, Abigail makes her own accusations seem more believable. Possibly, Abigail faces Tituba when she accuses her of lying, and turns to face Hale when she makes her further accusations, thereby symbolising the way she has 'turned her back' on Tituba.

Abigail continues to build up the evidence against Tituba, causing Tituba to question the reason for this (turn 17). Her question, 'Why you say that . . . ?' implicates that Abigail's accusations are not true, since it is not normally necessary to justify oneself for telling the truth. The question suggests that Tituba knows that Abigail is lying for a reason. Abigail does not answer Tituba, and she and Hale appear to talk 'over her head', much as adults do in the presence of children. (The questioning from Hale is also suggestive of the kind of language employed by adults to children. His questions seem to be 'known-answer questions', inferring that he only asks them to have them confirmed.) Abigail is allowed a long 'turn' (turn 18) where she elaborates on the case against Tituba. These statements could be true, and could again be taken as an admission of her guilt, yet she suggests a powerlessness in such phrases as 'I find myself', claiming that Tituba is 'bewitching her'. Her accusation 'tempting me' reinforces the impression that she is a passive victim of Tituba's power. Tituba attempts to interrupt with a denial, directed at Hale since Abigail is relentless in her accusations, 'Mister Reverend I never . . .' (turn 19). She is herself interrupted by Hale who is now 'resolved' about Tituba's guilt (turn 20). His commands to Tituba indicate his belief in her power over the girls, since, despite the fact that Tituba denies his accusations (turn 21), Hale is 'certain' as indicated by his question, 'When did you compact with the Devil?' (turn 22). The presupposition (You did compact with the Devil) is difficult for Tituba to deny, and the chain of inferences built up over the previous lines has led to a certainty of Tituba's guilt which allows Parris and Putnam to feel justified in threatening her if she does not confess:

> You will confess yourself or I will take you out and whip you to your death . . . (turn 24)

> This woman must be hanged . . . (turn 25)

Tituba's response, 'I tell him I don't desire to work for him, sir' (turn 26) is ambiguous, since the accusers are not told who 'he' is (one could speculate that it could even refer to Parris). However they infer that she means the devil (turn 27), and conclude that she 'saw him' (turn 28). Tituba does not in fact need to make a confession since her accusers supply the information which Tituba omits in order to justify their belief in her guilt. Tituba's utterances are denials, not admissions, yet her claim that '. . . somebody else be witchin' these children' (turn 29) is seen as confirmation of her guilt, since it suggests that she can supply information about other witches. That Tituba is unable to do so is evidenced by her underinformative utterances (turns 31, 48, 50, 52). She is apparently unable to provide any further information, yet this is taken by her accusers as proof of a need to 'save her', not as proof of her innocence. The accusers are oblivious to the fact that it is Tituba's powerlessness and not her power which leads to her (non-) confession. Their belief in their own superior knowledge of the truth of Tituba's wickedness leads them to infer from her denials and underinformative answers that she is guilty.

The accusers' belief that Tituba has power over the girls can be seen to be misguided, however. It is the result of Abigail's manipulation of the conversation. Tituba's powerlessness to control the direction of the conversation leads to the implication of her guilt, and her powerlessness in this situation is symptomatic of her powerlessness in Salem, casting doubt on her ability to exert any control over Abigail and the other girls. That the characters do believe in her power may be explained by the fact that they are predisposed to believe that she is wicked. Their 'superiority' over Tituba is based on their belief in their own contrasting 'godliness', a belief which the reader/audience does not necessarily share, Even without the background information of the previous conversation between Abigail, Mary and Mercy, and Miller's comments that Abigail has '. . . an endless capacity for dissembling', (Act I, p. 18) it is likely that the reader/viewer's cultural knowledge of the relationship between black slaves and their white 'superiors' would lead them to doubt the ability of Tituba to 'make' Abigail 'do' anything. Abigail is able to manipulate the conversation to the extent that those present believe paradoxically that she is in Tituba's power. The distribution of turns between Abigail and Tituba follows a pattern of accusation and denial, and if the speech act values of the characters' utterances are examined it is evident that Tituba is in the unenviable position of being always on the defensive. If we contrast the typical speech acts of the white people with Tituba's, it is apparent that the conversation follows a pattern of accusations and questions from the white people against which Tituba must defend herself (see Table 4 below).

TABLE 4: TYPICAL SPEECH ACT VALUES OF CHARACTERS' UTTERANCES

Speech Act	Abigail	Hale	Parris	Putnam	Tituba
Accusations	10	1			
Threat			1	1	
Questions		10	6	1	
Denials					5
Pleas					1
Counter-accusations					2

It is apparent that the white people's speech acts are the, most powerful, with Tituba having to defend herself. At times this is impossible for Tituba to achieve as she is denied her 'turn' in the conversation. She is unable to answer Hale's question 'Are you gathering souls for the Devil?' (turn 11) as this is followed by Abigail's supporting move (turn 12) which is in turn supported by Parris (turn 13) and is followed by Abigail's further accusation (turn 14). When Tituba eventually manages to respond, it is to Abigail's accusation, not to Hale's question, which means that in effect she has failed to complete the 'adjacency pair'. Coulthard (1977: 70), discussing Sacks' work on the structural units of conversation describes 'adjacency pairs' as part of the turn-taking mechanism which enables a speaker to 'select next action and next speaker'. A question should normally be followed by an answer from the person to whom it is directed: if not, the adjacency pair appears incomplete since 'the first part provides specifically for the second, and therefore the absence of the second is noticeable and noticed'. Hale's question is, in effect, 'answered' by further 'evidence' from Abigail supported by Parris. Tituba's counter accusations against Abigail are interrupted by Abigail who accuses Tituba of lying (turn 16). Tituba interrupts Abigail once (turn 19) but is herself interrupted by Hale (turn 20). The other characters support Abigail's position by indicating their belief in her accusations. This culminates in Hale's question which indicates his certainty in Tituba's power, 'I want you to wake this child' (turn 20) pre-supposing Tituba's ability to do so.

Tituba's attempts at counter-accusation are unsuccessful. She is denied opportunities to speak, and many of the questions asked of her contain presuppositions which are difficult to deny. In addition her own beliefs are subsumed under the white peoples' certainty that her actions are wicked, apparently causing her to believe that this must be the case. This is partly due to the presuppositions contained in such questions as 'When did you compact with the Devil?' (turn 22). This is apparently all the evidence of guilt required by Parris, who threatens Tituba: 'You will confess yourself or I will take you out and whip you to your death, Tituba!' (turn 24), a threat which is supported by Putnam; 'This woman must be hanged!' (turn 25). The stage directions tell us that Tituba is 'terrified' and 'falls to her knees'. Her utterance 'No, no, don't hang Tituba!' is evidence of the duress which has culminated in the explicit threat. Yet her 'confession' consists of the ambiguous statement, 'I tell him that I don't desire to work for him, sir' (turn 26). This leads to Parris' question 'The Devil?' (turn 27) and Hale's statement, 'Then you saw him!' (turn 28) which presupposes that Tituba saw the devil. Tituba's ambiguous utterance implicates that she has 'seen the Devil' and is therefore guilty of witchcraft. She may have been 'just saying something', yet her accusers place a speech act value of 'confession' on her utterance. Hale's statement 'Then you saw him!' is followed by the stage direction, 'Tituba weeps'. Tituba's weeping is an index of her despair. Faced with her accuser's belief in her guilt, and the threat that she will be hanged if she does not confess, she has no alternative but to allow herself to be implicated in witchcraft, and her weeping suggests the sadness and inevitability of her predicament. As the questioning continues, the stage directions tell the reader/audience about Tituba's state of mind, confirming the 'duress' under which the 'confession' is elicited; she is 'terrified', (turn 26) 'frightened', (turn 29) 'fearful', (turn 32) and 'sobbing in terror' (turn 39). This may be contrasted with her reactions when she receives the 'promise' of salvation after her 'confession'; she 'kisses Hale's hand' (turn 56) 'deeply relieved' (turn 58). The perlocutionary effect of Hale's 'promise', 'You have confessed yourself to witchcraft . . . and we will bless you, Tituba', (turn 57) is to persuade Abigail to 'confess' ('I want to open myself'), and is followed by Betty's miraculous 'recovery' and 'confession' (Act I, p. 49). The fact that the stage directions tell us that Tituba is kneeling down (turn 26) and is forced to look up into Hale's eyes (turns 32, 44) may be seen as symbolising the way she is forced to look up to her white accusers and accept their will.

8   Conditions for 'unhappy' performatives

The physical interpretation of the stage directions during a performance of the play would make the pressure on Tituba to confess even more noticeable. The contrast between the confident Abigail and the progressively more fearful Tituba would serve to accentuate the asymmetrical power relationship between them. Given the 'extenuating circumstances' it would not be surprising for Tituba to 'confess' in order to save herself from hanging. A 'confession' of guilt in Tituba's case would not only perform the action of saving her life but would exonerate the other girls from blame. Yet according to Austin's description of 'explicit performatives', Tituba's 'confession' fails. Describing the act of 'apologising', Austin suggests that the description of the acts includes the notion that the apologizer 'repents':

Explicit Performative	Not Pure (half descriptive)	Descriptive
I apologize	I am sorry	I repent (Austin, 962: 83)

Similarly, a confession of guilt in *The Crucible* does not only appear to entail being guilty, but suggests an emotional attitude of the 'confessor'; namely that she is 'sorry' and 'repents'. Austin suggests that we could ask the question, 'But did he *really?*' The same question could be asked of Tituba: even if she 'confessed', does she *really* believe she is guilty, and if not, how can she be sorry and repent? If we examine the 'confession' in accordance with Searle's felicity conditions for Directives, (Searle, 1975: 71) Tituba's 'confession' complies with the first two:

Preparatory Condition	Tituba is able to confess
Sincerity Condition	Hale wants Tituba to confess

Her confession also fulfils the 'Propositional Content' and the 'Essential Condition' if these are taken to refer to the act of confessing itself. However if the 'future act' that Hale predicates is that of 'repenting', it is evident that Tituba cannot repent if she has nothing to be sorry for.

Preparatory conditions for confessions in *The Crucible* appear to change according to the status of the individual involved. Since Tituba's status is relatively low, her 'confession' similarly need not conform rigidly to the constitutive rules which are enforced for the other characters. John Proctor, by contrast, must not only confess in front of witnesses, his 'confession' must be written down and signed, and used as proof of his guilt for the other citizens of Salem. It may be tempting to interpret this difference as a deliberate irony by Miller to show the hypocrisy of those who accuse others in an attempt to deflect criticism from themselves. However, analysis of Tituba's (non-) confession is complicated by the fact that Miller apparently also believed that she confessed. Miller argues (1956: 39) that 'Devil worship' was practised in Salem and that 'one certain evidence of this is the confession of Tituba, the slave of the Reverend Parris, and another is the behaviour of the children who were known to have indulged in sorceries with her' (Act I, p. 39). This poses the question of whether or not Miller intended to show inequalities of power in Salem, in which case the invalidity of the 'confession' is deliberate: or whether he actually believed that he had written Tituba's confession, in which case it is accidental. Thus the fact that we can interpret Tituba's 'confession' as void may itself either be perlocutionary object of Miller's writing, or an unintended sequel.

9 Conclusion

Speech act theory provides a useful framework for an analysis of *The Crucible* due to the explicit performatives of the characters. It is possible to explain the feeling of dissatisfaction associated with Tituba's 'confession' due to the 'unhappiness' of the circumstances in which it occurs. Austin's rules for 'happy performatives' allow me to argue that Tituba's confession is void and highlights important issues concerning the differential treatment of individuals according to social status. In addition it is possible to pose the question of Miller's intentionality, i.e. to discuss whether Tituba's (non-) confession is deliberate or accidental. Miller argues that 'ours is a divided empire in which certain ideas and emotions and actions are of God, and their opposites are of Lucifer' (Act I, p. 37). This explains Salem's perception of Tituba as 'other', as different from themselves and therefore 'wicked'. Hence her 'confession' is simply a matter of 'going through the motions', since her guilt is taken for granted and she is not afforded the opportunity of denying the charge of witchcraft.

The reader/audience is in the privileged position of being aware of the intentions (and 'unintentions') of the characters, something which is not always possible in everyday conversation, and the problems associated with speech act theory are those which form the plot of the play. The uncontrollability of perlocutionary effects is exemplified by the unintended result of Abigail's accusation and Tituba's subsequent 'confession'. Abigail's original intention may have been to rid herself of her rival by drinking a 'charm to kill Goody Proctor' but the consequence was to have devastating results for the population of Salem.

Notes

The Crucible Copyright © 1952, 1953 by Arthur Miller. I wish to thank Greene & Heaton Ltd. Literary Agents, for permission to reproduce copyright material, The Crucible is published by Penguin Books Ltd.

References

Austin, J. L. (1962) How to do things with Words, Oxford University Press, London
Brown, G. (1977) Listening to Spoken English, Longman, London
Burton, D. (1980) Dialogue and Discourse, Routledge and Kegan Paul, London
Coulthard, M. (1977) An Introduction to Discourse Analysis, Longman, London
Elam, K. (1980) The Semiotics of Theatre and Drama, Methuen, London
Fowler, R. (1986) Linguistic Criticism, Oxford University Press, Oxford
Grice, H. P. (1975) 'Logic and Conversation' in Cole, P. and Morgan, J. L. (eds) Syntax and Semantics (Vol. 3), Academic Press, London, pp. 41–58
Levinson, C. (1983) Pragmatics, Cambridge University Press, Cambridge
Miller, Arthur (1956) The Crucible, Penguin, Middlesex
Searle, J. R. (1975) 'Indirect Speech Acts' in Cole, P. and Morgan, J. L. (eds) Syntax and Semantics (Vol. 3), Academic Press, London, pp. 41–58
Short, M. (1989) 'Discourse Analysis and the Analysis of Drama', in Carter, R. and Simpson, P. (eds) Language Discourse and Literature, Unwin Hyman, London, pp. 139–168.

JOHN S. SHOCKLEY

Death of a Salesman *and American Leadership:* *Life Imitates Art*

D_{eath} *of a Salesman* hit the American stage in 1949, catapulting Arthur Miller into the status of the "greats" of American dramatists. While the play was never without its critics, who agreed over whether the play could appropriately be called a "tragedy," whether the writing was a bit stilted, and whether Miller's message about American capitalism and the American dream was a bit garbled, it still was an enormously popular play among theater-goers and critics. All of them seemed to find something of the American creed, and of themselves, in the play.[1]

But more than 40 years have passed since the play was written. Should we now view the play as a dated relic of another age, or does it still resonate with the American character? Is the play primarily the personal problem of an aging playwright whose formative years were spent in the Great Depression, and who therefore could never "trust" American capitalism again?[2] If so, do we have little need to understand *Death of a Salesman* or come to terms with it? On the contrary, I shall argue that *Death of a Salesman* still resonates powerfully in American life and culture and that in a fascinating and chilling way life has imitated drama. Willy Loman shares a number of important traits with the most successful American politician of the late twentieth century, Ronald Reagan. To understand American culture and American politics, one must come to grips with the phenomenal success of Ronald

From *Journal of American Culture.* © 1994.

79

Reagan. Arthur Miller's perspective in creating Willy Loman and *Death of a Salesman* can help us do this.

I.

The Similarities of Willy Loman and Ronald Reagan

In the first place, both Willy Loman and Ronald Reagan are salesmen. Both understood that a salesman has got to believe in himself and his product before he can sell it to others. Both were selling themselves and the American dream. Ronald Reagan, of course, was a salesman for General Electric, "living well electrically" while touting the corporation's conservative political agenda. But most of all, as he gave "The Speech" to 250,000 GE employees while traveling all over the country, he sold the American dream.[3] And he was selling that both before and after his years as a GE salesman.

After he was dropped by GE, he became a salesman for the conservative ideas of Southern California businessmen, who recognized in him the best spokesman for their ideology that they could find. "A salesman has got to dream, boy. It comes with the territory."[4] So says Charlie, Willy's neighbor, at Willy's funeral. Both Willy and Reagan dreamed the American dream and believed that in America a man could, and should, fulfill himself.

Second, both also had to deny basic points of reality in order to believe in the dream. Willy tried desperately to deny that his sons were failures and that he was failing as a salesman. His son Biff is always about to be a success, about to land a good job. And Willy lies to Linda about the source of his income, telling her the money is coming from sales when in fact Charlie down the street is lending him the money. Throughout the play he is always lying about how important he is and how many "friends" he has. Ronald Reagan, as the son of a failed, alcoholic, shoe salesman, was forced to deny his family's problems from an early age. Ronald Reagan is the adult child of an alcoholic. Yet his father's skills as a raconteur and his mother's encouragement of his acting and entertaining abilities channeled the denials and "stories" into more acceptable outlets than Willy had. As Willy loved telling jokes to highlight his personality, Reagan loved entertaining others.[5] Denials continued throughout Reagan's life: denying that Hollywood had engaged in a blacklist; denying that the MCA (Music Corporation of America) was involved in bribery and "payola" while Reagan dealt with them as president of the Screen Actors Guild; denying that his tax cuts could be responsible for the mounting federal deficits; denying that his cuts in low-income housing subsidies could be responsible for the rise in homelessness; denying that he sold arms for hostages; and forgetting virtually everything about the Iran-Contra diversion scandal.[6]

To scholars of the Reagan era, one of the most striking features of Reagan the man was his lack of interest in facts, which were often misstated or completely wrong. His view of "facts" was entirely utilitarian, in service to his ideology of the American dream and American foreign policy. Willy too had great difficulty absorbing facts that did not fit the view he wanted to have of himself and his life. The entire play is basically a struggle within Willy's mind between his vision of himself and the painful reality of facts intruding upon his "dream." Perhaps the most painful and poignant moment in the play comes when his son Biff tries to tell Willy that he's not now and will never be the "success" Willy imagines for him. Willy cannot hear him. Actually, in denying basic facts each man was trying to create himself from myth.[7] One was of course more successful at doing this than the other.

Third, Ronald Reagan and Willy Loman also had to fantasize in order to avoid the realities they could not handle and to give themselves the confidence they otherwise would lack. Willy was "well liked" and known all over New England, and at his own funeral his boys would be impressed at how many "friends" would show up (Miller 764, 796). Ronald Reagan moved more than a dozen times during his childhood, and had to learn to survive without close friends. He wanted to play football but was never any good (his eyes were too poor). Yet he was "the Gipper," Notre Dame's great football hero, throughout his political career. His movie career and political career often blended, sometimes consciously as in the above example, and sometimes unconsciously. The "Gipper" was a kind of double fantasy, in that George Gipp himself was a mythical hero based heavily on fantasy. While "Win One For the Gipper," Reagan's favorite movie and political line, probably was said by George Gipp on his death bed, most likely Gipp thought he was talking to his doctor (qtd. in Lippman). In reality, George Gipp was a rather unsavory character who bet on his own games and by today's standards would have been expelled from the sport.[8] But, as with so much of Ronald Reagan and Willy Loman, facts were not allowed to get in the way of the myth. And in another kind of chilling rehearsal for life (politics) imitating art (the movie), the Reagan movie helped make Gipp into "a teflon hero."

Fourth, while both Willy and Reagan wanted to be well liked, and wanted to have the personalities to "win friends and influence people," neither was successful at forming close personal friendships.[9] In both cases, only their wives stood by them, and in both cases their wives tried to protect them and sustain their husbands' illusions in the face of reality.[10] Each man tried to make sure his "image" presented an air of leadership and success, but both men in fact were more passive than they wanted to appear.[11]

Both men also faced severe problems with their children and denied these problems to themselves and the outside world. Willy's pained relationships with his two sons is one of the basic themes running through *Death of a Salesman*. With Reagan, his relationship with his adopted son Michael (detailed in Michael's autobiography, *On the Outside Looking In*) has been extremely strained. His daughter Patti barely has been on speaking terms with her parents since the publication of her autobiography (thinly disguised as a novel) several years ago (*Home Front*). Both men lacked strong fathers who could nurture them, although their father relationships also contained important differences. In a poignant moment, Willy asks Ben (his older brother) to tell him more about "Dad," who left when Willy was still young, because "I still feel kind of temporary about myself" (Miller 770). Reagan had a much longer relationship with his father, but Reagan's stay in any one place was "kind of temporary." Jack Reagan was also "footloose." He moved constantly, changed jobs, and was usually a failure as a salesman. In addition, Reagan's father's alcoholism was a source of worry and shame. But Ronald Reagan also described his father as "the best raconteur I ever heard," and this surely must have helped Ronald's own skills as a salesman and storyteller.[12]

Fifth, both men had brushes with the uglier side of capitalism, and yet seemed unable to recognize or condemn this brutal side. To Willy it was his older brother Ben, who became a millionaire at a young age and kept admonishing Willy: "Never fight fair with a stranger, boy. You'll never get out of the jungle that way" (Miller 770). Yet Willy constantly wants Ben's approval and is asking him how he managed to be so successful. Willy even views his son Biff's stealing as "initiative."

Reagan was called before a grand jury investigating the seamier side of Hollywood capitalism, the bribery and monopolistic practices of the Music Corporation of America. Its special sweet deals with the Screen Actors Guild while Reagan was president of the Guild and simultaneously getting what looked like kickbacks from MCA nearly resulted in his indictment.[13]

Later, as President, Reagan was surrounded by corruption, influence peddling, indictments, trials and convictions of his aides and associates— Michael Deaver, Lynn Nofziger, John Poindexter—the HUD scandal, the Savings and Loan scandal and the spectacular corruption of some who became multimillionaires during his era. But throughout his administration and throughout *Death of a Salesman* neither Reagan nor Willy ever criticized or condemned any actions by these people. As Willy refused to condemn son Biff's stealing or brother Ben's ruthlessness, neither did Reagan condemn the stealings and illegalities of any of his aides. Neither had a moral code of what were fair and unfair practices, what were proper ways to get rich and what were improper ways. To both, the American creed meant success and riches, but *how* these were obtained neither wanted to examine too closely. Perhaps they did not want to examine this too closely because the truth would have been too painful. To both men America and the American creed seemed to have no place for failure. How one succeeded was therefore not a moral question.

Both the Reagan presidency and *Death of a Salesman* then are dramas about the power of the American dream and the self-deceptions necessary for the kind of American dream believed. These are both potent forces in American politics and culture. But Willy Loman and Ronald Reagan are obviously not identical. Their differences are too important to ignore.

II.

The Differences between Willy Loman and Ronald Reagan

From the beginning, Ronald Reagan had physical traits and a personality that made it more likely that he would succeed in America. His personality was a more marketable commodity, both for Hollywood and in politics. He was physically handsome, meticulous about his appearance and successful at entertaining others. His "self-deprecating humor" was in marked contrast to Willy's braggadocio (Cannon 32). Reagan had the ability to inspire others and to make people feel good about themselves. This allowed others to enjoy being around Reagan and gave him the self-confidence Willy wanted but lacked. Yet, like Willy, Reagan was essentially remote from others and could be highly manipulative (229, 218).

As the "good guy" in so many Hollywood movies, Reagan had a clearer sense of the "bad guy" than Willy had. Demonology—the Sandinistas, the Communists, terrorists, etc., abroad and welfare queens and government at home—served Reagan well both in defining himself and explaining the world to others.[14] Willy didn't really know what was happening to him. *Death of a Salesman* is a desperate search to find out what is killing Willy, and Willy never figures it out. The final "Requiem" scene shows that the remaining characters are divided over what the cause was as well. If Willy had had a scapegoat, or a clearer sense of what was killing him, he could have fought back and found a greater reason for living. But Willy never questioned the social, economic or political order. Broader institutional forces are more remote from him, givens in a system where he's searching for fame, success and the American dream.[15] Reagan, however, translated his personal values and dreams into politics and was the defender of the American dream from threats both external and internal.

While both Willy Loman and Ronald Reagan had to confront failure, their responses to their failures were different. Like Willy, Ronald Reagan faced career problems with middle age. He was dumped by Hollywood after a string of B-grade movies. Near the end he was even forced to co-star with a chimpanzee in *Bedtime for Bonzo*. General Electric rescued him from obscurity in Hollywood and honed his speaking skills. But he was dropped on 24-hours' notice by the company when *G.E. Theater* was cancelled, and Reagan was forced to take a salary cut in hosting *Death Valley Days*. By 1964 Reagan was in debt and owed back taxes to the U.S.

Government.[16] Willy of course was also failing financially and with age. But here the differences in the two men are too important to ignore. Willy had no one to rescue him, save his neighbor Charlie, who in fact did help. But Willy was too proud to give up his salesman's job (or admit that he had been fired) to work for Charlie. Ronald Reagan, however, was quite willing to accept help and funds from anyone, including wealthy admirers of his conservative views:

> A group headed by Justin Dart (Dart Industries; Rexall Drugs; Kraft Foods), Holmes Tutle (a Los Angeles Ford dealer), William French Smith (a wealthy Los Angeles attorney), and A. C. (Cy) Rubel (Chairman of Union Oil Co.) formed the Ronald Reagan Trust Fund to take over his personal finances. . . . (Dye 71)

Willy didn't have anyone to set up the Willy Loman Trust Fund to take over his personal finances. In addition, Reagan was given a ranch. Willy needed one. This difference allowed Reagan never to lose self-confidence (at least for long), while Willy's self-worth was collapsing around him (Dye 72).[17]

Other differences follow from ones already mentioned. As Willy's psychological condition deteriorates, he is more obsessed with the meaning of life and his place in history than Ronald Reagan. In his struggle, Willy is engaged in a battle with himself. But that is only because he has to be. Willy is not by nature any more introspective than Ronald Reagan. Reagan seeks love less desperately because he is a more successful salesman. He has enough of what he needs. And while Willy is haunted by his failed relationship with his sons, there is no evidence that Ronald Reagan is. Willy, however, in his own failures, must live more through his sons. Ronald Reagan doesn't need to. These differences thus emphasize that through his more obvious and painful confrontations with failure, Willy has been forced to become more introspective than either Willy or Reagan would have desired. But deep down both men were solipsists. Neither was interested in learning from other people. Neither wanted the real world to intrude upon his fantasy world.

Ronald Reagan, in sum, was what Willy Loman wanted to be: well-liked, at least in a superficial way; entertaining without being a bore; successful; handsome; and not fat. Reagan's attributes allowed him to be rescued by wealthy individuals who realized they could use him for their own purposes, as he used them for his own purposes. But Willy had no Southern California businessmen to come to his rescue when he was washed up, abandoned, aging and unsure of his value to society.

III.

Arthur Miller's Vision of the Power of the Dream

Willy Loman committed suicide. Ronald Reagan became President of the United States. Yet this difference hides greater truths. Each believed in the American dream. That Reagan was elected President twice, and was widely liked by the American people during his tenure, ultimately says more about the American people than about Ronald Reagan. Here Willy Loman and Arthur Miller can help us. That Arthur Miller understood the power of the American dream, and the need of little people to believe in it, helps us later explain the rise and success of Ronald Reagan in American politics when America itself was undergoing a crisis of confidence.

Of course, the American dream has meant different things to different people. Tom Paine ("We have it in our power to begin the world over again"), Franklin Roosevelt and our "rendezvous with destiny" and Martin Luther King ("I have a dream that one day this nation will rise up and live out the true meaning of its creed: 'We hold these truths to be self-evident, that all men are created equal' ") all evoke feelings of the New Adam in the New Eden. In this new world the sins, hatreds, unfreedoms and inequalities of other lands can be changed and history can be forgotten.[18]

But Arthur Miller (through Willy Loman) and Ronald Reagan are focusing on an altered dream: the self-reliant individual, Jefferson's yeoman farmer, gradually became the man who could make a lot of money. And to do that, marketing, salesmanship and image became the road to the dream. The defense of heroic individualism became the defense of competition, capitalist exploitation and, in Reagan, also virulent anti-communism. Willy never examines his values and how these values don't fit with his true, more agrarian personality. While Ronald Reagan mouthed the potent cliches of the business ethic as the ultimate form of freedom, he examined the values in hardly any greater depth than Willy. But he did have the advantage, once he entered politics, of being someone who had spent his life, including his professional life, presenting himself as an image, a role to be seen by others.

The rewards of being successful for both men were to be well liked and to be rich. To be rich for both seemed to mean 1) having a place where they can get away from it all—a ranch or "a little place out in the country" and 2) consuming the products of a bountiful business society. To be rich is thus to be "free" in the two senses above, with the added self-confidence of being admired, a model for others.

Willy Loman and Ronald Reagan share this new, salesmanship understanding of the American dream. Miller's purpose, however, is very different from Willy Loman's and Ronald Reagan's. While he wanted to show the power of this dream, he also wanted to show the dangers, the costs and the emptiness of it. In his autobiography, *Timebends*, Miller says that in writing the play he had as a motive "in some far corner of my mind possibly something political; there was the smell in the air of a new American Empire in the making . . . and I wanted to set before the new captains and the so smugly confident kings the corpse of a believer" (184). He does this in many unsubtle ways, including letting us know early on that the Loman family is caught up in mindless consumerism ("whipped cheese"), and that these new products disrupt attempts at meaningful human interaction. Miller shows the power of advertising and consumerism, and the contradictions of attitudes toward products in the Loman family by having Willy call his Chevrolet both "the greatest car ever built" and "that goddamn Chevrolet" in the space of only a few minutes, and in Willy's remark that "Once in my life I would like to own something outright before it's broken!" (Miller 765, 766, 777). But while Willy utters these remarks, he still is completely caught up in the pursuit of the dream.

Miller understood the power of the belief in a New Land, a New Eden, where the normal rules and motives for other countries and other peoples would not apply. Even in its competitive, "get rich" meanings, Miller understood the continuing force of the dream in mobilizing and inspiring people.

"Can we doubt," said Reagan in accepting the Republican nomination for president in 1980, "that only a Divine Providence placed this land, this island of freedom, here as a refuge for all those people in the world who yearn to breathe freely. . . . ?" This is Reagan's belief. But where does this belief lead? Is God a white American, willing to countenance the near genocide of millions of the original Americans and willing to sanction the death and slavery of millions of blacks so that the economic system of white America could grow stronger and be "free"? Reagan's encomium to the American dream can be as soaring and inspirational as it is in part because he never asks or answers these questions, any more than Willy does. Similarly, with American power abroad Ronald Reagan sees only altruism, not imperialism, manifest destiny or messianic causes unwanted by others: "I'd always felt that from our deeds it must be clear to anyone that Americans were a moral people who, starting at the birth of our nation, had always used our power only as a force for good in the world" (qtd. in Wills 3).

Reagan's is a view deeply soothing to a nation questioning its self-confidence after Vietnam, Watergate, stagflation and energy crises. The blinders and the fantasies are not only necessary for the laudatory rhetoric; they also do not prepare anyone for failure. Both Willy and Reagan believed; each was an incurable optimist always wanting to paint a "rosy scenario."[19] And the downside of this view is that there is no place for failure. If in the face of such boundless opportunities ("just check the want ads"), a person does not succeed, there must be something wrong with that person.[20] It is this downside that is so hard for Willy to confront, because he believes so strongly in the American dream. Willy is unable to let go of it, unable to change in the face of reality, and commits suicide in the hope that he is helping his family.

Arthur Miller, through Willy Loman, presages the Reagan prototype through 1) emphasizing the power of the capitalist-consumerist-get-rich-and-be-well-liked dream, and the hold it has on the American people. Miller shows us the power of the myth. 2) He also understood the need for selective perception, fantasy and denial, and the tenuous hold on reality necessary for this strident view of the dream. He prepares us for the Reagan denials, misstatements and lies, and the gap between appearance and reality.[21] To both Willy and Reagan, uttering the cliches of success is virtually the same thing as bringing these cliches into actuality. To both, "saying makes it so," and thus they are an evasion of the truth. Arthur Miller helps us understand that Ronald Reagan succeeded not in spite of but because of all his paradoxes and contradictions. As the defender of the little man's dream, he succeeded because millionaires could use him to champion a dream that benefited primarily themselves. If he had been truly committed to helping the little Willys of the nation fulfill their dreams, he would have been dumped by his financial backers. Instead, Reagan was the "sincerest claimant to a heritage that never existed . . . —a perfect blend of an authentic America he grew up in and of that America's own fables about its past."[22] As political analysts have written of Reagan: "He had been in some measure the Wizard of Us, a fabulist presiding over a wondrous Emerald City of the mind . . . people wanted to believe in it" (Goldman and Mathews 32).[23]

Miller also seems to understand that 3) as pressures on the dream close in, the desire to believe in it will intensify rather than weaken. The American people did not want to hear Jimmy Carter (or John Anderson or Walter Mondale or Bruce Babbitt, etc.) any more than Willy wanted to hear Charlie. A "realist," willing to talk of limits, taxes, sacrifice and mixed motives in a complex world isn't what Willy or the American people wanted to hear. Arthur Miller understood this form of the American psyche and its power.

Surely all writers—political analysts as well as dramatists—recognize the need of people to find meaning in their lives. But Miller understood the particular nature of the American need for meaning. Through giving us Willy Loman, Miller helped us better understand the successful Willy Loman when he appeared on the American stage: Ronald Reagan, the super salesman, everything Willy and our nation of Willys wanted to be. Ronald Reagan understood American fears, hopes, lies, vulnerabilities and the need for optimism better than many political scientists, and he understood the role of the salesman in selling us our dreams better than others did. He had the confidence the rest of us wanted.

But whether we should assess Reagan as critically as son Biff assessed Willy—"He had the wrong dreams. All, all wrong" (Miller 797)—is less clear. After a decade of Reagan and Reaganism we have record budget deficits, record trade deficits, increased dependence upon foreign lenders in the world economy, a crumbling infrastructure and, most poignant and ironic of all, a growing gap between rich and poor. It is now harder, not easier, for the little Willys of society to reach the American dream. To criticize Reagan, we, like Biff, would have to condemn part of ourselves, condemn part of our own dreams, and condemn part of our identity and meaning as Americans. We Americans are a long way from being ready or able to do that. But we should not forget that both Willy Loman and Ronald Reagan embody what ought to be a debate about the essence and direction of America.

NOTES

1. For reviews of the play, see Harold Bloom, ed., *Arthur Miller's Death of a Salesman*, 1982. For a review of Arthur Miller in general, see Neil Carson, *Arthur Miller*, 1982. As Carson notes (13) the play ran on Broadway for 742 performances and "transformed Miller's life," elevating him "to a position of prominence where he became exposed to both adulation and criticism of a kind he had not previously experienced."

2. The play is in many ways autobiographical, for Miller's father, Isidore, lost his business and his fortune in the Great Depression and was blamed by his son for an inability to cope with these changes. See the review of Miller's autobiography, *Timebends* (1987), in The New Republic, Feb. 8, 1988, 30–34, "All My Sins," by David Denby.

3. These points are mentioned many places, including Lou Cannon, *Reagan*, 1982, 93.

4. Arthur Miller, *Death of a Salesman*, *The Bedford Introduction to Drama*, Lee Jacobus (ed.), 797. William Heyen, "Arthur Miller's *Death of a Salesman* and the American Dream" in Bloom, *supra* note 1, p. 51, has said, quoting Leslie Fiedler, that American industry produces "not things . . . but dreams disguised as things."

5. Lou Cannon, the journalist who has observed Ronald Reagan the closest over the past three decades, comments in his latest biography of Reagan, "Acting took early hold of him, and never let him go." *President Reagan: The Role of a Lifetime*, 1991, 39.

6. On Reagan denying the Hollywood blacklist, see Victor Navasky, *Naming Names*, 1980 p. 87; for Reagan's relationship with the MCA, see Garry Wills, *Reagan's America*, 1988, chapters 28 and 29. For his confused views on taxes and deficits, see David Stockman, *The Triumph of Politics*, 1986; for the severe cuts in low- and moderate-incoming housing, see Charles Moore and Patricia Hoban-Moore, "Some Lessons from Reagan's HUD: Housing Policy and Public Service," *PS: Political Science and Politics*, Mar. 1990, 13–18; for denying that the diversion of funds took place and for forgetting nearly everything about the Iran-Contra scandal, see *Newsweek*, Apr. 2, 1990, 36 ("A Diminished Ron, a Refurbished Jimmy"). *Newsweek* reports that "Reagan pleaded loss of memory some 150 times in two days of testimony [at the Poindexter trial]—and he had forgotten the conclusion of his own Tower Commission, that funds were diverted to the Contras." In a chilling parallel with the Iran-Contra scandal, Garry Wills reports (325) that as the Justice Department proceeded with the investigation of MCA and the Screen Actors Guild's favorable treatment of them, "Reagan's strategy was to retreat toward constantly expanding areas of forgetfulness." At one point in his grand jury tes-

timony in 1962, Reagan said, "And all of this, including the opinions of myself, is vague at the Guild on everything that took place for all those years all the way back including whether I was present or not" (Wills 323).

7. David Broder, "Reagan Memoir Fails to Tell All," *Minneapolis Star-Tribune*, Nov. 23, 1990, editorial page, comments that "Reagan has devoted most of his eight decades to remaking, not the nation or the world, but himself." Sidney Blumenthal, *Our Long National Daydream: The Political Pageant of the Reagan Era*, 1986, p. xiv, has written, "The essential quality for any actor is to induce in his audience a willing suspension of disbelief . . . [he] must also suspend disbelief within himself, giving himself over to the role and the scene. Reagan's grip over the nation partly lay in his ability to maintain his grip over himself. Above all, he was a true believer in his role. He used that role to persuade that willing was doing, that saying something made it so." Michael Rogin, *Ronald Reagan, The Movie*, 1987, 3, argues that Ronald Reagan "found out who he was through the roles he played on film."

8. Lippman also reports that after the Notre Dame coach invoked George Gipp's name at half-time, Notre Dame did win 12 to 6, but Army was on the Notre Dame one-yard line as the game ended, and Notre Dame lost the rest of its games that season to finish 5–4 overall. Comments Lippman, "Another few seconds and . . . Ronald Reagan might never have become president."

9. The string of "kiss-and-tell" books from Reagan's closest aides, starting with Michael Deaver and continuing through David Stockman, Larry Speakes and Chief of Staff Don Regan, makes this point painfully clear.

10. Nancy, however, was a greater help to Ronald than Linda was to Willy. As an entertainer herself, she better understood the needs of her husband, but both actively intervened to try to defend their husbands. See Garry Wills, "The Man Who Wasn't There" [a review of Lou Cannon's *President Reagan: The Role of a Lifetime*], *The New York Review of Books*, June 13, 1991, 3–7.

11. Fred Greenstein, "Ronald Reagan—Another Hidden-Hand Ike?" *PS: Political Science and Politics*, Mar. 1990, 7–13 concludes that Reagan was surprisingly passive and remote from the specifics of politics and policy, although he did have strong general beliefs. He quotes Chief of Staff Donald Regan that Reagan's outgoing personality and infectious likeability are based on a "natural diffidence."

12. Wills, *supra*, note 6: 15, quoting Reagan's autobiography, *Where's the Rest of Me?* (1965): 14.

13. Wills, *supra* note 6: 322. Wills also concludes (322) that "it seems that Reagan's political career would not have emerged at all if the circumstances of a 1962 investigation had become known at the time; if an indictment of Reagan, seriously considered for months by the Justice Department, had been brought or even publicly threatened; if a civil suit of conspiracy against the MCA had not been settled by a divestiture."

14. One does not appoint master spy and covert operator William Casey as campaign manager unless one has a strong sense of the need for action against "enemies." Michael Rogin, *supra* note 7, argues that demonology was an essential part of Reagan's persona.

15. Helene Wickham Koon, "Introduction," *Twentieth Century Interpretations of Death of a Salesman*, 11, says of Willy that he "accepts the world without question and never seeks to better it, who reacts without thought, who substitutes dreams for knowledge, and who is necessarily self-centered because unanalyzed feelings are his sole touchstone to existence." Willy does, however, protest the surrounding of his house by apartment buildings and the loss of sunlight and space that comes with it. He also pro-

tests how things are constantly breaking down. But these protests are completely devoid of meaningful human action. He is apolitical.

16. These events are discussed in Thomas Dye's *Who's Running America? The Reagan Years*, Third Edition, 1983, 69–73 and Garry Wills, *Reagan's America*, 1988, 338–39. Wills, however, states that "Reagan was financially secure by 1962," which seems not to account for the need for his trust fund to be set up by wealthy benefactors.

17. Dye notes other investments for Reagan as well.

18. The first two men are quoted in Ronald Reagan's speech accepting his party's nomination in 1980, which can be found in *Ronald Reagan Talks to America* (1983) 77. But Reagan does not quote Martin Luther King. For contested meanings of the American dream, see David Madden, *American Dream, American Nightmare* (1965), who argues that the American dream comes in an older agrarian and a newer urban form. John Cawelti, *Apostles of the Self-Made Man* (1965), describes three main competing versions: the first came from a more conservative tradition of middle-class Protestantism and stressed piety and honesty; the second stressed more secular qualities of initiative, aggressiveness and competitiveness; the third tied individual fulfillment to social progress more than wealth or status, along the lines of Emerson's self-reliant man. Alfred Ferguson, "The Tragedy of the American Dream," *Thought* (1978) 83–98 explores the "New Adam" in the "New Eden" in greater detail, arguing that the dream now means "it is possible for everyman to be whatever he can imagine himself being" (88). "[T]he wish is father to the fact" (90).

19. William Heyen, *supra* note 4: 49, speaks of Willy Loman as "an incurable yea-sayer, painting everything rosy, prophesizing empire . . . for the Lomans . . . He is insatiable. He so much needs to believe in his dream." David Stockman, *supra* note 6: 385, recounts a story President Reagan would tell of a boy who is an optimist that gets a roomful of horse manure for a Christmas present: "He's delighted. He digs around the room for hours on end. With all that horse manure, he figured there just had to be a pony in them somewhere!" Stockman uses the term "rosy scenario!" to describe President Reagan's constant belief that the nation would "grow" itself out of the deficit problems.

20. John Cawelti, *supra*, note 25, discusses this in more detail. He notes (217) that "positive thinkers like Norman Vincente Peale and Dale Carnegie seem to accept the American business world wholeheartedly. If it has flaws, they are the result of some failure to assume a positive "attitude." Cawelti argues provocatively (217), however, that "positive thinking is . . . a revelation of the failure of the dream," because these books are full of eloquent testimony of anxious, neurotic people and "the failure of the business world to fulfill human needs."

21. To say this is not to say anything as precise as that from Miller we can sense that *Ronald Reagan* would launch a "war on drugs" while secretly dealing with Manuel Noriega, or condemn "terrorism," while secretly dealing with Iran. Rather, the point is that when these gaps between appearance and truth appear, most Americans will want to believe their leader, especially one who can evoke the symbols of the dream as powerfully as Reagan. If the leader can maintain his self-confidence and affability, even as the truth is (partially) revealed, he will likely survive and be "well liked."

22. Lou Cannon, Ronald Reagan, *supra* note 5: 793, quoting Garry Wills, *supra* note 6.

23. See also Sidney Blumenthal, quoted in footnote 6, *supra*.

Works Cited

Cannon, Lou. *Reagan*. New York: Putnam, 1982.

Dye, Thomas R. *Who's Running America?—The Reagan Years*. Third ed. Englewood Cliffs, NJ: Prentice Hall, 1983.

Goldman, Peter Louis, and Tom Mathews. *The Quest for the Presidency, 1988*. New York: Simon & Schuster, 1989.

Lippman, Theo. "Let Reagan Have Role He Was Born to Play: Rockne." Minneapolis *Star-Tribune*, date unknown (1988) quoting sportswriter Jim Murray.

Miller, Arthur. *Death of a Salesman*. Ed. Lee Jacobus. New York: Bantam Books, 1955.

Wills, Garry. "Mr. Magoo Remembers." *New York Review of Books* 20 Dec. 1990.

SUSAN C. W. ABBOTSON

Issues of Identity in Broken Glass: A Humanist Response to a Postmodern World

The final quarter of the twentieth century has been marked by a popular insistence on the evaporation of meaning in people's lives. Arthur Miller responds to this mood with a resounding "No"—he insists that meaning still exists and through the plays he has written during this period suggests how it can be reinstated. His plays, from *The Archbishop's Ceiling* to *Broken Glass*, form a counter-tradition and attractive alternative to the influential, but increasingly unsatisfying, de-humanizing theories of postmodern critics such as Frederic Jameson and Jacques Derrida.

Though set in 1938 in the wake of "Kristallnacht," *Broken Glass*, Miller's most recent play, responds to problems which have not evaporated for a 1994 audience, but have become more urgent. As Miller tells Charlie Rose: "In each of us, whether recognized or not, is that same bloody ethnic nationalism. This is not coming from the moon. This is coming from us. And we have not come close to even confronting this thing."[1] The notion of difference, when pursued too stringently and unalloyed with the acceptance of universal humanity, can lead to unnecessary fragmentation, harmful restrictions of the individual, and the destruction of society as a whole. Written in the shadow of atrocities in Rwanda and Bosnia, *Broken Glass* conveys the necessity of a humanistic response to the contemporary world we inhabit.

From *Journal of American Drama and Theatre*. © 1999.

Miller sees Nazism as defined by its strong conformist pressure, chilling technological power, and erosion of autonomy—all of which led to people being stripped of their humanity. Such a description all too closely resembles the objectified picture the postmodern critic, Jameson, creates of our contemporary society in *Postmodernism, or the Cultural Logic of Late Capitalism*, where he announces the death of individualism, "symbolized by the emergent primacy of mechanical production"[2] by which all becomes identical and exists without individual identity, choice, or spirit. Yet Miller clearly resists such forces, just as he insists the Nazi regime should have been resisted.

Miller's plays affirm the presence of a moral and humanistic impulse which is absent from the social vision which passes "beyond man and humanism" described in Derrida's *Writing and Difference*.[3] "My effort, my energy, my aesthetic," Miller has declared, " is to find the chain of moral being in the world."[4] As the threat of an amoral, alienating world has escalated, so has Miller's resistance become more focused and forceful. His later plays are fruitfully read as an artist's efforts to redefine the postmodernist trend toward disjunction and otherness into a culture of connection and self. Such a direction corresponds with a more positive mode of postmodernism which is developing among critics like John McGowan and Alan Wilde. It is a mode which maintains a humanistic and ultimately optimistic outlook through social commitment and irony, while acknowledging the contingencies and uncertainties of modern existence.

Aware of critics like William Spanos, who reject humanism as an excuse for imperialism, Alan Wilde in *Middle Grounds* calls for a more flexible "contemporary humanism" which can claim, in answer to such criticism, "not that man is the measure of the world's meaning but that he is its agent or partner in the task of bringing meaning into being."[5] Thus, we move away from a culture which privileges the individual above social concerns toward a culture which John McGowan describes in *Postmodernism and Its Critics* as "semi-autonomous," where the individual and the communal society bear equal importance.[6] Indeed, each is dependent upon the existence of the other. Without the diversity inherent in individual input, any society becomes stagnant and lifeless. However, a protective social structure is necessary for individuality to flourish. Miller's plays, which present characters striving to understand this complex balance between individual and social needs and interests, clearly fulfil the demands of both Wilde and McGowan. A moral responsibility for others and the self is the core of Miller's lesson: to neglect either personal or social responsibility is tantamount to self-destruction. But a moral responsibility can only be fully recognized by those who have an understanding of their own identities as individuals and as members of a society.

In order to act purposively and meaningfully people need to recognize their own identities, which involves, McGowan tells us, "a reconciliation to

the necessary social bases of the self, a construction of identity that manages
... to tie together the self's various social roles."[7] Thus, we acknowledge that
individual and social identities are first, inextricably connected, and second,
humanly created constructs. As Miller states: "I'm under no illusions that
people really invent themselves. They do to a degree, but they're working in
a social matrix."[8] Social identities tend to be externally imposed and defined
by the "community," while, as McGowan suggests, "the self-identity is for-
mulated in relation to others," but is ultimately controlled by the experience
and choices of the individual." If a subject is unable either to recognize her
relation to others or to make the necessary independent choices in creating
her own identity, the consequences are damaging, both to the self and to the
community. In the premiere production of *Broken Glass* at Long Wharf, each
scene began with a single freezing spotlight on the scene's central character
before raising the other lights. This served to highlight the idea that we are
individuals first and need to come to terms with our individual identities;
only then can we become effective in the community at large, a community
which is shown to stretch beyond the shores of America.

In Miller's world, it is important that one take responsibility even
for things one cannot control, as a refusal of responsibility is ultimately a
refusal of humanity. Ignoring responsibilities, either personal or social, will
interfere with an individual's ability to connect. Miller has declared that,
through his plays, he tries "to make human relations felt between individuals and the larger structure of the world."[10] Citing the sense of connection
evident in Elizabethan drama, he admits that such a sense is lacking in the
contemporary world, but suggests it can be reformulated: "We have to invest
on the stage connections that finally make the whole. For they exist, however
concealed they may be."[11]

An event like the Holocaust involves everyone; there can be no turning away without cost. The denial, resignation, or ignorance we observe in
Broken Glass is tantamount to complicity. Non-action, Miller informs us,
whatever its rationale, becomes destructive when it allows certain other
actions to occur. Thus the theme of potency vs. impotency is central to the
play. Though Miller represents this theme mainly as a sexual problem, he
wishes it to be seen as affecting every aspect of life. Of what use is Doctor Harry Hyman's evident potency when he himself is incapable of true
commitment or fidelity to either his culture or his wife? Of what value is
Phillip Gellburg's commercial success when he understands so little of who
he is and what he does? Of what use is even Sylvia Gellburg's compassion
when she has lost touch with her own selfhood so much that she no longer
retains even the capacity to stand? This play explores the complex notion
of humanity's dual identity and points out the necessity of balancing self-
awareness (individual identity) and a sense of security through connection

to others (social identity), a balance which allows people to live with dignity and direction.

Neither Hyman, Gellburg, nor Sylvia have attained a proper balance, and each represents a different aspect of failure. Miller wants us to recognize and learn from their mistakes. Their reactions to "Kristallnacht" are indicative of their failures and differences. Though managing to be somewhat self-aware, Hyman refuses to acknowledge the true identity of others and views the Germans with nostalgic pleasure rather than seeing them as dangerous killers. His sense of connection is severed by his own selfish needs. Gellburg may accept the truth of events, but he refuses to allow them any relevance in his own life for he lacks both self-awareness and community spirit. Sylvia fully recognizes her *communal* identity and insists upon a connection, both personally and humanistically. However, she has lost touch with herself, which has led to a symbolic, but also literal, paralysis.

In contrast to the pinched, repressed Gellburg, Hyman seems full of life, a romantic hero, who even rides a horse. But as Stefan Kanfer observes, Hyman's horsemanship may also be revealing "some conflicts in his own life. The physician turns out to be an embodiment of Isaac Babel's observation, 'Put a Jew on a horse and he's no longer a Jew.'"[12] We should take early warning when Hyman informs us that doctors are often "defective" and look for Hyman's defect. Christopher Bigsby points out that Hyman's "appetite for life" makes him "vulnerable to his own passions."[13] Hyman is a selfish man. John Peter declares: "Miller knows that those who are good at questions are not always good at answers; behind Hyman's breezy articulacy there is a barely perceptible undertow of hesitation, of vulnerability . . . Healers, Miller is saying, can be as frail as their patients."[14] Hyman enjoys asking questions of others, but he finds it far harder to question himself, preferring to remain in ignorance of his own selfish motivations.

Hyman may have a capacity to enjoy life (which the Gellburgs have lost a long time since) but he is dissatisfied with the quality of that life, a dissatisfaction which leads him to flirtation and adultery. Partly a reaction against encroaching mortality (an attempt to relive and revive the youthful vigor with which he pursued girls like Roslyn Fein), his adulterous behavior is also an attempt to boost his dwindling feelings of self-importance. As he tells Gellburg: "Some men take on a lot of women not out of confidence but because they're afraid to lose it."[15] We need to question Hyman's sexuality and sense of responsibility, for both are highly suspect. For all his life force, his marriage is as barren of children as it is of true commitment. Hyman may be self-aware, understanding his insecurities as much as he fears them, but he is unable to do more than build a smoke screen with that knowledge because he is unable to make any real connection. Hyman admires Sylvia's sense of connection and is drawn to it, but how she achieves it is a mystery to him.

Hyman is left hanging at the close as an illustration of those individuals for whom answers are ever out of sight, despite their ability to ask questions, due to a fundamental lack of commitment in their lives.

Hyman is, as described by Michael Kuchwara, "the spokesman for complacency in the play."[16] When problems loom, be it his wife's displeasure or Nazi oppression, he creates an illusion to protect himself and to prevent him from having to really address the problem. Hyman has a history of infidelity and it becomes increasingly clear that he is little better as a doctor than as a husband, despite all of his pretensions to care. Hyman's wife Margaret suffers as much from her husband's potency as Sylvia does from her husband's impotency. Hyman's psychiatric treatment of Sylvia, telling her to focus her concentration on her legs to awaken their power, borders on the immature. Telling Gellburg he needs to show his wife a little more love is like placing a band-aid on a gangrenous wound.[17] He needs to dig deeper to uncover the true extent of the disease, but such digging might necessitate real commitment; so his diagnoses tend toward inaccuracy as he simplifies issues to suit his own narrow, personal view of the world. This is hardly surprising from someone who so patently lacks a true vision of social obligation.

Hyman acts at being a part of the community by taking on a neighborhood practice, but as his wife points out: "Why, I don't know—we never invite anybody, we never go out, all our friends are in Manhattan" (6). His capacity to create illusions makes him attractive, but it also leads him to hide from certain necessary truths, such as what was really going on in Germany. His simplification of opera ("either she wants to and he doesn't or he wants to and she doesn't. Either way one of them gets killed and the other one jumps off a building" [94]), is an indication of his reductive level of response to everything; it precludes any necessity for deep commitment and leads to an easier (if somewhat shallow) life. Like too many early reviewers of the play, he looks for easy answers and thereby vastly simplifies the couples' problems, stereotyping them and reducing the fundamental importance of what they must both attempt to face.

The play's title invokes the idea of the multiple reflections one sees in a broken mirror, each related yet unique in its own perspective: a powerful symbol to illustrate the relationship between the individual and society.[18] The glass on stage in both the New York and London sets was significantly never broken since the Gellburgs' resentments and worries are continually bottled up as neither seeks to understand the other. Their suffering stems in fact from their inability to break the glass which surrounds them. Appearances are upheld and personal feelings repressed as they try to live their lives as good middle-class "Americans." As the Gellburgs' lives constrict, we see a connection between them and their Jewish counterparts in Europe who were being frozen into ineffectuality in the ghettos *and* the millions outside who refused to get involved. The Gellburgs need to face and overcome both the chaos of a dehumanized world as represented by the escalating Nazi horrors and their own inhuman relationship, inhuman for its lack of true communication and connection. To do this, each needs to face and come to terms with his or her own identity.

For people supposedly trying to be frank with each other, the play's characters are poor communicators. Though Sylvia, finally, will speak openly and directly to her husband, we must remember that this is only after twenty years of self-imposed silence. Gellburg and Hyman are equally self-restricted in their attempts to communicate. At one point Gellburg attempts to dismiss Hyman, mainly as a result of his self-consciousness regarding his impotency. Hyman's passionate response, instead of calming Gellburg, serves to make him even more uneasy. Failing to communicate, Hyman does not react to Gellburg's fears but to his own: he feels guilty for having flirted with Sylvia and thinks Gellburg may suspect. Each isolates himself from the other by his own self-involvement, and confusion results as each fails to recognize the other's feelings of guilt and inadequacy. It is such failures of communication that lie at the heart of the play's aura of ambiguity. There are declarations and conversations throughout the play which are filled with ambiguity as unresolved as the ending. For example, Sylvia's sudden cry, "What is going to become of us?" (106), leaves us wondering whether she refers to humanity, her relationship with her husband, or her relationship with Hyman.

Both Gellburgs avoid their personal needs and fears by immersing themselves in either work or the home. Their problems fester and grow, perpetuated by their mutual silence. Each secretly holds the other to blame: Gellburg sees his wife as emasculating and Sylvia sees her husband as tyrannical. As John Lahr points out: "They're both right, and they're both wrong. What's true is the psychological dynamic, in which blame becomes a way of not dealing with unacceptable feelings."[19] Neither has been fully honest or supportive of the other. Gellburg is too wrapped up in his own divisions to tell Sylvia how much he loves her, or allow her the freedom she wants. Allowing her to work would have broken the control he feels he needs to assert to give him a sense of security. Having married a provider for the sake of her family, Sylvia is full of regret, but instead of speaking out, she maintains a twenty year silence during which she helps drive her husband to impotency.

Gellburg's problem is far more complicated than Hyman's picture of him as a self-hating Jew. Declaring himself and his son to be the first or only Jews to do this and that, he seems not embarrassed but proud of his Jewishness. But is he proud of his achievements as a Jew or *despite* his Jewishness? The answer to this question is kept deliberately ambiguous. Partly due to his recognition and fear of American anti-Semitism,[20] Gellburg has tried to sever his connection with other Jews, yet his own Jewishness is unvoidable:

he has a Jewish wife, he speaks Yiddish, he is prone to Jewish folk beliefs, and his achievements mean more, either way, *because* he is Jewish. But also, like Hyman, Gellburg is so self-involved that he has no place for a community in his life. Even though he has striven to be accepted there, he cannot feel comfortable in the anti-Semitic American community, nor is he happy in the Jewish community for which he feels such antipathy. What is worse, Gellburg has no place in the larger community of mankind, for, unlike Hyman, he has no sense of himself anymore, and has lost touch with his own humanity.

The play's lessons regarding how to be a good Jew are as much an illustration of the wider issue of "how to be a human being, to live a human life, grasp the shames and responsibilities of being human and deal with the fears inherent in being human."[21] This places Gellburg's difficulties into the more universal framework Miller continuously has in mind. As Miller has said, *Broken Glass* is a play about people who are "fleeing from their identity and trying to go toward it at the same time. . . . In this case they're Jews, but this is obvious, I think, it's anybody's identity."[22] Gellburg may have problems as a Jew, but they stem from his problems as a human being.

In one sense, Gellburg's inner mirror has become shattered; he has lost touch with who he is, and even whom he would like to become. Louise Doughty suggests that Gellburg sees everything—Kristallnacht, his wife, and the world—"through broken glass," which is why he cannot make the right connections.[23] Furthermore, he breaks down whenever he is pushed to a point where he may have to break his self-imposed silence and speak out and face his problems. He is doubly caught: first, between his own Judaism and the popular idea of America as a melting pot and second, between his own rejection of his Jewishness and the anti-Semitism he sees around him. Anti-Semitism is not something he has created; it lies all around him. His response to it is to try to see himself as unique, insisting on his unusual name and Finnish origins. However, such a response is inadequate, for it is done to avoid becoming part of communities he views with ambivalence; it is an empty identity he is creating.

The blackness of Gellburg's dress and the paleness of his complexion emphasize the emptiness inside the man. He is, as Miller says, "in mourning for his own life," and it is a life he himself is largely responsible for stifling. Reservedly stiff and "proper" (until the more truthful realities of his life start to insist on recognition) Gellburg offers up glimpses of inner torments in his outbursts of anger and his hesitancies. His pent up anger conveys an increasing sense of threat. Even in silence, his dark, brooding presence on stage commands attention as we wait to see if he will explode. Internally, Gellburg is a mass of contradictions he finds it hard to control. He has lost the ability to connect and communicate to Sylvia how he feels about her. We are constantly told that he loves and even adores his wife, and the difficulty he has admitting this to Sylvia is related to his fear of such uncontrollable feelings that he stifles and twists but is incapable of destroying. Revealing flashes of violence as he throws a steak at his wife or pushes her up the stairs, he is also capable of great tenderness, but he continually suppresses both sides of his humanity. The point is, he is human, and every human (including the Nazis) has the capacity to be both violent and tender, it is the individual's responsibility to choose how to respond.

Concentrating on his work, Gellburg allows himself no personal side. He is ever on duty as the foreclosure man. He acts a part in which he conceals and suppresses his own humanity. Unable to trust himself, he has lost the capacity to trust others. This inability to trust leads him to fail even at work, for it is instrumental in his losing the property his boss had wanted. Gellburg's growing nervousness when questioned and his inability to look anyone in the eye indicate the erosion of his sense of self at the same time that it shows him trying to conceal the fact.

Gellburg desperately desires a sense of control in his life to protect him against the chaos he sees around him. He acts like a "dictator" (26) at his grandmother's funeral and even, on occasion, plays the tyrant at home in order to seem in control, but to no avail. His work had given him a sense of power and control, but he loses even that as he comes to realize how empty his work actually is. By the close of the play, as he recognizes that it is impossible to separate himself from his community, he can no longer find pride in a job which is based on dispossessing others. A conscious suppression of his uncontrollable love for Sylvia has been another result of his mania for control. As Lahr points out, "Gellburg is devoted to his wife, but idealization is not intimacy."[24] By refusing to allow his love any freedom, Gellburg has grown as distant from his wife as from their wider community.

Both Gellburg's and Hyman's self-obsessed concerns may seem trivial in the face of the more important matter that Sylvia introduces, but they are concerns which do need to be addressed. Gellburg and Hyman try to rationalize the events taking place overseas in an effort to defend and preserve their own fragile beliefs. Their failure is an indication of the innate wrongness of the beliefs they had adopted and the need for them to discover something more worthwhile in which to believe. We should also note that it is not just Gellburg and Hyman who dismiss concern for the German Jews, but the majority of Americans. Sylvia's sister Harriet and Harriet's husband both agree that Sylvia's worries are not real concerns and that she should not be worrying about people three thousand miles away.

Miller cites the Holocaust as the period when the world learned to turn away, "And we're still doing it . . . There is the sense that we feel helpless to affect anything in Bosnia or Africa now and we learned how to do that then."[25] Miller insists that we combat this tendency to ignore what is unpleasant in life and involve ourselves before another Holocaust can occur. Humanity is "in a boiling soup," Miller tells us "We change the flavor by what we add, and it changes all of us."[26] Therefore, it is not acceptable to refuse to act on the grounds that a single person's action cannot make a difference.

In direct contrast to her husband, Sylvia has been in touch with the community all along but so much so, that she has lost her sense of self. As she exclaims: "I'm here for my mother's sake, and Jerome's sake, and everybody's sake except mine" (44). She has lived her life so long for others she has lost all connection with her own selfhood, but she begins by blaming *others* for this. With Gellburg dominating every scene he is in, Sylvia tends to get pushed to the side, but this marginality only reflects the way she has *allowed* her life to run.[27] In a way, Sylvia's outer mirror has been shattered. Through "Kristall-nacht" Sylvia's sense of community is challenged by both the behavior of the Nazis and the apparent apathy all around her. But this challenge provokes Sylvia to embody a mixture of rage and regret, disgusted at *herself* as much as others.

Sylvia has let herself become as pale and drained of vitality as her husband. Even her laugh is "dead" (41). Having withdrawn from their marriage as much as Gellburg, she "punished" her husband when he would not let her work by refusing to have another child. Despite her condition, she has shown no interest in healing the relationship with her husband and mocks him when he feebly attempts to reconnect. She tells Hyman that she pities Gellburg, but not once in the play does she ever speak of loving him. She has failed to consider his private nature when speaking to her father about their sex life, a conversation which has not helped but only exacerbated Gellburg's feelings of guilt and embarrassment. Caught up in her own confusions and feelings of betrayal, she has failed to recognize that *he is suffering too.*

Miller is not writing a case study of Sylvia's illness, as Lahr points out: "He is aiming at something much more ambitious: an anatomy of denial . . . Her private sense of humiliation is projected onto her fury about the public humiliation of the Jews."[28] Sylvia has settled for and accommodated herself to her situation to a point which ultimately becomes untenable even for her self-effacing spirit. Her having reached her limit manifests itself in her objections to the Nazis' treatment of Jews in Europe. When Sylvia rises for the first time in the play, she is driven to do so by her fear that no-one will do anything about the suffering in Germany. This is the first time in her whole life, Miller tells us, that Sylvia has taken her life into her own hands. It marks an important turning point in her relationship with Phillip. She may have allowed herself to be a victim, like so many of the Jews in Europe, "but she is also a revolutionary." Miller concludes, "Finally, it is Sylvia who is giving the orders, not Phillip."[29]

For a time Sylvia is distracted by Hyman's vitality, and she is fooled into believing that she has a stronger connection to the doctor than to her husband. However, she eventually acknowledges the truer connection which exists between her and her husband which they have been stifling. This acknowledgment, coupled with her decision to face up to her own responsibility for the way she is, gives Sylvia the strength to rise. Sylvia's paralysis has been an emblem of her loss of control, related to a denial of certain responsibilities she had to herself as much as others. She comes to realize her own complicity in her condition, declaring "What I did with my life! Out of ignorance . . . Gave it away like a couple of pennies—I took better care of my shoes" (112). She finally takes responsibility for her condition and ceases to blame others. It is the acceptance of such responsibilities that offers a person real control in life.

Much has been made of the various endings of the play and Miller's difficulties in finalizing the piece. Miller has stated a final preference for the ending that the 1996 BBC filmed production uses.[30] Arguably, it is the nature of the play and its themes which have caused the problem in the ending. First, it hardly matters if Gellburg dies or not, as the focus is now on Sylvia; she rises to her feet in *every* version. Gellburg attracts our attention throughout the play, but Sylvia now insists that we look at *her* as she faces certain truths and allows *herself* to take center stage. Progress has been made, admittedly minor, but enough to suggest the possibility of hope. But beyond that, the play's ambiguity and lack of closure are essential to its message. The play cannot (and should not) be resolved by the playwright, for he has already passed on the "baton" to his audience; it is up to them to create a happy ending—if they can.[31] Any disappointment on the audience's part becomes their responsibility and an indication that they have failed, perhaps, to learn the play's lessons. To see the play as incomplete is to hold back from engagement and therefore to resist and prevent the play's completion, by refusing to join the circle (of humanity) and involve oneself in ways that the play demands. After all, Miller's intention is not to tell a tale of other folk so much as to tell us our own lives and thereby involve us, the audience, in our own moral resuscitation.

It is hard to resist comparing *Broken Glass* to a Greek drama. Miller declares that its relatively short length was an intentional emulation of such dramas.[32] Also, its evident concern with people's identities and place in society are issues which lie at the heart of most Greek plays. One can even begin to see how *Broken Glass*'s predictability, about which many critics have complained, is yet another aspect of its structure which relates it to Greek dramas whose impact largely depended upon the audience knowing what would happen next. *Broken Glass* uses the same type of classical structure which Miller used for *A View from the Bridge*, where the predictability of the outcome is an important part of the play's message. Coincidence lies at the heart of such dramas as *Oedipus Rex* and should be seen as positive proof that we do, indeed, all connect and live in a world capable of coherence. Miller describes such plays as revealing "some unreadable hidden order behind the amoral chaos of events as we rationally perceive them . . . there are times when things do indeed cohere."[33]

Numerous reviews of the play discuss how dissatisfied critics felt on leaving the theater.[34] Rather than a failing of the play, this may be an indication of its effectiveness. Miller intends to discomfit his audience: the repetition of the eerie cello music is an indication of this. There is a sense of menace from the start as the strident cello fills the auditorium with its pulsing rhythms. In *Timebends*, Miller points out how audiences, in America particularly, have a tendency to resist plays which challenge them and ask them to judge themselves. Maybe the final dissatisfaction with *Broken Glass* stems from learning that this menace is not so much the expected Nazism, as the common failings within each and every one of us, which all too often prevent us from fully connecting with our fellow human beings. After all, the lesson of Kristallnacht was not heeded until *after* the elimination of six million Jews—there is a guilt attached to that neglect which we all must continue to share. The Gellburgs may begin to uncover the roots of their problems, but they are still a long way from solving them. Sylvia regains her feet by the close of the play and seems to have regained her sense of balance; however, although she stands, it remains unclear what she stands for, and where her first steps might lead. Miller is suggesting that it is partly the audience's responsibility to help create a world in which Sylvia can safely walk.

FOOTNOTES

1. Arthur Miller, interview with Charlie Rose, *The Charlie Rose Show*, Public Broadcasting System, 31 August 1994.

2. Frederic Jameson, *Postmodernism, or The Cultural Logic of Late Capitalism* (Durham: Duke University Press, 1991), 15.

3. Jacques Derrida, *Writing and Difference*, Alan Bass trans. (Chicago: Chicago University Press, 1978), 292.

4. Arthur Miller, quoted in *Arthur Miller and Company*, Chris Bigsby ed. (London: Methuen, 1990), 178.

5. Alan Wilde, *Middle Grounds: Studies in Contemporary American Fiction* (Philadelphia: University of Pennsylvania Press, 1987), 128.

6. John McGowan, *Postmodernism and Its Critics* (Ithaca: Cornell University Press, 1991), 154.

7. Ibid., 246.

8. Arthur Miller, quoted in James J. Martine, *Critical Essays on Arthur Miller* (Boston: Hall, 1979), 180.

9. McGowan, 244.

10. Arthur Miller, quoted in *Conversations with Arthur Miller*, Matthew C. Roudané, ed. (Jackson: University Press of Mississippi, 1987), 171.

11. Ibid., 172.

12. Stefan Kaner, "On Stage: A Hit and Three Misses," *New Leader* 75 (May 1992): 21.

13. Christopher Bigsby, "Miller's Journey to *Broken Glass*," in program notes for production of *Broken Glass* at Long Wharf (1 March 1994–3 April 1994), 23.

14. John Peter, "A Raw Slice of Humanity," *Sunday Times*, 14 August 1994, sec. 10, p. 21.

15. Arthur Miller, *Broken Glass* (Harmondsworth: Penguin, 1994), 78. All subsequent references cited parenthetically in text.

16. Michael Kuchwara, "Review of *Broken Glass*," *Associated Press*, 25 April 1994, [n.p.]

17. Hyman is not the voice of appropriateness or a model of behavior as certain critics have intimated. See Benedict Nightingale, "Smashed Certainties," *Times* (London), 6 August 1994, sec. E, p. 5; John Simon, "Whose Paralysis is it, Anyway?" *New York*, 9 May 1994, in *New York Theatre Critics' Review* 55 (1994): 128; and Linda Winer, "Arthur Miller's Morality Soaper," *New York News Day*, 25 April 1994, in *New York Theatre Critics' Review* 55 (1994): 132.

18. The "Broken Glass" of the play's title has been variously interpreted. It is certainly intended to bring to mind the shattered windows of Kristallnacht. David Richards suggests that it alludes to a marital row where dinnerware gets smashed. See David Richards, "A Paralysis Points to Spiritual and Social Ills," *New York Times*, 25 April 1994, in *New York Theatre Critics' Review* 55 (1994): 129. However, we realize that one of the Gellburg's main problems is that they have never allowed themselves to release their frustrations so satisfyingly. It may allude to the glass the bridegroom breaks at a Jewish wedding ceremony as Jeremy Gerard suggests, although he is incorrect in explaining the act's symbolism as a "celebration of the hoped-for performance of the marital vows." See Jeremy Gerard, "Review of *Broken Glass*," *Variety*, 25 April 1994, in *New York Theatre Critics' Review* 55 (1994): 128. The various Rabbinic explanations for the breaking of the glass—from being a reminder of the destruction of the Temple in Jerusalem to being a symbol of our imperfect world—all seem to involve some sadness. This symbol of sadness, so prominently displayed on a joyous occasion, serves as a reminder of the duality of human existence. We may celebrate, but others are mourning; we may enjoy peace, but others are suffering war. This world view is not pessimistic, but basic to Judaism, which recognizes that all is not perfect. This is why observant Jews feel commanded to work for the improvement of this world and the enrichment of the lives of all its inhabitants. This altruistic aspect of Judaism is something both Gellburgs have forgotten.

19. John Lahr, "Dead Souls," *New Yorker*, 9 May 1994, in *New York Theatre Critics' Review* 55 (1994): 125.

20. As a character, Stanton Case, Gellburg's ruthless boss, seems rather stereotyped as the WASP anti-Semite, a not-so-subtle inversion of the more usually stereotyped minority, such as the Jew. He passes his time at the yachting club while Gellburg does all his dirty work, then discards the Jew swiftly after his usefulness is over. Thus the play points out that while we bemoan (and some even try to deny) the Holocaust, America herself was at the same period a hotbed of anti-Semitism so strong as to even turn Jews like Gellburg against themselves.

21. Peter, 21.

22. Miller, interview with Charlie Rose.

23. Louise Doughty, "Shard Time: Night and Day," *Mail on Sunday*, 14 April 1994, p. 30.

24. Lahr, 124.

25. Arthur Miller, quoted in Sara Villiers, "Tried in the Crucible," *The Herald* (Glasgow), 15 May 1995, p. 11.

26. Miller, quoted in Martine, 178.

27. Alice Griffin feels that Sylvia's complacency is very reflective of the time in which she was raised, when Women were encouraged to be amenable to others and not to insist on their own independence. See Alice Griffin, *Understanding Arthur Miller* (Columbia: University of South Carolina Press, 1996), 186.

28. Lahr, 124.

29. Arthur Miller, quoted in Griffin, 186–7.

30. Miller told me his preference when I asked him about the confusion over the various endings. Audience discussion, Williamstown, 1996.

31. It seems that Miller retains something of his early education in agitprop in which the onus for action is forced onto the audience, although he has evolved it into a far more subtle and sophisticated form.

32. Miller, interview with Charlie Rose.

33. Arthur Miller, *Timebends: A Life* (London: Methuen, 1990), 135.

34. For example, Gerard declares it is "an unfinished work whose power has only been partly realized" (128). Michael Phillips sees it as too "reductive," "simple," and lacking in "dramatic instinct." See Michael Phillips, "Broken Glass Makes Things Perfectly Clear," *San Diego Union-Tribune*, 25 April 1994, sec. E, p. 1. Frank Schenk complains "You feel that there's a great play buried in *Broken Glass*, but like its heroine, it can't seem to rise to its feet." See Frank Schenk, "Grains of a Good Play Exist in Arthur Miller's Strained *Broken Glass*," *Christian Science Monitor*, 27 April 1994, in *New York Theatre Critics' Review* 55 (1994): 127.

BRENDA MURPHY

"Personality Wins the Day": Death of a Salesman and Popular Sales Advice Literature

One of the primary characteristics of Willy Loman's character is his penchant for self-contradiction: "Biff is a lazy bum! . . . There's one thing about Biff—he's not lazy" (16). One area where this is evident is Willy's attitude toward business and success. As he tells his boss Howard Wagner, he is aware that in 1948, the "real time" of the play's action, business is "all cut and dried, and there's no chance for bringing friendship to bear—or personality" (81), but he still longs for the days when "there was respect, and comradeship, and gratitude in it" (91). As Brian Dennehy's performance in the 1999 production of *Death of a Salesman* reminds his audience, Willy is a "born" salesman. In the scene between Willy and Howard, he nearly sells Howard on the myth of Dave Singleman before he sabotages his sales pitch by losing his temper. Willy Loman is a very confused man, but his confusion about what it means to be a salesman and what it takes to succeed at the job is as much cultural as personal. In the character of Willy Loman, Arthur Miller has established a metonymic representation of the contradictory beliefs and value-systems that were at the heart of American business culture in the decade after World War II. In his own memory and experience, Willy encompasses three generations of American salesmen, that of his father and his hero Dave Singleman, that of Willy, his brother Ben, and his friend (or brother-in-law) Charley, and that of Willy's sons and his boss, Howard Wagner. In the play, Miller

---

From *South Atlantic Review.* © 1999.

creates a history of the career of the traveling salesman in America through the references to these characters, and in doing so, he suggests the extent to which social and cultural forces have figured in Willy's business failure, and his personal disintegration.

The occupation of traveling salesman began in the United States with the Yankee peddler, in the early nineteenth century. The peddler would buy up cheap, portable manufactured goods in the early industrial centers of the Northeast, pack them in a wagon or peddler's pack, and set off for the rural South or the frontier villages of the West, where he would travel from small town to small town, selling his wares at a high profit. Peddlers were entrepreneurs, operating completely on their own, free to buy and sell whatever they wanted and to travel wherever they liked. Willy Loman's father, born in the mid-nineteenth century, is a peddler, a "very wild-hearted man," according to Ben, who would "toss the whole family in the wagon" and drive right across the country, through Ohio, Indiana, Michigan, Illinois, and all the Western states (49).[1] Miller emphasizes the elder Loman's independence by indicating that he even manufactured the products that he sold, the flutes that he made along the way. According to Ben, he was also a great inventor, who made more in a week with one gadget than a man like Willy could make in a lifetime (49). It is the elder Loman that Miller evokes with the play's flute music, "small and fine, telling of grass and trees and the horizon" (11). It expresses nostalgia for a lost age when the traveling salesman was free and independent, living by his wits and his own hard work.

It is significant that Willy's father traveled west, away from the urban centers of the country, and eventually left his family to go to America's last frontier, Alaska. During Willy's childhood in the 1890s, the Yankee peddler was already an outmoded figure, living on the fringes of society. He had been replaced by a figure who served the interests of the larger manufacturers more efficiently, the drummer. Beginning in the late nineteenth century, the drummer, usually a young man with a pleasant personality, was sent by a large manufacturing firm or wholesaler to greet small retail merchants who came from outlying areas to the industrial centers in order to buy their stock. The drummers would go to hotels, railroad stations, and boat landings, greet the merchants, help them to make their way around the city, and offer them free entertainment in hopes of securing their orders for merchandise. As competition between wholesalers intensified, the drummers were sent on the road with sample cases and catalogs, going out to the merchants rather than waiting for them to come to the city. These were the original "commercial travelers" or "traveling salesmen," and they spent six to nine months a year on the road, living in hotels and sleeping cars.

Dave Singleman, Willy's hero, is Miller's example of the drummer. As Willy tells it, he met Dave Singleman when he was young, in the first decade of the twentieth century. Singleman, a salesman who had drummed merchandise in thirty-one states, was eighty-four years old at the time that Willy met him, and still making his living as a salesman. According to Willy, he could go into twenty or thirty different cities, pick up a phone, and call the buyers, who would give him orders. Willy says that he decided then that he wanted to be a traveling salesman because he wanted to become like Singleman, and be "remembered and loved and helped by so many different people" (81). In the early part of the century, it was character that was considered to be the paramount factor in sales success. Aspiring salesmen were urged to develop the qualities of character that would make customers respect and want to buy from them. A prototype for Dave Singleman, James Fenelon, an eighty-nine year veteran of the traveling sales force in 1916, attributed his success to the fact that "he never used tobacco in any form and that he always acted as a gentleman should" (Geyer 53). His virtue was rewarded when he became ill and the president of the company wrote that "he wanted to keep the dean of the force on the pay roll as long as he lived, even if he never made another trip" (Geyer 53). Willy's generation remembered the time when there was "respect, and comradeship, and gratitude" (81) in business.

In the first two decades of the twentieth century, salesmen were urged to improve sales by improving their character, often as a kind of religious exercise. Self-tests to see whether one had the requisite strength of character for the job were common in popular magazines. One expert suggested a self-examination at the end of each day:

> The salesman should possess the ability to review carefully his work at the close of each day, and decide just where and how he has been weaker than he should have been. There is some reason for the loss of every sale. The salesman may not be at fault, but it is safer for him to assume that he is and to endeavor to put his finger upon his weakness. Such a practice will foster in him the habit of holding himself strictly accountable for errors. He should also at the same time review the essential qualifications of a salesman and decide in which of them he is lacking. (Jones 170)

The salesman was urged to be thoroughly honest with himself when performing his "task of introspection," for "the salesman can develop only by earnestly striving to discover and eliminate his negative qualities, while at the same time he makes every effort to strengthen his positive ones" (Jones 170–71).

Willy's own career as a salesman begins in the early part of the twentieth century, when it was, as Willy tells his sons, "personality" that was considered the salesman's greatest asset. His job was to make friends with the buyers and merchants, so they would buy what he was selling. The product itself was not all that important. With the growth of mass production, however, the pressure increased on the salesman to move merchandise in order to keep up the volume of production. Consequently, as Willy's generation came into its maturity, married, and raised children during the 1920s, there was a good deal of pressure to sell merchandise, but it was relatively easy to do since the American business economy was enjoying one of its greatest periods of prosperity.

Salesmen at this time debated the best approach to selling merchandise. While there were many like Willy, who put all their faith in personality, friendship, and personal loyalty—"Be liked and you will never want" (33)— there was a new way of thinking about salesmanship. The earlier assumption had been that salesmanship was an essential quality, an innate character trait that could be nurtured and developed, but not created by the aspiring salesman. During the teens and twenties, salesmanship was beginning to be treated as a profession to be learned. The new interest in psychology led experts to think about the psychology of the buyer, and how best to manipulate it, as well as the psychological traits that made for the best salesmen. With mass production and increased competition, buyers and merchants began to think more about profit margins and customer satisfaction than their own personal relationship with the salesman. There was more interest in the quality of the product and the salesman's knowledge about it. Companies began to train their salesmen in the methods of salesmanship and to educate them about the products they were selling. As one writer put it:

> Salesmanship is not trying to persuade people to buy something they do not want. That kind of salesmanship is, indeed, practiced, but not for very long; and no one makes any money out of it. Real salesmanship is demonstrating an article, or whatever it may be, in terms of the person who, it is hoped, will buy it. It is the development of a need, that already exists, into a present want. It is an operation performed first on the intellect and only secondly on the pocketbook of the prospect. (Hopkins 29)

With the stock market crash in 1929, and the Great Depression that followed it, the competition among salesmen became more and more cutthroat. As Willy tells Ben in one of the daydream sequences that takes place in 1931, "business is bad, it's murderous" (51). Using all of the tricks that Willy has learned in a lifetime of selling, including seducing the buyer's secretary and bribing her with stockings, Willy is barely able to eke out a living for his family. The salesman was up against an unforgiving business climate that placed the blame for failure squarely on the individual. Business writer J. C. Royle, for example, maintained that all that was needed to increase sales in 1931 was better salesmen: "The sales of the born salesmen have not suffered terribly during the Depression, but the amount of goods handled by the poor salesmen or those who need training has been pitiable." In 1929, he contended, American salesmen did not sell sufficient goods to justify themselves, and "they are urged to do so now under spur of necessity. They are not being asked the impossible either" ("Wanted" 41–2).

During this period, the prevailing idea was still that, as Willy puts it, "the man who makes an appearance in the business world, the man who creates personal interest, is the man who gets ahead" (33). As J. George Frederick suggested in his *1000 Sales Points: The "Vitamin Concentrates" of Modern Salesmanship* (1941), the first element of good salesmanship was to "Polish Off Your Personality." A salesman's personality "must not be rough-hewn. It must feel agreeable and bland to all who contact it, or else it is a handicap. Therefore the first sales fundamental is to present *an acceptable personality*—in neatness, cleanliness, clothes, manner, deportment, expression, etc." (17). Once his own personality was attended to, the salesman could concentrate on the psychological manipulation of the customer.

With most of the younger men in the military, middle-aged salesmen like Willy made an adequate living during World War II, despite the fact that the manufacturing of consumer goods was severely restricted. In the post-war period when the real time of the play takes place, there was a pent-up demand for things like new cars, tires, brand-name liquor, and nylon stockings, which had not been available during the war. The enormous American war industry was being retooled to produce consumer goods, and the advertizing business was expanding rapidly as Americans were "educated" into desiring things like vacuum cleaners, television sets, and air conditioners, which had not been manufactured in large quantities before the war. The newly invigorated American business sector seized on the youthful and energetic workforce of young men returning from the military, displacing the women and older men who had been employed during the war. Men like Willy Loman, sixty-three years old in 1948, were being displaced by the younger generation everywhere.

Hap Loman and Howard Wagner represent typical members of this younger generation. Hap is not a salesman, but one of two assistants to the assistant buyer of a large department store. His job is more secure than Willy's, and it carries a regular salary rather than the precarious commission that Willy lives on. Unlike his father, though, Hap does not use his salary to support a family. Instead, he lives a carefree bachelor life, more interested, as Linda tells him, in his apartment and his car and his women than in helping his family, soon to become the ideal consumer of Hugh Hefner's *Playboy*. His final response to his father's death is to proclaim that he is "not licked that easily. I'm staying right in this city, and I'm gonna beat this racket! . . . Willy Loman did not die in vain. He had a good dream. It's the only dream you can have—to come out number-one man (138–39). Howard Wagner, who has taken over the business that employs Willy after the death of his father Frank, is pragmatic and impersonal in his treatment of the aging salesman. When Willy admits that he can't handle the road anymore, Howard refuses to consider finding him something to do in New York as his father might have done, explaining, "it's a business, kid, and everybody's gotta pull his own weight" (80). When Willy loses control, showing his desperation, Howard fires him, telling him that he is not in a fit state to represent the firm.

The profession of selling underwent a tremendous change after the war. In the late forties, a movement to professionalize the salesman began, promoting sales as a career for college graduates. An important part of this movement was to emphasize the salesman's expertise and downplay his personality. Students were taught in business courses that the salesman's job was to learn everything he could about his product, and about the market, to gather all the data he could and analyze it using the most sophisticated statistical methods—in Willy's words, "today, it's all cut and dried, and there's no chance for bringing friendship to bear—or personality" (81). A number of books were written about "salesmanship" in the late forties and early fifties, attempting to codify the knowledge that was the fruit of a lifetime of experience for a Willy Loman or a Dave Singleman. Unfortunately for the veteran salesmen, the knowledge was expressed in a new lingo they didn't always understand, and it was based on different values, Howard Wagner's values, where the bottom line was everything.

During the forties and fifties, the professional salesman became increasingly driven by things like market studies and demographics. Willy's plea for loyalty and humane treatment—"you can't eat the orange and throw the peel away—a man is not a piece of fruit!" (82)—is irrelevant to Howard's way of thinking. The prevailing view in the post-war business culture was that a salesman's job was not to sell a product—any product—to a buyer because he was liked and trusted by him, but to learn as much as possible about a particular product, identify its market, and bring the product to the buyer, any buyer. The two human beings, salesman and buyer, were becoming the least important elements of the transaction. Willy's complaint that salesmanship was becoming "cut and dried" is meaningless to a man like Howard, who is interested only in the bottom line of profit and loss. That is exactly the way he wants it to be.

A good example of the popular application of the new ideas about salesmanship is Harry Simmons' *How to Sell Like a Star Salesman* (1953). Simmons' description of the first two necessities for salesmanship are "application to the job—keep everlastingly at it" and "complete knowledge—knowing not only the rules of the game, but the reasons behind the rules and the smart application of the rules to the situation at hand. This also includes every single bit of knowledge about your product that it is possible to acquire; you never know when the smallest fact will develop into a big factor that will turn the tide in your favor" (Simmons 12).

Simmons' book includes "Twenty-eight pint-size capsules that hold a gallon of helpful sales advice" for the salesman operating in the post-war business environment, several of which speak directly to Willy's failings. For example: "Reach for the order instead of applause. Many a man mistakes sociability for sales ability. He spends his time being a good-time Charley instead of a brass-tacks salesman. And then he complains about business being slow!" and "Tall tales make funny stories, but sound selling talks its way to the cash register! It's just a question of whether you want your sales manager to laugh with you or at you" (Simmons 94). The modern salesman, in Simmons' post-war view, is a serious businessman emphasizing "product information" and "helpmanship"—"helping your customer to buy properly, to use correctly, and to sell efficiently will fill both your pockets with more profits" (Simmons 98).[2]

The successful representatives of Willy's generation in the play, Charley and Ben, are hard-nosed capitalists, who have never allowed themselves to succumb to the sentimentality of the Dave Singleman myth as Willy has. Ben's creed is "never fight fair with a stranger, boy. You'll never get out of the jungle that way" (49). Although Charley is a loyal friend to Willy, he understands that the business world operates by different rules than human relations: "You named him Howard, but you can't sell that. The only thing you got in this world is what you can sell. And the funny thing is that you're a salesman, and you don't know that" (97). Unlike Willy, Charley has been able to adapt to the prevailing business culture. Willy's reaction to his failure in business during the real time of the play is similar to his response to his sense of failure in the other areas of his life. He retreats from present reality into nostalgic daydreams of the past, until he can no longer separate daydream from reality, past from present. His response to Charley's blunt statement of reality is a nostalgic reference to the bromides of the sales literature of the twenties: "I've always felt that if a man was impressive, and well liked, that nothing—" (97).

From the point of view of men like Howard and Charley, Willy's failure in business is a failure to adapt his old-fashioned sales technique—based on the buyer's personal loyalty to the salesman—to the new post-war business climate where salesmanship was based on knowledge of the product and service to the customer. Willy is a dinosaur. Howard fires him because "Business is business," and Charley offers him a job out of charity because he is an old friend, a gesture Willy recognizes and rejects. Through his representation of the three generations of businessmen in the play, however, Miller suggests that Willy's failure is also due to a deep cultural dissonance in the messages he has heard throughout his life. Willy has heard the hard truth from the capitalists, but he has chosen to believe in the Dave Singleman myth, widely reflected in the popular literature of his day, that it was humanity that mattered—whether it was measured in sterling traits of character, as in the early part of the century, or in a pleasing personality, as in the twenties. Despite the fact that Biff has won the chance to play in Ebbets Field through his accomplishments on the football field, Willy really believes, as he tells Ben, that "three great universities are begging for him, and from there the sky's the limit, because it's not what you do, Ben. It's who you know and the smile on your face! . . . that's the wonder, the wonder of this country, that a man can end with diamonds here on the basis of being liked!" (86). The play's overwhelming message is that this is a lie, and that Willy is a fool to believe it. It is one of the things that destroys him. Willy is not alone, however, as the popular sales literature demonstrates. His belief that innate superiority will win out is the other side of the "strive and thrive" message of the American Protestant success ethic. Willy never ceases to believe that Biff is "magnificent," that he is one of the elect. It is imagining "that magnificence with twenty thousand dollars in his pocket" (135) that Willy goes to his death, destroyed, in one sense, by the salesman's creed of the twenties, from which he has never deviated.

Notes

1. See Barry Gross, "Peddler and Pioneer in *Death of a Salesman.*" *Modern Drama* 7 (Feb. 1965): 405–10 for a discussion of these themes.

2. For similar views, see also Paul Ivey and Walter Hovarth, *Successful Salesmanship*, 3rd ed., New York: Prentice-Hall, 1953; Melvin S. Hattwick, *The New Psychology of Selling*, New York: McGraw-Hill, 1960.

Works Cited

Frederick, J. George. *1000 Sales Points: The "Vitamin Concentrates" of Modern Salesmanship.* New York: Business Bourse, 1941.

Geyer, O. R. "The Oldest Traveling Salesman." *The American Magazine* 81 (Mar. 1916): 53.

Hopkins, George W. "The Real 'Star Salesman' in Modern Business." *The American Magazine* 93 (Apr. 1922): 28–9, 70.

Jones, John G. *Salesmanship and Sales Management.* New York: Alexander Hamilton Institute, 1919.

Miller, Arthur. *Death of a Salesman.* New York: Viking, 1949.

Simmons, Harry. *How to Sell Like a Star Salesman.* New York. Henry Holt, 1953.

"Wanted: Salesmen." *The Literary Digest* 113 (21 May 1931): 41–2.

JEFFREY MEYERS

A Portrait of Arthur Miller

In the 1970's I wrote two literary biographies, one on Katherine Mansfield, a short-story writer from New Zealand who died early at the peak of her career; the other on Wyndham Lewis, an original novelist, great painter and incurable outsider who died blind and neglected in 1957. As I began to consider a new subject, my biographer's antennae quivered at the thought of Arthur Miller. His opposition to the infamous House Un-American Activities Committee (HUAC) in the 1950's had earned him lasting political prestige. His plays were a staple of the American theater repertory, and he'd also written classic film-scripts of his own work. Though his normal, commonsensical, intellectual life rarely made headlines, in the late 1950's he had been married to Marilyn Monroe, a conjunction that made heads spin at the time and now seemed the stuff of myth. I was full of respect for him, and curiosity as well.

In September 1980 I wrote to sound him out. I couldn't help noting in my letter the similarities between his early life and mine. We both came from Jewish families, grew up in New York, had a father in the coat business, were adored by our mothers (who slept late while the maid served breakfast), were taught by Irish spinsters in public schools, rebelled against piano lessons and Hebrew school, and graduated from the University of Michigan.

From *The Virginia Quarterly Review*. © 2000.

Not surprisingly, Miller didn't want to be distracted from his current work by contemplating the shape and pattern of his entire life. He did not want a sleuth to comb through his private papers for unwelcome revelations. Nor did he want to give away material and ideas he still might use in his own writing. But he replied courteously and, as I learned to expect, modestly: "I would be loath to begin a project such as you suggest for several reasons. I am really writing more now than ever in my life and I don't want to interrupt. I've never kept anything like an orderly file of all my correspondence, most of which, in any case, is hardly worth reading. And finally, I guess, I don't think I'm all that fascinating"—though he was about to write his own autobiography.

This last remark might seem disingenuous. Miller's life, lived at the center of American cultural history, had been a starring role, not a walk-on part. But he was making a distinction between the complex external events and his straightforward inner character. As an enormously successful playwright he must have had extraordinary ambition and drive, been innovative, even rebellious. He must have made personal sacrifices and taken infinite pains. Did he, in fact, retain the human sympathy and self-respect that had sparked his imagination and informed his greatest work? Was there a modest man, an ego under control, inside his creative personality? If so, he must be quite different, I thought, from the selfish, driven, often tragic artist that lies at the heart of most literary biographies. This distinction made him all the more interesting to me.

My letter began our relationship. He asked me to send him my book on Mansfield and read it attentively. "Though I usually distrust biographies," he wrote, "to the point of avoiding them whenever possible, yours I believe. . . . She is one of those tragic persons launched on a short trajectory, the self-consuming rocket." He invited me to visit him in Connecticut, and in June 1981 I made the first of nine visits, extending over the next 17 years.

Arthur had bought this rustic house in 1956, a retreat from Manhattan and the theater, but close enough to New York to keep an eye on the city. Down a country lane, surrounded by 40 acres of woods and meadows, it was set on a rise above a swimming pond. He came out to meet us, six feet tall, as straight-backed as a soldier, his white hair crowning his tanned bald head and his Jeffersonian face, familiar from many press photographs. He was as unpretentious as his house, a comfortable place with oriental rugs on the floor, colorful sofas, books overflowing the bookcases and scattered around the rooms. He had a carpentry workshop and separate studios for himself and his wife, the photographer Inge Morath. As we walked through the grounds he pointed out the plants and vegetables in their garden, and moths laying eggs in the grass.

Arthur was a powerful physical presence. I was aware of his large capable hands, his denim workshirt, his shorts and muscular legs, his bare feet in moccasins. He mowed the huge lawn himself, replaced the cement on the patio and made his own furniture. He was proud of his new custom-built Finnish woodstove, made of soapstone; and had been using the left-over material to carve building blocks and had assembled them to look like minia-ture stage sets and a modern city filled with skyscrapers. He cut a lot of wood and for him trees had distinctive characters: he showed me his "wolf tree," which dominated and devoured all the other trees around it. It had seeds that flourished only if they drifted far away.

Though he tried to "hide out" in Connecticut, many people came to see him, and he had some illustrious neighbors: Alexander Calder, Richard Wid-mark, Dustin Hoffman, Philip Roth, and William Styron (on whose court Arthur played tennis). Norman Mailer had once lived nearby. In this quiet, seemingly remote place he seemed more a countryman than a sophisticated New Yorker. (In 1984, when Arthur was in China, a fire from a defective oil burner destroyed the main house, along with his books and personal posses-sions. Fortunately, his studio was unharmed and his papers were safe. His insurance was excellent and, though it took six months to restore everything, the new house was much better than the old one. He called it "one of the best fires I ever had.")

He probably earns more money from books and plays than any other serious writer. His plays, produced all over the world, are staged more fre-quently than those of any other dramatist save Shakespeare. (Though his agents, he told me, were lucky to collect half of what was owed in Asia and Africa; in Europe and South America he did well. He sometimes has five plays on in England in one year.) He had a new Mercedes and a Rabbit con-vertible in the garage, and we talked about driving into Manhattan. He was pleased to have found a cheap place to park, but liked it even more when he was chauffeured into town for a premiere and could sleep on the way back. He had one of the new wireless phones, run off a battery, which he carried around while he did the chores, and was delighted by the convenience when it rang and actually worked.

Rich he must be, but he didn't act rich, didn't seem in the least acquisitive or flashy. Fame, too, had a price. Ruefully, he told me his nice-guy reputation inspired ten to 20 letters a week from strangers, asking for, even demanding, large sums of money for all kinds of needs—school tuition and medical expenses. Though his face is not so famous that he stands out in the crowd, he had recently been stopped in the street in New York by a man who recognized him and insisted that Arthur help him publicize a new theory about light refraction. The light in the man's own pale gray eyes was disquiet-ing, and Arthur had gotten rid of him with difficulty.

The table was set for lunch out in the sunshine, and as we sat down Inge appeared, in a hurry to drive across the countryside to New Haven. She was taking a course in Chinese at Yale in preparation for their long trip—she to take photographs, he to direct *Death of a Salesman* in Beijing. Thin, bird-like, and dynamic, Inge welcomed us warmly, said goodbye to "Arr-toor" and departed in a cloud of energy. We had smoked salmon, a rich salad and home-made rye bread. Arthur's Austrian mother-in-law, round, placid, and charming, had baked a superb strudel.

Sitting across the table, Arthur looked strong and handsome. He'd injured his knee in a youthful football game and been rejected by the Army in World War II. Recently, he'd fallen off a ladder and broken his ankle. (With it still in a cast he'd sailed up the Nile in Sadruddin Khan's yacht to see the Pharaonic monuments.) Just before a trip to South America a tear in his retina almost blinded him. During a seven-hour emergency operation, performed the next day, the surgeon took the eyeball out of the socket and fastened a "buckle" around it to keep the tear from spreading. Though Arthur continued to be bothered by mist in his distant vision and had to rest his eyes in the afternoon, the operation saved his sight and gave him 20/20 vision with glasses. Apart from his ankle and his eyes, he was in remarkably good shape for a man of 66.

Tilting back his chair, pushing back his glasses and jutting out his lower jaw as he talked, Arthur was warm, friendly, even paternal. At ease with him-self, if not with the world—for he could be surprisingly severe—he made me feel immediately at ease, as if I had known him forever. It was hard to imagine him ever playing the temperamental artist or pompous great man. A social being, who seemed to like visitors, he spoke genially and naturally about everything, though it was tacitly understood that I would not interrogate him. I didn't associate such repose with writers. His plays dramatized univer-sal themes, common to all men in all languages: unconscious fears, domestic and political conflicts. His reputation was secure, he showed no arrogance. He was actively engaged in writing and getting his new plays produced, yet he didn't seem competitive. He talked all afternoon, listened attentively and asked me to come back on my next trip east.

II

On my second visit we exchanged life stories, as people getting to know each other do, and Arthur talked more extensively about his past and present. His father, he said, had been barely literate but prosperous, his mother a high school graduate. They had lived comfortably in Manhattan, with servants and a chauffeur. When Arthur was 14, his father lost everything in the Wall Street Crash and never recovered his business or his wealth. He moved the family to Brooklyn and, cushioned by his remaining jewels and property, drifted slowly into poverty. This was the crucial experience of Arthur's life—the Depression, the ugly side of capitalism made manifest—which devastated the lives of his family and friends, but inspired his poignant portrayal of Willy Loman. For the rest of his life he would sympathize with those who were exploited and then found themselves used up and discarded.

Arthur married for the first time in 1940, Mary Slattery, a lapsed Catholic classmate at the University of Michigan who became a school psychologist. In 1956 they had a bitter separation, and he had not seen her for 20 years. Reflecting on the houses he had lived in (so important to a writer, whose home is his workshop), he told me that after his first success in the theater he had bought a Brooklyn Heights brownstone for $32,000 and lived there with his wife in the early 1950's. She had recently sold it for $650,000.

He bought the present Connecticut house, his second, when he married Marilyn Monroe. I pictured him in my mind's eye in all the photographs of the period, when the flashbulbs popped incessantly and Arthur Miller's face appeared next to Marilyn's in *Picture Post* and *Photoplay*. At 41, in the prime of his life and achievement, he was thinner then, tense and bespectacled. He didn't seem to go with the fluffy, artificial, lipsticked timebomb he had married. I thought of the photos of the group on location for *The Misfits* in the Nevada desert—Clark Gable, Montgomery Clift, Monroe, all doomed to die within the year—and Arthur, watching his screenplay develop as Monroe unraveled. Sitting in the lush quiet of the garden, I said surely this place must have made Marilyn happy. "Nothing could make Marilyn happy for very long," he flatly observed.

He spent so much on her treatment that he had to sell his literary manuscripts to the University of Texas. "Wasn't she rich, couldn't she pay for her own doctors?" I asked. He explained that, on the contrary, she was broke. She'd signed a seven-year contract with Fox that kept her on the same low salary after she became famous and earned them a fortune. Her photographer Milton Greene had formed a joint corporation with her, literally owning 49% of her. Arthur prevented him from getting majority control, but eventually Marilyn had to pay $100,000 to get rid of him.

From talk of Marilyn it was a short step to Norman Mailer, Arthur's bete noire, and to all the books about her "by trashy writers who never took her seriously." I then realized why Arthur was so sceptical about biography. He was particularly severe about his once close friend and collaborator Norman Rosten, who wrote the screenplay for *A View from the Bridge*, and called his book on Marilyn "superficial, vulgar and self justificatory." (Rosten had begun his career by winning a Yale Younger Poets prize, but never fulfilled his promise.) Mailer's bizarre *Marilyn* (1975), a fantastical fiction masquerading as biography, claimed that Miller lived off her earnings, though Mailer could easily have found out the reverse was true. Mailer invented witty and satiric remarks, directed against Miller, and put them into Marilyn's mouth. Arthur considered suing him, but finally decided that would only help promote the book. At this point he was more disgusted than angry.

Arthur also thought the theory that the Kennedys had Marilyn murdered was absurd. She was probably sexually involved with them, but they were unlikely to have told her anything incriminating. In any case, she was loyal, and they had no reason to kill her. As for Arthur's own relationship with Marilyn, which he did not talk about, I had the feeling that his happiness must have been brief, and that he'd spent most of his time trying to help a talented, wounded woman. Abused by so many men on her way to the top, she'd had several abortions and miscarriages. When they met, she was suffering from depression and addicted to prescription drugs. The odds were against them, the decision to marry her an impulsive gamble for someone as self-controlled and self-respecting as Arthur Miller.

Inge Morath, by contrast, was and is eminently sane, strong, capable, and self-reliant. Always warm and welcoming—not the self important dragon-guardian, like some literary wives—she is a cultured and sophisticated European intellectual, critical and alert. Her career and travels mesh with Arthur's, and she admires his work without lionizing him.

On a later visit I mentioned that the publisher of my Hemingway biography had asked for an author's photograph. Inge responded immediately and enthusiastically. She brought out several cameras, told Arthur to continue our conversation so we'd have more natural expressions and took several rolls of pictures.

Arthur has two children from his first marriage and one from his third. His son, Robert (born in 1947), who lived in California and worked in television, was a driving force in the recent movie of *The Crucible*. To raise money for this project, Arthur had sold in advance the rights to show the film on network television and HBO. Sixty directors, including Arthur Penn, had turned the film down because it had to be made in 30 days and none of them thought it could be done. Arthur's agent, Sam Cohn of International Creative Management (ICM), reputedly the best in the business, had grave doubts they'd ever sell such a serious work in the age of "bang-bang" films. Finally, Robert asked if he could have the rights for six months. Within a few weeks he sold it to Twentieth Century-Fox and was made executive producer. John Briley, the scriptwriter of *Gandhi*, had done a screenplay. Arthur didn't like it and did one himself, writing half of the 140-page script in two weeks. He also went to Los Angeles to consult about the cast and director, and had wanted Kenneth Branagh for the leading role. *The Crucible* was Arthur's great money-maker. Even before the film came out, the play had sold eight million paperback copies in America and was Penguin's best-selling book.

Arthur's older daughter, Jane (born in 1944), was married to a sculptor and lived in New York. In the early 1990's she and her husband built a house near Arthur's on land he gave them. He was proud of Rebecca, his daughter with Inge, born in 1962. Beautiful and talented, educated at Choate and Yale, she learned three languages and graduated cum laude. Two of her paintings appeared on the covers of the English editions of Arthur's *Collected Plays*, and she had several exhibitions in New York. She had a successful career as an actress, writer, and director, and justifying Arthur's belief that an actor did not need formal training of the Lee Strasberg kind. In 1996 Rebecca married Daniel Day-Lewis, son of the poet C. Day-Lewis and star of the movie version of *The Crucible*.

III

Arthur's life has a creative rhythm. He usually works for a few hours in the morning, then reads, does farm chores and carpentry, answers letters and (in the summer) swims in his pond in the afternoon. He used to have a secretary, but gave her up when he had to follow her schedule, not his. He switched to a computer for his autobiography, *Timebends*, and found it effective for revisions. He usually writes slowly, and is preoccupied with the dramatic expression of his ideas.

Over the years Arthur often talked about his plays that were being revived. The idea for an early social protest play, *The Man Who Had All the Luck* (1944), came from Mary Slattery's rich and successful cousin in Ohio who hanged himself at the age of 28. Arthur had alternate endings: in one the suicide was caused by fate, in the other by self blame. *Focus* (1945), his novel about anti-Semitism, was published by an innovative firm, Reynal and Hitchcock, which folded when Hitchcock died young. Since Reynal supplied the money and they were not dependent on sales, they did as John Lehmann had done and as New Directions does today, publishing only books they liked to read.

Arthur's achievement came early in his life—though not quite so early as that of Fitzgerald or Hemingway—and many theater critics in the 1980's seemed to assume that his work was somehow "over," that there are no second acts for American writers. But the constant revivals show that his early plays still resonate, still matter. His first great success in the theater, *All My Sons* (1947), became popular in both Israel and Egypt after the war of 1967. Prime Minister Shimon Peres, who sat next to Arthur at the opening, told him it could have been a contemporary Israeli play. Some of his countrymen were also profiteering from arms sales while others risked their lives in the air. To the Israeli audience the play was not of mere entertainment and, as a mark of respect for the solemnity of the occasion, they did not applaud at the end.

Arthur said he wrote the famous scene in *The Misfits* (1961) in which Roslyn flirtatiously plays with a ball and paddle in a bar, but Marilyn did some improvising and gave it final form in the movie. He liked and admired

John Huston, the director. He described him as tall, gangling, lively, macho, and adventurous, an expert with horses—an important skill in the movie—both sensitive and brutal. A good writer, with discriminating taste, he was less interested in the finer points of acting than in the composition of the scene.

The masterpiece of Arthur's late years is undoubtedly *Timebends* (1987). In a letter of April 1987 he said he was surprised and pleased with its reception: "I dreaded that its serpentine form . . . would put people off, but incredibly Book-of the-Month has taken it," and it was translated into 15 languages. Arthur had complained to me of the lack of historical background in the American reviews. My own review did not discuss the political side of Miller's life, but I noted the book's dominant themes: "the origins of creativity, the dangers of fame, the temptations of the flesh, the corruption of Hollywood, the commercialization of Broadway and the betrayal of American idealism." I explained that I was writing for William Buckley's conservative *National Review*—a magazine that would normally ignore the book—and that was not the place to discuss the Communist witchhunts of the 1950's.

The plot of the ironically titled film *Everybody Wins* (1990), originally called *Almost Everybody Wins*, was based on his one-act play *Some Kind of Love Story* (1984). In a New England mill town a woman in her mid-30's hires a private detective, an Irish ex-Chicago cop, to free a convicted murderer she knows to be innocent. The story explores the woman's multiple personalities which, for the detective, make all reality provisional. Though Arthur originally wanted Jack Nicholson for the leading role, the movie was made with Nick Nolte and Debra Winger. Though he's been in and out of the film business for years, Arthur remains psychologically detached from it. Movie stars who accumulate $50 million, he wryly observed, "become strange."

The Ride Down Mt. Morgan (1991) portrayed the confrontation of a wife and mistress around the hospital bed of a man who has had a car accident on an icy road. Arthur said it concerned the point at which an unpleasant but attractive man recognizes he's made a moral transgression. The play, like so many of his late works, is a mixture of the personal and subjective, the realistic and fantastic. He'd written more than a thousand pages of dialogue over a period of nine years before he knew where the play was going and could finish it—an interesting aside that tells us something of Miller's capacity to follow his urge, stick with an idea, and patiently develop it. The play was performed in London and Williamstown, and by the Public Theater in New York.

Arthur gladly signed all his books for me, and four of his inscriptions were illuminating. He wrote that *Situation Normal* (1944), his early book of military reportage, was "the first trigger pull." *In the Country* (1977), a charming book about Connecticut, with photos by Inge, he called "This by now rare book and a favorite." He described the inspiration for *Everybody Wins* (1990) as "Things sometimes go whizzing off by themselves." And he linked the two settings of *The Archbishop's Ceiling* and *The American Clock*—an unnamed East European country (presumably Czechoslovakia) and the United States—by describing them as "two dangerously shaky, promising countries."

When I was writing the life of Scott Fitzgerald and describing his ill-fated career in Hollywood, I discussed the art of the screenplay with Arthur. He agreed with me that Joseph Mankiewicz was a much better screenwriter than Fitzgerald and had helped him by revising the script of Erich Remarque's novel *Three Comrades*. In 1981 I had enthusiastically suggested that Arthur write a screenplay of Joseph Conrad's *Victory*—one of my favorite books. The system, he replied, did not encourage even an established dramatist to write for the movies. A major studio might pay him to do a script, but unless he owned the rights, the director could change it at will. In today's climate, it was highly unlikely such a film would ever be made. Arthur could also raise the money privately, but it would be risky. Investors expected to earn a 20 percent return, the cost of making a film like *Victory* would be too high, its audience too small. And the star would always be more important at the box office than Conrad or Miller.

IV

Arthur didn't like teaching or lecturing, though he'd done a fair amount of both. He found Columbia students lively, those at Harvard and Yale surprisingly dull. He was pleased when a Columbia student paid him a compliment by calling him truly "plugged in." At the Harbourfront Writers' Conference in Toronto he addressed 4,500 people in Symphony Hall—the first writer to speak there since 1938, when Thomas Mann lectured after his arrival in North America. When I tried to lure Arthur to the University of Colorado, he recalled that he'd once attended their World Affairs conference and been given hospitality in a house where the marriage was clearly breaking up. He was unwilling to return to Boulder because being lionized was boring, and he dreaded the petty squabbles about the right to monopolize him.

While on the subject of the academy, he remarked that none of the biographical or critical books about him was any good, and that several of them were unreliable. Benjamin Nelson (1970) had mistakenly said Arthur's mother had been a schoolteacher. James Goode (1963) had missed the real story of *The Misfits*. His Japanese bibliographer, Tetsumaro Hayashi (1959), had hopelessly confused him with a cinematographer of the same name and made a hash of the attributions. Arthur was especially critical of the Yale professor and New Republic drama critic, Robert Brustein. He had no sense of the theater but enormous power to condemn a play, which was an expensive investment and had to attract an increasingly cautious audience. Two critics Arthur approved of were Harold Clurman, who'd co-produced *All My Sons* and directed *Incident at Vichy*, and was for many years drama critic of the *Nation*; and the younger English academic Christopher Bigsby, who ran the Arthur Miller Theatre Studies Centre at the University of East Anglia in Norwich.

Arthur always showed a friendly interest in my books, noted the good reviews, and was generous with praise and letters of recommendation. He even wrote a rare blurb for my life of Edmund Wilson, which read in part: "I found it a fascinating exploration of a period and the man who probably personified its critical intelligence and—most of the time—its artistic conscience. Drunk or sober, in or out of love, employed or not, Wilson was engaged with his time."

When he praised my book, I seized the opening to raise once again the subject of his biography. He had a good excuse to turn me down—his personal papers, in seven big filing cabinets that he daren't open, were in a terrible mess. I countered, helpfully, that a good scholar or librarian could do the organizing for him, and he admitted that Texas had done an excellent job with his literary manuscripts. But this wasn't the real reason for his reluctance. After two unhappy marriages and a barrage of unfavorable publicity about Monroe, he couldn't face it. Nor had he made any provision for a biography in his will, which Inge would execute. He thought his remaining papers might go to the Library of Congress or to the University of Michigan, where he got his start as a playwright. Though he was at work on *Timebends* when we had this conversation, he still maintained that his own life was dull. The big problem, he said, was to make sense, form, and meaning of it all. Leave it to me, I said, that's what biographers do! He agreed that his potential biography was important and that it ought to be done properly. I suggested he let me interview his family and friends (before it was too late) and get started on a first volume that would take me up to 1949. Superstitiously, he shook his head, exclaiming, "That's death!"

V

Just as the New York theater had changed for the worse in the course of Arthur's career, so had the climate in publishing. He had had the same agent for nearly 40 years, and in that time ICM had been sold three times. They had two rooms full of his records, so he couldn't leave them, even if he wanted to. But he did leave his publisher. Though Arthur's books had sold in the millions, he complained of the way Viking was treating him. The company had been bought by Penguin, an English firm owned by a German multi-national corporation. Viking was run from London, with no one at the helm in New York. They had adopted a cost-accounting mentality and projected sales were estimated by marketing men who cared only for profits. His editor, Elizabeth Sifton, now lacked the power to push his work, and in this environment the author of quality books was no longer important. The day Arthur called Viking to discuss these issues, no one answered the phone for 30 rings. Neither the operator nor the secretary recognized his name.

He was furious that Viking didn't advertise *In the Country* (1977) after it received a negative review in *The New York Times Book Review*. At the same time that Graham Greene left Viking for Simon & Schuster and Saul Bellow left for Harper & Row, Arthur left them for Farrar, Straus & Giroux, which published *Chinese Encounters*, with photos by Inge, in 1979. But he was lured back to Viking with volumes of his *Theater Essays* and a second volume of his *Collected Plays*. He thought Viking's design of "Salesman" in Beijing (1984) was good, but the paper for the photographs was poor and so was the marketing. Voicing a complaint of all authors, he said the reviews were favorable, but the book was not available in the stores. He published with Aaron Asher at Grove Press between 1984 and 1990, when he again returned to Viking, which brought out his last three plays. *Homely Girl* (1995), his novella, had a first printing of only 6,000, but there was a surprising demand for the second printing of 25,000. It was being made into a film by a French company.

Over the years I often asked his opinion of other writers. For him, the positive and negative qualities of Wyndham Lewis' character cancelled each other out, and he found it impossible to sympathize with him. Describing how Lewis, Hemingway, and many other modern writers felt obliged to kill the father-figures in their fiction, he contrasted the European respect for the authoritarian father with the American desire to destroy the father and inability to assume his role. He thought this was partly why most English and American writers lacked the "staying power" of a Thomas Mann. He recalled how he met Mann at a performance of *Death of a Salesman* in the late 1940's. Very formal in manner, Mann said in good but heavily accented English that he'd looked in vain for some philosophical statement in the play. Miller replied that he took pride in conveying his meaning through the action, without directly expressing a "message."

He acknowledged Hemingway as a stylistic, if not personal, influence when he first started writing. In his view, Hemingway transformed the American idiom into a literary language and virtually every American writer, except for the Southerners who followed Faulkner, was influenced by him. Arthur didn't know that Edmund Wilson had written eight plays and been married to the actress Mary Blair, who'd appeared in many O'Neill plays, but called Wilson "the best critic we ever had." He described Wilson's late mistress, the screenwriter and film critic Penelope Gilliatt (who'd been married to John Osborne), as not especially attractive and a very heavy drinker. He thought Wilson's surprising connection with Lillian Hellman was based

on mutual love of gossip. He blasted Hellman for her intellectual dishon-
esty—and felt she fully deserved the attacks by Mary McCarthy, Martha
Gellhorn, and Diana Trilling. Hellman was also an imperious hostess on
Martha's Vineyard. When Styron invented an excuse to avoid her dinner
party and she discovered the truth (at the store where they both shopped for
fancy desserts), she didn't speak to him for a year.

When he talked about writers, he seemed especially concerned with
personal character, and he made shrewd judgments about the contrast
between art and message, between the quality of an author's work and his
literary reputation. Wise and benign himself, Arthur was fascinated by good
writers, like V. S. Naipaul, who were famous for being nasty. John Osborne
and Philip Roth, desperate to antagonize their audience, were deliberately
offensive in their work and behavior. (He was sure none of these nasties
received as many begging letters as he did.) But he liked .Roth (a summer
neighbor) personally, was amused by his nasty side, and didn't presume to
judge him.

Describing a dinner with Alexander Solzhenitsyn at the Connecticut
house of his translator Thomas Whitney, Arthur said the Russian spoke no
English and only a little German, and the host translated for him. Imperious, authoritative, and dictatorial, he was unappealing but impressive. His
didactic manner, inherited from Tolstoy, made him more concerned with
message than with art, but his honest vehemence and personal courage gave
him real power. Arthur praised his noble vision, but he felt living under his
government wouldn't be pleasant. He thought East European writers like
Solzhenitsyn and Kosinski, more ideologues than artists, craved power for
themselves even as they criticized the powers that be.

I was interested in Arthur's appraisals of the contemporary theater,
and asked him to reflect on the playwrights of his youth. He said the popular, melodramatic, and now neglected playwright, David Belasco, actually
taught the influential Russian director Konstantin Stanislavsky a good
deal about theatrical realism. In the 1930's Eugene O'Neill, who had been
so great in the previous decade and lived until 1953, seemed completely
dated and had dropped into oblivion. *A Moon for the Misbegotten* (1957),
like many of his plays, had flat language and a stale plot. But his greatest work was the posthumously published *Long Day's Journey Into Night*
(1956).

Clifford Odets had suffered the same fate as O'Neill. Though Odets
had invented contemporary realistic New York speech, and was often
imitated, he didn't transcend his time and was now dull and dated. Odets
knew Miller slightly, but resented him for eclipsing his star. Arthur disliked the long biography of Odets (1982) by the psychoanalyst Margaret
Brenman-Gibson, and felt it was too long, doting, and subjective a book.

By contrast, he admired Tennessee Williams—with whom he had a passing acquaintance and who seemed to have mainly homosexual friends—and believed his works would last. Unlike Williams, Edward Albee had been relatively silent at the time of our interview. Both had had to find their way into a heterosexual world from the suppressed homosexual one.

Harold Pinter, a close friend, was by temperament always angry and embittered. But in 1993 he had a new play, *Moonlight*, coming out in London, which Arthur had read in typescript and thought was very good. *Glengarry Glen Ross* (1983) by David Mamet, one of the stars of contemporary American stage and film, had powerful language and theatrical effects, including crude and shocking language. But, unlike Arthur, brought up in the idealistic 1930's, the much younger Mamet had by main force to create some kind of "moral vessel" into which he could distill his ideas.

Saul Bellow was an old friend. In 1956, when they were both waiting in Reno for divorces, they lived in neighboring cabins. Their common editor at Viking, Pascal Covici, suggested they go west together and keep each other company. (At that time the place seemed remote, and they were surrounded by Indians. A few years later, he returned to film *The Misfits*, and Reno was booming.) He was impressed by Bellow's erudition, which Bellow casually tried to hide. Though part of the academic establishment at the University of Chicago, Bellow disliked the scholarly and academic world. In May 1986, after learning about yet another divorce, Arthur wrote: "I was sorry to hear about Bellow, had thought from reports that was a reasonable marriage, but I guess he will have to go on to the end writing new chapters."

Like most writers, Arthur was fascinated by the manic character of Robert Lowell, whom he'd met in the political turmoil of the 1960's. A wildly disconnected speaker, a terrible snob, sometimes crazy and cruel, Lowell also had a winning and sympathetic personality. When I sent my book *Manic Power: Robert Lowell and His Circle* (1987)—which was dedicated to him—Arthur saw (as few others did) the significance of the interwoven chapters that I had used to structure the work: "I found that by reflecting Lowell's illness in and among that group of writers a kind of epochal sense emerged, and in a way that was otherwise impossible one got the feeling that his illness was something more than personal."

I was curious to ask Miller, a veteran insider, panel member and literary judge, about how prizes to writers were awarded. This topic made him smile with a gentle cynicism. Some prizes, he said, were finally given because the committee had failed to reach an agreement by five o'clock and, desperate for a pee and a drink, simply gave in to whoever persisted with his pet candidate. We got on to Mailer's Pulitzer Prize for *The Executioner's Song* (1980) and the prize awarded to a journalist who had falsified her stories. Basically, he said, prizes were useless. No one today would recognize 98 percent of the plays that had won the Pulitzer. He'd won it for *Death of a Salesman*, but not for *The Crucible*—considered too left-wing.

For years I had wondered why certain obviously great writers, Miller especially, did not win the biggest one of all, the Nobel Prize. Arthur agreed that many undeserving authors had won it, and thought that Graham Greene was the most overlooked contender. (He felt Greene's artistic failure in *Monsignor Quixote* [1982] was caused more by his preachy Catholic doctrine than by lack of literary inspiration.) Arthur told me how, during the run of one of his plays at the National Theatre in London, the publicity office heard a rumor that he'd won the Nobel Prize. As they started to exploit the story the rumor proved false. He had never expected to receive the prize, despite his worldwide success and the enduring appeal of his classic plays, but he'd heard that some writers (Octavio Paz, for example, who won it in 1990) had actively electioneered for it. He predicted a Chinese writer would get it soon. I added that coming from a major country that had never won the prize was a great advantage, and considered Margaret Atwood of Canada and Jorge Amado of Brazil strong candidates. Because political persecution was another important (and non-literary) criterion, I thought Salman Rushdie, Ariel Dorfman, and Vaclev Havel were also in the running. Arthur was amused by this Nobel racecard, but clearly wasted no sleep over it.

VI

The McCarthy period had cost Arthur a close friend and colleague, Elia Kazan. Unlike Miller, he'd named names before the HUAC, and the two had quarreled bitterly. Kazan's *A Life* (1988) was full of gaps, lies, and self justifications. He said that Miller had "walked away from" their film *The Hook*. In fact, Miller had refused to turn the gangsters into Communists, as the Columbia Pictures mogul Harry Cohn and the Hollywood union bosses wanted him to do. The film was later rewritten that way by Budd Schulberg (another self serving "friendly witness") as *On the Waterfront*. Kazan, still racked by guilt about his betrayal of close friends, once stared at a fellow writer and asked: "you're thinking about it, aren't you?" He ascribed his behavior to some mystical racial memory. As a Greek in Turkey, Kazan said, he had to learn the art of survival. Morality, honor, and personal courage—or so his story went—were much less important than looking after oneself.

Far from doctrinaire, however, Arthur saw the moral and human complexities of these times. In 1996 I was writing a life of Humphrey Bogart, who in 1947 first opposed and then recanted his opposition to HUAC, and sought Arthur's opinion of his behavior. (Arthur himself appeared before the Committee in 1956, when anti-Communist hysteria was at its height.) He thought Bogart had been misled by the Hollywood Ten, who'd been called before the Committee but did not tell him that they were in fact Communists. Bogart rightly feared the witch-hunt would end his career and Miller was "reluctant to judge him in this two-edged story."

VII

Perhaps the most sensitive issue I discussed with Arthur, and to me the saddest, was the question of his literary reputation at home. American theater critics had savagely expressed the belief that since *After the Fall* in 1964 Miller's plays—like those of O'Neill, Odets and Osborne—had abruptly declined. For many years Arthur has been in the unique position of being more appreciated, and certainly more performed, in England than in America. In June 1984, on a triumphant visit, he read from "Salesman" in Beijing to overflow audiences at the National Theatre and the University of East Anglia, where he received an honorary degree. He dined with the novelist Angus Wilson, and had a penetrating radio interview on the BBC's "Kaleidoscope." He contrasted the well-prepared English journalists with the Americans, who barely glanced at a book before the program went on the air and didn't have a clue what questions to ask. The most intelligent reviews of his work appeared in the *London Spectator*. On his 80th birthday, in 1995, Oxford University awarded him another honorary degree.

We often discussed the difference between the American and English theater. He thought English directors, like Bill Bryden, tried to bring out the best in a play, while the more egoistic Americans wanted to put their personal stamp on it. He contrasted the elevated style of English acting to the limited realism of the Americans. Expressive actors, like Dustin Hoffman, Robert De Niro, Al Pacino, and Harvey Keitel, were very good at confrontational parts, but British players, trained on Shakespeare, had much greater range and skill. He particularly admired Anthony Hopkins in the National Theatre production of *Pravda* and the film *The Silence of the Lambs*.

Arthur emphasized the comparatively low cost of putting on plays in England. Cameron Macintosh, producer of the phenomenally successful Andrew Lloyd Webber musicals, told him that New York theaters cost three times as much as the ones in London. The London production of O'Neill's *Mourning Becomes Electra*, with Glenda Jackson, cost $100,000. When the play came to New York, the backers had to pay $600,000 before the curtain went up. Noting that Lincoln Center was currently dark, he concluded that there was simply much greater opportunity for serious theater in England.

In the late 1940's, he recalled, he'd visited his college roommate in Little Rock, Arkansas, and heard great backwoods storytellers, who attracted large crowds. NBC found out about them, but they refused to come to New York. The problem today is that such regional artists no longer exist; and even if they did, nobody would be interested. Literary and theatrical life has become purely commercial. Citing the recent New York closing of Pinter's play, *The*

Hothouse, which got rave reviews, Arthur said it was now impossible to make money on intellectually challenging drama. Theater tickets in New York now cost as much as a night at the Stork Club and customers expected the same kind of fun for their money. The serious audience has almost disappeared. During the last decade, however, the tide has turned strongly in his favor. The Tony Award for the revival of *A View from the Bridge*, its transfer to Broadway from a limited run at the Roundabout, and its national tour have led to a new appreciation of his artistic achievement.

Though Arthur has not lost his idealistic belief in the social importance of the theater, he is pessimistic about the future of books and plays in a world that regards every literary work as an investment, meant to generate cash. He laments the alienation of artists from society and from each other in the cutthroat, fearful atmosphere of today. In his view, the discontinuity in American intellectual life reflects the wider lack of a collective memory and a collective culture.

JULIUS NOVICK

Death of a Salesman:
*Deracination and Its Discontents**

> To me the theater is not a disconnected entertainment. . . . It's the
> sound and the ring of the spirit of the people at any one time. It is where
> a collective mass of people, through the genius of some author, is able to
> project its terrors and its hopes and to symbolize them.
>
> —Arthur Miller [1]

A primary function of the theater is to perform social fact, to express
it in terms of fictive yet truthful personal experience. With the passing of
the years, social fact becomes historical fact, and the drama, particularly
the realistic drama, stands as an often-invaluable record of what history felt
like to those who actually lived it. The great subject of American Jewish
drama—defined for our purposes as plays written in English by American
Jews about Jewish experience—is the great subject also of the historians and
sociologists of American Jewry: the encounter with America, the complex
question of Americanization, acculturation, assimilation.

America is famously a nation of immigrants. In Oscar Handlin's words,
"the immigrants were American history." The "history of immigration," he
went on to say in his most famous book, significantly called *The Uprooted*,

> is a history of alienation and its consequences. . . . Emigration
> took these people out of traditional, accustomed environments

From *American Jewish History*. © 2003 Johns Hopkins University Press.

and replanted them in strange ground, among strangers, where strange manners prevailed. The customary modes of behavior were no longer adequate, for the problems of life were new and different. With old ties snapped, men faced the enormous compulsion of working out new relationships, new meanings to their lives, often under harsh and hostile circumstances. . . . The shock, and the effects of the shock, persisted for many years; and their influence reached down to generations which themselves never paid the cost of crossing.[2]

American Jewish drama reflects Handlin's insight. It is not primarily about the immigrants themselves, but about their legacy to their descendants. It dramatizes the wound of immigrant uprooting as it throbs down the generations, the continuing effect of the "alienation," the shock," that Handlin speaks of.

Where in this new world do we find beliefs and models to tell us what is important and good, to show us how to *be*? And even beyond America, beyond ethnicity, most people today are living in a different world from that of their immediate ancestors. We all live in the tension between what we came from and what we have come to; we are all faced with the challenge of making some accommodation between them. American Jewish drama chronicles and analyzes the American Jewish version of an all-but-universal, historically determined experience.

Arthur Miller (1915–2005) is manifestly the most eminent Jewish playwright who ever lived (unless you believe the rumor that Shakespeare was a Marrano.)[3] *Death of a Salesman*, produced on Broadway in 1949 for a run of 742 performances, starring Lee J. Cobb in a celebrated performance as Willy Loman, is universally considered his most important play (as generations of high school students can attest). But what has *Death of a Salesman* to do with American Jewish drama as we have defined it? In what sense is Arthur Miller a Jewish playwright? Allen Guttmann, in an otherwise admirable book about American Jewish writers, placed Miller with Nathanael West and J. D. Salinger as "nominally Jewish, but . . . in no sense Jewish writers."[4] That was in 1971— Guttmann would probably not say that today—but the question of Jewishness, or the lack of it, comes up frequently in discussions of Miller's work. Thus Morris Freedman wrote about several Miller plays, including *Salesman*,

The ethnic anonymity of these plays is striking, if only in comparison with the plays of Odets and O'Neill, whose Jewish and Irish Catholic families in *Awake and Sing!* and *Long Day's Journey Into Night* are so plainly identified for us.
It is difficult to find ethnic clues in Miller.[5]

Difficult, but not impossible, as Freedman went on to make clear. Christopher Bigsby, perhaps the world's leading Millerologist, has stated categorically that "Willy was not Jewish."[6] But in 1951, one George Ross went to Brooklyn to see Joseph Buloff in *Toyt fun a Salesman*—*Death of a Salesman* in Yiddish—and wrote in *Commentary*, "What one feels most strikingly is that this Yiddish play is really the original, and the Broadway production was merely—Arthur Miller's translation into English"—even though, as Ross acknowledged, Yiddish has no word for "salesman." "In many places, said Ross, "one felt in the English version as if Miller was thinking in Yiddish and unconsciously translating. . . ." He added that the play lost a lot in this English "translation":

> The vivid impression is that translating from his mixed American-Jewish experience Miller tried to ignore or censor out the Jewish part, and as a result succeeded only in making the Loman family anonymous. What we saw on Broadway was a kind of American Everyman, an attempt at generalization which in fact ended in limitation. . . . Arthur Miller, one feels, has almost deliberately deprived himself of some of the resources of his experience. . . . Buloff has caught Miller, as it were, in the act of changing his name. . . .[7]

Note the peculiar quality of personal *accusation* here: Miller is caught in the act of trying to hide his origins. Ross was perhaps unaware that in 1945, before his first success as a playwright, Miller had published *Focus*, a novel about anti-semitism that sold 90,000 copies.[8] He could not know that Miller's first play, a student work, was about a Jewish family (his own), that Miller would publish short stories about Jewish characters, or that in later years he would write very specifically about Jewish protagonists and Jewish issues in his plays *Incident at Vichy* and *Broken Glass*.

A number of very high-powered critics picked up Ross's main point. Mary McCarthy, not generally noted as an expert on Jewish affairs, wrote,

> A disturbing aspect of *Death of a Salesman* was that Willy Loman seemed to be Jewish, to judge by his speech-cadences, but there was no mention of this on the stage. He could not be Jewish because he had to be "America." . . . He is a capitalized Human Being without being anyone. . . . Willy is only a type. . . .[9]

And Leslie Fiedler, the Jewish wild man of American lit. crit., wrote that Miller creates crypto-Jewish characters; characters who are in habit, speech, and condition of life typically Jewish-American, but who are presented as something else—general-American say, as in *Death of a Salesman*. . . . Such pseudo-universalizing represents, however, a loss of artistic faith. . . . The works influenced by pseudo-universalizing lose authenticity and strength. [10]

The matter is complicated. Miller has said that as a young man he "was struggling to identify myself with mankind rather than one small tribal fraction of it," [11] implying a desire to transcend his Jewishness—a desire shared by other young American radicals of the 1930's, and perhaps not entirely discarded by Miller when he wrote *Salesman*. When Fiedler's attack was brought up by an interviewer in 1969, Miller replied, somewhat grumpily, that in his plays, "Where the theme seems to require a Jew to act somehow in terms of his Jewishness, he does so. Where it seems to me irrelevant what the religious or cultural background of a character may be, it is treated as such." [12]

The generalizing impulse that Miller's detractors make so much of is certainly there. The lack of specific ethnic markers in *Death of a Salesman* is paralleled by a lack of specific chronological markers. The play takes place "today," say the stage directions, [13] which presumably means 1949, the year of its premiere. But there is little that is 1949 about it: no memories of the Depression or World War II, no postwar prosperity, no Cold War, no atomic anxiety, no television (just a couple of references to radio). Does this make the play merely vague, inauthentic, and ahistoric, or does it silently emphasize that the process we are seeing is not the product of one historical moment, but a looming possibility over many decades, and even now? Whether the generalizing impulse is a fault or a virtue is an open question. Is *Death of a Salesman* indeed "pseudo-universalized," or is it genuinely universal? Elia Kazan, who directed the original production, was only the first of many who found in Willy Loman an image of their own fathers; [14] Kazan was a Greek American from Turkey. When Brian Dennehy played Willy, with his broad geniality and his big grin, the Lomans seemed as if they might be Irish Americans. (Miller reports that when the road company, with Thomas Mitchell as Willy, played Boston, *Salesman* was hailed as "the best Irish play ever.") [15] There have been productions with all-African-American casts. [16] "*Death of a Salesman*," says a Miller scholar, Brenda Murphy, "has been produced on six continents, in every country that has a Western theatrical tradition, and in some that have not. . . . There is no need at this point to demonstrate *Salesman*'s universality." [17]

And yet, some of the Loman "speech cadences"—especially the famous "attention must be paid," as Mary McCarthy pointed out—can indeed be thought of as typically Jewish, even as translated from the Yiddish. What the Lomans are and do and suffer is never uniquely or parochially Jewish. Crucially, they are Americans. But there is reason to think of them as Jewish.

Certainly the real people and the personal experiences that provided the germ of the play were Jewish. In his autobiography, *Timebends*, Miller tells us that his own salesman uncle, Manny Newman, was a primary model for Willy. [18] But the little Loman house in Brooklyn, with two brothers, and a father humiliated by financial failure, more than coincidentally resembles the little house in Brooklyn where Arthur Miller and his brother Kermit lived as teenagers after their father lost his business in the Depression.

If the Lomans are thought of as Jewish, then *Death of a Salesman*, like so many American Jewish plays, can be thought of as a sequel to *Fiddler on the Roof*, although *Fiddler* was written some fifteen years later. The musical begins with a song about "Tradition!" expressed visually in Jerome Robbins's choreography as a circle-dance. "Because of our traditions," says Tevye, the spokesman for the Russian Jewish community of Anatevka, "everyone knows who he is and what God expects him to do." [19] But by the end of the show, the circle-dance of tradition is broken, and the villagers must leave to start, somehow, a new life in a new country. It becomes very difficult for them to know who they are and what God expects them to do. Willy and his family are, so to speak, their descendants, still subject to the "shock," the "alienation," that Handlin described. Miller says that all great drama addresses the question, "How may a man make of the outside world a home?" [20] —a question with special poignance for immigrants, for many Jews, and, agonizingly, for the Lomans.

In a new preface to the fiftieth-anniversary edition of *Salesman*, Miller for the first time, as far as I know, explicitly identified the Lomans as Jews—but as Jews who had lost their Jewishness. By 1999, the melting pot in which ethnic differences were dissolved was no longer the American paradigm. The general awareness of ethnicity—the very concept of ethnicity—was far more widespread, and Miller was ready to comment on the ethnic implications of his play. And so he wrote of the Lomans: "As Jews light-years away from religion or community that might have fostered Jewish identity, they exist in a spot that probably most Americans feel they inhabit—on the sidewalk side of the glass looking in at a well-lighted place." [21] Thus their lack of explicit ethnic markers is not merely an attempt at universality, but an integral part of their characterization. Their separation from their roots, their isolation, the absence of ethnic, religious, or cultural context that so many critics have complained about—this is what makes them so terribly vulnerable to the false values that undo them; nature abhors a vacuum. The Lomans are assimilated but not assimilated, and they have the worst of both. Uprooted, cut off from their past (Willy's father, like many Jewish immigrants, was an itinerant peddler, and Willy evidently grew up in a wagon), lacking the traditional beliefs that would order their lives and tell them what to do, they are trying to be "American." But how? (The only exception is Linda Loman, who has found her identity and her moral compass in preserving, protecting, and defending her husband.) Allen Guttmann, in his book *The Jewish Writer in America*, placed Miller among writers whose work does not "deal significantly with the process of assimilation and the resultant crisis of identity."[22] But that is precisely what *Death of a Salesman* deals with.

For Willy, desperate to break into that "well-lighted place," the model to be emulated is his hallucinatory brother Ben, who says, "when I was seventeen I walked into the jungle, and when I was twenty-one I walked out. [*He laughs.*] And by God I was rich." "We'll do it here, Ben!" Willy says. "You hear me? We're gonna do it here!" (33 , 66) In the words of the critic Ronald Bryden, he "has been lost in that jungle all his life."[23] And as Benjamin Nelson has written, "Willy is . . . in some respects, the archetypal diaspora Jew, a stranger in a strange land, clutching at his dream with fervent, if illogical, valor, as if the American success myth is his new Jerusalem.[24]

Isaiah Berlin once said, "There isn't a Jew in the world known to me [and Berlin knew some very eminent and powerful Jews] who somewhere inside him does not have a tiny drop of uneasiness vis-à-vis them, the majority among whom they live."[25]

The "success myth" can be seen as Willy's defense against this "uneasiness," but in his case it brings terrible consequences. America is famously the land of opportunity, the golden land, where anyone can make good, meaning make money. But if anyone can, then everyone should, and what excuse is there for those who don't? "Don't live, just make success," is old Jacob's grumpy summary of American values in *Awake and Sing!*, Clifford Odets's benchmark Jewish family play[26] —with "success," as so often, meaning money. Willy Loman, says Miller, "has broken a law . . . which says that a failure in society and in business has no right to live."[27] This is a common American situation, of course, but perhaps exacerbated for Jews, who have historically been so good at "making success."

The business of America is business," said Calvin Coolidge. Willy might or might not put it that way, but in practice he agrees. The Jewish social ethic of "repairing the world" means nothing to him; he or some ancestor lost it along the way. For Willy, "the business world" (20) is the America that counts, that will validate him, that will bring him and his sons the money, status, and love that are so terribly mixed up in his mind. Part of Willy's problem is that the business world to him is not *just* about making money: it is the context in which he expects to become, or imagines he is, "well-liked," a term that comes up over and over again, meaning accepted, embraced, a real American at last. America, to Willy, is not only a jungle: it is also a benign paradise, "the greatest country in the world." (6) "America is full of beautiful towns and fine, upstanding people." To his sons, this marginal man spins a feverish fantasy of acceptance:

> Well, I got on the road, and I went north to Providence. Met the mayor . . . . He said, "Morning!" And I said, you got a fine city here, mayor. And then he had coffee with me . . . they know me, boys, they know me up and down New England. The finest people. (18–19)

Fighting desperately for his job, he tells his boss how he was on the point of going to Alaska with his brother Ben, when he met a salesman named Dave Singleman, who was eighty-four years old and still selling.

> And when I saw that, I realized that selling was the greatest career a man could have. 'Cause what could be more satisfying than to be able to go, at the age of eighty-four, into twenty or thirty different cities, and pick up a phone, and be remembered and loved and helped by so many different people? Do you know? When he died—and by the way he died the death of a salesman, in his green velvet slippers in the smoker of the New York, New Haven, and Hartford, going into Boston—when he died hundreds of salesmen and buyers were at his funeral. (61)

(This is the only point in the play where the words "death of a salesman" appear.) "The wonder of this country" is "that a man can end with diamonds here on the basis of being liked." (65–66) Being well-liked enables you to make money, which, in turn, is the sign that you're well-liked. If you're well-liked, people will come to your funeral. Willy seeks in business the acceptance, the comradeship, that Ralph Berger in *Awake and Sing!* seeks in revolutionary action—both of them, in opposite ways, perhaps trying to salve the alienation inherited from immigrant ancestors. This is Willy's personal variation on the success imperative. Perhaps that is why he never got anywhere in business: looking for love, he lacks the ruthlessness of Uncle Morty in *Awake and Sing!*, or his own brother Ben, who says, "Never fight fair with a stranger, boy. You'll never get out of the jungle that way." (34) Willy believes that he is Ben's loyal disciple; he never quite realizes how different they are.

Willy's obsession with success for himself and his family through business is an extreme but not atypical Jewish adaptation to what Jews and non-Jews alike tend to believe is the American imperative. (Of course, so little is Willy's obsession *uniquely* Jewish that Willy's yearnings are often cited as exemplifying "the American dream." But this overlooks how many versions of the American dream there are, and how desperately self-contradictory Willy's version is.) Miller's novel *Focus* offers a vivid description of the barriers that American Jews faced, even toward the middle of the twentieth century, when seeking employment in Gentile-owned businesses; not permitted, in most cases, to rise through the ranks of big corporations, they generally achieved success in business, if they did, by going into business on their own, like Willy's neighbor, Charley, and his former boss, "old man Wagner."[28] Hence Willy dreams, "Someday I'll have my own business. . . ." (18) More important, he worries, like Miller's Uncle Manny, one of the models for Willy (and like so many Jewish fathers),[29] about making "a business for the boys." (25) The same words appear in *Timebends*, apropos of Uncle Manny,[30] and in *Salesman*: "a business for the boys." Willy has humiliatingly failed to meet this standard for Jewish fathers; killing himself for his insurance money is the only way he can provide a business for his favorite son. Biff, he thinks at the end, will compensate for all his disappointments, Biff will win the success that has eluded Willy, Biff will justify his father's life. "Can you imagine that magnificence with twenty thousand dollars in his pocket?" (108) In characteristically (but, again, not uniquely) Jewish fashion, his boys bear the crushing burden of his hopes for them.[31]

Biff, the favorite son, is repelled by business: "It's a measly manner of existence." He loves working outdoors. But Willy has the stereotypical Jewish contempt for country life and manual labor:[32] "How can he find himself on a farm? Is that a life? A farmhand?" (5) When Biff says, "We should be mixing cement on some open plain, or—or carpenters. A carpenter is allowed to whistle!" Willy replies, "Even your grandfather was better than a carpenter." (44) "*Even* your grandfather," as if grandfathers are the lowest of the low, except for carpenters. What a raging imperative to social mobility is implied in this flash of contempt for his own insufficiently successful—insufficiently American?—ancestry! Biff is not allowed to be a carpenter. That's no way to make success. Of course, the irony is that Willy, too, as Biff sees, gets his real satisfaction not by selling but by working with his hands, but Willy is too blinded by his dream to realize it. The demand to rise through the business world is as much a violation of his true nature as it is of Biff's.

But though Willy despises manual labor, in other respects he is strikingly at odds with the Jewish tradition of favoring mental over physical qualities. He tells his sons, "I thank Almighty God you're both built like Adonises." (21) He has them steal materials from a nearby building site: "I got a couple of fearless characters there." (35) He encourages them to be athletes, buys them a punching bag. Jewish boys, like other American boys, have frequently wanted to be athletes, but Jewish parents have traditionally been skeptical. As one father wrote to the *Jewish Daily Forward*, "It makes sense to teach a child to play dominoes or chess. But what is the point of a crazy game like baseball? The children can get crippled. . . . I want my boy to grow up to be a *mensch*, not a wild American runner."[33] That was in 1903, but it is still a mark of Willy's American-ness that the day Biff gets to play football in Ebbets Field for the high-school championship of the city, Willy is almost delirious with joy. It is as if he is running away with all his might from the ghetto/shtetl stereotype of the pale, intellectual, cringing, physically helpless Jew.[34] Who ever heard of nice Jewish boys named Biff and Happy?

Next door to the Lomans, however, lives Biff's more typically, not to say stereotypically, Jewish friend, Bernard, whose first words in the play are, "Biff, where are you? You're supposed to study with me today." (20) Willy thinks that good looks and athletic ability will make his sons "well liked," and therefore successful. He dismisses unathletic, studious Bernard as "anemic," "a worm." (20, 27) But when all three boys are grown up, Biff is "one dollar an hour" (106) (his words), Happy is a "philandering bum" (41) (his mother's words), and nerdy Bernard, now *a quiet, earnest, but self-assured young man* (69) (according to the stage directions), is married with two sons, is a lawyer, is about to go to Washington to plead a case before the Supreme Court, and to stay with friends who have their own tennis court. In every way—even athletically!—Bernard has achieved the success that eludes Biff and Happy. The emptiness of the great American Jewish success story is a theme of American Jewish fiction from Abraham Cahan to Philip Roth, and it is far from unknown in American Jewish drama, but there is no suggestion in *Death of a Salesman* that Bernard's success is anything but genuine and fulfilling.[35] Evidently, then, according to this play, real success *can* be achieved in America, if not by someone like Willy, than by someone like Bernard, through studying hard, being smart, and playing by the rules—a combination well known to American Jews. *Death of a Salesman* certainly takes its place in the great indictment of American values that serious American drama has produced, but at the same time it is kinder to the American dream than is often supposed. "The truth was," said Miller in *Timebends*, "that I had always lived in the belief that a good man could still make it, capitalism or no capitalism."[36] And that possibility, too, is a central fact of American Jewish history.

Notes

* An earlier version of this essay appeared in the *Forward*.

1. Arthur Miller, "The Contemporary Theater," *Michigan Quarterly Review* 6 (Summer, 1967), reprinted in Robert A. Martin and Steven R. Centola (eds.), *The Theater Essays of Arthur Miller*, revised and expanded (New York, 1996), 311.

2. Oscar Handlin, *The Uprooted* (Boston, 1951), 4–6.

3. See Bonnie Graber, "'Non-writer' Basch Offers Provocative Views of Shakespeare," *University of Connecticut Advance*, February 14, 1997. See also http://www.ucc.uconn.edu/~ADVANCE/021497PF.htm, and http://www2.h-net.msu.edu/~judaic/articles/shylock.basch.

4. Allen Guttmann, *The Jewish Writer in America: Assimilation and the Crisis of Identity* (New York, 1971), 13.

5. Morris Freedman, *American Drama in Social Context* (Carbondale and Edwardsville, Ill., 1971), 48.

6. C. W. E. Bigsby, *A Critical Introduction to Twentieth-Century American Drama*, 2 vols., (Cambridge, England, 1984), 2:174.

7. George Ross, "*Death of a Salesman* in the Original," *Commentary* II (February 1951), reprinted in Arthur Miller, *Death of a Salesman, Text and Criticism*, ed. Gerald Weales (New York, 1967), 259 , 260.

8. Malcolm Bradbury, "Arthur Miller's Fiction," in Christopher Bigsby (ed.), *The Cambridge Companion to Arthur Miller* (Cambridge, England, 1997), 215.

9. Mary McCarthy, *Sights and Spectacles: Theatre Chronicles, 1937–1956* (New York, 1957), xiv–xv, xvi.

10. Leslie A. Fiedler, *Waiting for the End* (New York, 1964), 91.

11. Arthur Miller, *Timebends: A Life* (New York, 1987), 70.

12. Robert A. Martin, "The Creative Experience of Arthur Miller: An Interview," *Educational Theater Journal* 21 (1969); reprinted in Matthew C. Roudane, *Conversations with Arthur Miller* (Jackson, Miss. and London, 1987), 183.

13. Arthur Miller, *Death of a Salesman* (New York, 1998), xxviii. Subsequent quotations from *Death of a Salesman* are from this edition; page numbers are noted parenthetically in the text.

14. Brenda Murphy, *Miller: Death of a Salesman* (Cambridge, England, 1995), II. David Mamet also felt that Miller "had written the story of my father and me"; Miller said that Chinese audiences told him the same thing. Quoted by Christopher Bigsby in *Arthur Miller and Company* (London, 1990), 64. However, I know no record of anyone saying that Miller had written "the story of my son and me." Like most family dramas, *Salesman* is written from the son's point of view, not the father's.

15. Miller, *Timebends*, 322.

16. Murphy, *Miller*, 83–87.

17. Ibid., 106.

18. Miller, *Timebends*, 126–31.

19. Joseph Stein (book), Jerry Bock (music), Sheldon Harnick (lyrics), *Fiddler on the Roof* (New York, 1964), 2–3.

20. Arthur Miller, "The Family in Modern Drama," *Atlantic Monthly* 197 (April, 1956), reprinted in *The Theater Essays of Arthur Miller*, 73.

21. Arthur Miller, *Death of a Salesman*, Fiftieth Anniversary Edition (New York, 1999), xii.

22. Guttmann, *Jewish Writer in America*, 13.

23. Ronald Bryden, "A Model for the Future," *The Observer,* London, February 19, 1967.

24. Benjamin Nelson, "Arthur Miller," in Joel Shatzky and Michael Taub, *Contemporary Jewish-American Dramatists and Poets: A Bio-Critical Sourcebook* (Westport, Conn. and London, 1999), 53–54.

25. Marylin Berger, "Isaiah Berlin, Philosopher and Pluralist, Is Dead at 88," *New York Times,* November 7, 1997.

26. Clifford Odets, *Awake and Sing!,* in *Six Plays of Clifford Odets* (New York, 1979), 66.

27. Arthur Miller, "Introduction to the *Collected Plays,* reprinted in *The Theater Essays of Arthur Miller,* 149.

28. "'The Jewish businessman is traditionally a small businessman, in his own or a family-owned firm." Nathan Glazer and Daniel Patrick Moynihan, *Beyond the Melting Pot: The Negroes, Puerto Ricans, Jews, Italians, and Irish of New York City,* second edition (Cambridge, Mass. and London, 1970), xxx.

29. "'The story of Jews in the South,' Eli Evans has written, in a formulation that applies equally well to the North, 'is the story of fathers who built businesses to give to their sons who didn't want them.'" Charles E. Silberman, *A Certain People: American Jews and Their Lives Today* (New York, 1985), 121.

30. Miller, *Timebends,* 30.

31. Charles E. Silberman quotes Alfred Kazin: "It was not for myself alone that I was expected to shine, but for them [his parents]—to redeem the constant anxiety of their existence." Silberman, *A Certain People,* 138. Silberman also cites, inevitably in this context, *Portnoy's Complaint* by Philip Roth.

32. Among the Jews of Eastern Europe, "Manual labor was frequently regarded as a mark of social disgrace, a badge of coarseness and ignorance." Irving Howe and Eliezer Greenberg, eds., *A Treasury of Yiddish Stories* (New York, 1953,), 5.

33. Irving Howe and Kenneth Libo, *How We Lived, A Documentary History of Immigrant Jews in America, 1880–1930* (New York, 1979), 51–52.

34. "Franz Kafka's friend Felix Weltsch wrote in the Prague Zionist journal *Self-Defense* that the Jews must 'shed our heavy stress on intellectual preeminence . . . and our excessive nervousness, a heritage of the ghetto. . . . We spend all too much of our time debating, and not enough time in play and gymnastics.'" Sander L. Gilman, *Smart Jews: The Construction of the Image of Jewish Superior Intelligence* (Lincoln, Neb. and London, 1996), 23.

35. In the Introduction to his *Collected Plays,* Miller writes, "And even as Willy's sons are unhappy men, Charley's boy, Bernard, works hard, attends to his studies, and attains a worthwhile objective." Reprinted in *The Theater Essays of Arthur Miller,* 150.

36. Miller, *Timebends,* 397.

JEFFREY D. MASON

Arthur Miller's Ironic Resurrection

And somehow we are now "post-dread." Something fell down. Nobody's
quite sure what it was or is, and whether a structure is re-asserting
itself—a new one. But things ain't what they used to be. I think
something did fall down, a structure which we look at sometimes
comically. . . . Now what we have is a flow; one thing happening after
another without any sensible form or shape.
                                   —Arthur Miller, 20 October 1996 [1]

Power changes everything.
                                   —Arthur Miller, 26 March 2001 [2]

Arthur Miller's *Resurrection Blues* (2002) closes with a renunciation of
expectations, of any belief that the future could constitute progress beyond
the present.[3] After struggling over how to respond to a man who might be
the new Messiah, the characters stand together, staring up into the bright
light that he radiates as he rises above them, and they cry out, in unison,
"Please go away." The light fades, and they say good-bye, "immensely relieved
and sorry."[4] If he is the Messiah, they are giving up on salvation, but if we
take his messianic status as metaphorical, interpreting him in a secular sense
as the one who would lead them to change society and rectify injustice,
then they are rejecting activism. From this perspective, the play constitutes

From *Theatre Journal.* © 2003 The Johns Hopkins University Press.

Miller's cynical denunciation of a post-millennial age when the values and aspirations he so long defended are, perhaps, no longer viable.[5]

Activism involves working to change and improve the existing order; as such, it requires taking a position that is antagonistic or even subversive in relation to established structures of authority and power. The activist defines a goal, a vision of what society could be, then maps out a strategy for reaching this goal in opposition to the resistance of those who would sustain the status quo. As dramatist and essayist, Miller has taken an activist approach most frequently by identifying a social problem and calling, through either direct or poetic means, for change, and although many characterize him as a social dramatist, both his work and his public life demonstrate a consistently political consciousness.

In *All My Sons* (1947), Miller indicts those who would profit at the expense of others' sacrifice and, more significantly, presents an understanding of community responsibility that goes beyond the conventional boundaries of the family. He attacks betrayal and political repression in *The Crucible* (1953), investigates the guilt for the Holocaust in *Incident at Vichy* (1964), and contemplates the dangers of censorship and surveillance in *The Archbishop's Ceiling* (1984). In these plays and others, Miller comes down firmly on the side of social action, placing his faith in resistance to oppressive authority, the right of the people to live free from tyranny, and the power of the individual to stand against the tide. Offstage, he served as an outspoken and highly visible president of International P.E.N. (1965–69), and he attended two national conventions of the Democratic Party, in 1968 as a delegate for Eugene McCarthy and in 1972 as a journalist sympathetic to George McGovern. In the course of his career, he has denounced Ezra Pound for supporting fascism, protested the burning of Vietnamese villages by American soldiers, censured the Greek government's oppression of writers, advocated for the release of Augusto Boal, and smiled at the prevailing American mistrust of Soviet Russia and the People's Republic of China.[6] He has urged the corrosive question of anti-Semitism in such plays as *Incident at Vichy*, *Playing For Time* (adapted 1980), and *Broken Glass* (1994), as well as the novel *Focus* (1945) and various articles.[7] In his many essays, he has argued that the intimidation of Salman Rushdie was not anomalous; warned that Congressional control of the National Endowment for the Arts would threaten freedom of expression; scolded Newt Gingrich for his position on the relationship of government to the artist; offered a mock-serious proposal that the government arrest and incarcerate each American citizen on her/his eighteenth birthday until a judge accepts evidence of the individual's allegiance; held up to ridicule the honesty not only of Richard Nixon but also of Lyndon Johnson, John F. Kennedy, and Dwight Eisenhower; and attacked a proposal that each American citizen carry an identity card.[8] In all, Miller's work provides a rich record of his response to certain major events and currents of his lifetime: the Great Depression, the Nazi invasion of Europe and the Holocaust, the anti-Communist repression of the 1950s, the anti-war movement of the 1960s, and the fall of the Nixon presidency. David Savran hails the playwright's political commitment: "Miller has consistently dedicated his writing to the exploration of manifestly political issues, including the alienation and commodification of the individual subject in bourgeois society, the mechanics of ostracism, and the ethics of informing on one's own colleagues."[9] Yet as an activist, Miller is more moderate than radical, highly cognizant of the intricacies and ambiguities in society and politics.

Outside the theatre, the most compelling staging of Miller's political persona and activist tendencies took place during his testimony before the House Committee on Un-American Activities on the morning of Thursday, 21 June 1956.[10] Although Miller's reputation as activist and social critic flowered due to his handling of the Committee and various journalists' reports on his testimony, his participation in the scenario did not truly establish him as an unequivocal leftist, activist, or opponent of oppression; rather, the dialogue revealed the subtleties and contradictions in Miller's thought. Early in the hearing, Richard Arens, the staff director for the Committee, asked a series of questions designed to establish that in 1947 alone, the playwright had supported the World Youth Festival in Prague, a *Washington Post* advertisement protesting punitive measures directed against the Communist Party, a statement by the Veterans Against Discrimination advocating the abolition of the Committee, and three actions by the Civil Rights Congress: a rally against the Committee, a statement in support of the Communist Party as a legal American political party, and a press release in support of Gerhart Eisler, whom Arens characterized as "a top-ranking agent of the Kremlin in this country."[11] The Committee regarded all of these organizations and activities as Communist in nature; for example, they listed the Veterans Against Discrimination as a "subversive affiliate" of the Civil Rights Congress, itself "subversive and Communist" and included in a list of Communist organizations compiled from the Attorney General's official reports intended to protect the national security and provide a reference to guide anyone in the government who was reviewing a job applicant's background.[12] Miller asserted that he could not recall whether or not he had given the support that so concerned Arens. He remarked that "in those times I did support a number of things which I would not do now. . . . I would not support now a cause or movement which was dominated by Communists."[13] He agreed that he had exercised poor judgment; not only had he allowed Communists and their supporters to use his name, he committed a "great error" by not using his platform to defend those whom the Communists were persecuting. The Committee regarded his remarks as a confession and acceptance of guilt, but their interpretation aside, he was clearly backing away from embracing these past affiliations.

When the hearing turned to the Smith Act, a law intended to discourage and punish insurgents, Miller took a more aggressive position and offered his well-known defense of advocacy in literature:

> I am opposed to the Smith Act and I am still opposed to anyone being penalized for advocating anything. That doesn't mean that a man is a propagandist. It is in the nature of life and it is in the nature of literature that the passions of an author congeal around issues.
>
> You can go from *War and Peace* through all the great novels of time and they are all advocating something. . . . I am not here defending Communists, I am here defending the right of an author to advocate, to write. . . .
>
> . . . my understanding of [the Act] is that advocacy is penalized or can be under this law. Now, my interest, as I tell you, is possibly too selfish, but without it I can't operate and neither can literature in this country, and I don't think anybody can question this.
>
> ("TAM," 4672, 4673)[14]

To write, Miller argued, is to advocate; he traces the process from issues to the writer's "passions" to the consequent work. He evokes a powerful conception of writing as a form of speaking out, of setting out one's ideas for public scrutiny, and of entering into a contentious, engaged discourse. Although he agreed that one should "call out the troops" to subdue a man if he were urging people to blow up the building where the hearing was taking place, he insisted that the Smith Act placed in jeopardy "the freedom of literature without which we will be back in a situation where people as in the Soviet Union and as in Nazi Germany have not got the right to advocate." When Representative Gordon H. Scherer asked whether or not "a poet should have the right to advocate the overthrow of this Government by force and violence in his literature," Miller replied, "a man should have the right to write a poem [concerning] just about anything" ("TAM," 4673, 4674).[15]

Yet Miller equivocated in two respects. First, he cherished a view of the special nature of the artist, and the more Committee members pressed him, the more he limited his defense of advocacy to its literary uses, implying that if literature moves in its own space, then it is harmless, and one can write a poem about anything because the work is "only" a poem. This position rests on a distinction and a boundary between art and politics, one that tends to subordinate and debilitate art, but even the Committee members realized that a poem can serve as a vehicle whose artistic value is of less significance than the ideas it carries. Miller argued that advocacy is essential for literature, and he asked for a special constitutional shield because of literature's artistic nature. In other words, in spite of his defense of advocacy, Miller asks that we appreciate his work for its artistic merits more than for its meaning.

Second, Miller remarked that he had never read the law he disparaged. In fact, the Smith Act specified punishment for anyone convicted not merely of advocacy in general, or even of advocacy of ideas, no matter how aggressive, but specifically of advocating the violent overthrow of the government of the United States.[16] The law did interdict a variety of ordinarily protected activities—to teach, to advise, to print, to publish, to encourage—but only if turned to such a purpose. We are left with the question of whether Miller was acting in ignorance or taking a canny position on a highly sensitive and politicized matter. The Smith Act was undeniably an object of active concern: eleven Communist Party leaders were arrested in 1948 and subsequently convicted under the Act, and the Committee's chair, Francis E. Walter, defended the Act against the argument that the threat of Communist conspiracy was no longer strong enough to warrant the compromise to the right of free speech.[17] We may speculate either that Miller was responding to the Smith Act imperfectly on the basis of hearsay, or that he was turning the Act to his own purposes, finding in it an opportunity to advocate for a certain view of First Amendment rights.

In the course of his testimony, Miller took several carefully-selected positions. Although he claimed not to remember offering his support for specific, allegedly subversive causes, he admitted his past affiliation with organizations that the Committee regarded as linked to the Communist Party. However, he had never submitted to the "discipline" of the Party or its cause, and he regarded supporting Communism as a "great error" ("TAM," 4660, 4690). He denounced the Smith Act insofar as it penalized advocacy, but he agreed that the government should restrain someone who incited others to violence. Most significantly, although he insisted that a poet should be able to write about anything and he demanded the right of advocacy in literature, he rested these positions on a meaningful and substantive distinction between literature and political action, apparently implying that literature could have political content even though its writing and publishing were not necessarily political acts. The hearing concluded in a conciliatory mood; the playwright agreed that "it would be a disaster and a calamity if the Communist Party ever took over this country," acknowledged that "we are living in a time when there is great uncertainty," and assured the members, "I believe in democracy [and] I love this country" ("TAM," 4689–90). Miller had found a judicious middle ground: he had not cooperated in the manner of Elia Kazan, Clifford Odets, and Lee J. Cobb, but neither had he resisted as firmly as Lillian Hellman, Pete Seeger, and Zero Mostel.

We should interpret Miller's delicate dance in relation to the political operations and personal risks of the moment. In the very different political climate of the 1960s, Miller took a clearer, more openly activist position. In response to the assassination of Robert Kennedy, he issued a call for social action:

> It must be faced now that we are afraid of the Negro because we have denied him social justice and we do not know how to stop denying him.
>
> We are afraid of the poor because we know that there is enough to go around, that we have not made it our first order of business to literally create the jobs that can and must be created. . . .
>
> We are at war not only with Vietnamese but with Americans. Stop both. We are rich enough to wipe out every slum and to open a world of hope to the poor. What keeps us? Do we want peace in Vietnam? Then make peace. Do we want hope in our cities and towns? Then stop denying any man his birthright. . . .
>
> Between the promise and its denial—there stands the man with the gun. Between the promise and its denial stands a man holding them apart—the American. Either he recognizes what he is doing, or he will take the final, fatal step to suppress the violence he has called up.
>
> Only justice will overcome the nightmare. The American Dream is ours to evoke.[18]

Miller asks his listeners to embrace the moment, to assume responsibility for their society, and to act on the belief that action can lead to results; his is a clarion call to activism. He insists that the United States has the money and the power to effect radical social change, to rectify the wrongs of racism, poverty, and war, and in spite of the remonstrative tone, his message is ultimately optimistic. Here, perhaps, is Miller at his most outspoken, but by the time he wrote *Resurrection Blues*, his confidence in action seemed to have faded.

Resurrection Blues

Resurrection Blues is a political satire that takes aim at such twenty-first-century targets as the power and cultural values of broadcast media, the deceitful rhetoric and compromise of military dictatorship, the wary and unbalanced relationship between the United States and Latin America, and the virtually palpable force of money in a global and corporate economy. Miller brings together these elements in a crisis developing from an impending crucifixion, a plot element that threatens to dislocate the action back to the concerns that led to a hill outside Jerusalem two thousand years ago.

The events take place in what Miller describes simply as "a faraway country" but which appears to be a deeply troubled nation located somewhere in the Americas, south of the United States, a Spanish-speaking region whose people still remember the Conquistadors. The country has endured nearly four decades of civil war, and two percent of the people own ninety-six percent of the land. Fathers turn their eight-year-old daughters into prostitutes while small children kill old men for their shoes, and in the most swanky shopping district, pedestrians casually ignore a dead baby lying in the gutter. The air pollution is acrid enough to peel the paint off an eighteenth-century canvas, and a leaking underground aqueduct has so undermined the foundations of homes in one affluent neighborhood that the weight of a grand piano threatens to collapse the house that holds it. Children suffer liver damage from drinking water riddled with blood fluke, and even the powerful must fly to Miami for competent dental care.[19] This "faraway country" has no clearly recognizable model or analogue, although a passing reference to the Andes, late in the play, suggests that Miller might have been thinking of Chile or Argentina, with echoes of Augusto Pinochet or Juan Perón. Yet rather than dismiss it as a generic cartoon of a banana republic, we might do better to regard it as the inverse of the United States, or rather of the self-conceived image of the United States, what the United States, in Miller's satirical commentary, hopes it is not: poor, backward, abused, and abusive.[20]

The story is fairly simple. General Felix Barriaux, the leader of the military junta that rules the country, has captured an alleged rebel usually known as "Ralph" whom he proposes to execute by crucifixion. The largest advertising agency in the United States offers $25 million for the exclusive rights to televise the event, and an account executive, Skip L. Cheeseboro, comes to scout locations with Emily Shapiro, a director of television commercials. They meet Henri Schultz, Felix's cousin, who suffers from chronic guilt over the ruthless operation of his pharmaceutical corporation and who lacks Felix's knack for overlooking the fact that many of the peasants light candles to "Ralph" as the second coming of the Messiah. "Ralph," who never appears on stage, not only generates a dazzling white light, he is apparently able to perform curative miracles. In the end, the characters' various selfish interests drive the debate over whether "Ralph" should stay for his own execution or depart by means of his own transfiguration.

The Operation of Power

The play depicts social and political power as rooted in exploitation and managed through presentation. Miller has explored social power—as distinct from the political processes that frequently express it—most notably in *All My Sons*, *The Crucible*, *The Archbishop's Ceiling*, and even *Death of a Salesman* (1949), which is, in part, an exploration of how exclusion from the currents of power—in the community, in society, in a vocation—relentlessly beats down one man. Yet his concern with power extends well beyond the stage; while serving as president of International P.E.N. in 1966, he offered a perspective informed by what he was learning about oppression outside of the United States. He presents the concentration camp as an expression and consequence of power deployed ruthlessly:

> I have always felt that concentration camps, though they're a phenomenon of totalitarian states, are also the logical conclusion of contemporary life. If you complain of people being shot down in the streets, of the absence of communication or social responsibility, of the rise of everyday violence which people have become accustomed to, and the dehumanization of feelings, then the ultimate development on an organized social level is the concentration camp. . . . The concentration camp is the final expression of human separateness and its ultimate consequence.[21]

Just two years earlier, he had finished *After the Fall* (1964), with its dominant scenic image of "the blasted stone tower of a German concentration camp" looming over the entire action and mutely influencing the characters' behavior even while it seems to warn them of the possible consequences of their actions.[22] Here, Miller is suggesting a cluster of associations: concentration camps are productions of totalitarian states, which constitute the most extreme manifestations of institutionalized power, but they also represent the logical extension of an existence rife with violence and fraught with alienation. Power, especially too much power, can crush life. He goes on to explain his fundamental concerns:

> I'm in deadly fear of people with too much power. I don't trust people that much any more. I used to think that if people had the right idea they could make things move accordingly. Now it's a day-to-day fight to stop dreadful things from happening.[23]

Miller made these deeply cynical and pessimistic remarks two years *before* his inspirational response to Robert Kennedy's assassination, so we may conclude that even during the sometimes exhilarating 1960s, he struggled with the problem of how to respond to social calamity, swinging between hope and despair. In *Resurrection Blues*, he explores the option of surrender.

Felix Barriaux constitutes Miller's comic demonstration of the danger of power. He is a composite of every uniformed dictator from Fidel Castro to Saddam Hussein, and the playwright chooses to show not the public persona, the Felix that might appear on CNN, but rather the man behind the

scenes who speaks frankly to those who are close to him.[24] We hear, therefore, not the political rhetoric itself but the ideas, ambition, and cynicism that
drive it, so the character comes across as brutally and comically honest. He
is a ruthless pragmatist, completely free from illusions, who advises Henri to
"fuck them before they can fuck you" (RB, 4). He chooses his concerns and
loyalties according to the results he seeks; he knows that dying children are
politically insignificant compared with those who will profit if the British
erect a warehouse on the waterfront. He so completely scorns the populace
that he dismisses the very idea of land reform, assuring Henri that "in ten
years the land you gave away will end up back in the hands of two percent of
the smartest people! You can't teach gorillas to play Chopin" (RB, 16). He states
unequivocally that any government must cooperate with the "narco-guerrillas"
because they have money and discipline. As for politics in general, "there is
only one sacred rule—nobody clearly remembers anything," and since he
attaches value to others only insofar as he can use them, he plays everyone
he meets (RB, 21). Felix is Miller's vision of a despot, of the ostensibly actual
substance behind the constructed image, so he constitutes the playwright's
attempt to get at the truth of power structures in the worlds of commerce,
force, and politics that he explores.

Miller distorts Felix enough that we can choose to laugh at him and not
take him too seriously. By contrast, the playwright felt that Danforth, the
deputy governor and presiding judge in The Crucible, represented so palpable
a threat that he should have drawn a darker picture of him. Four years after
that play opened, Miller wrote:

> I was wrong in mitigating the evil of this man and the judges he
> represents. Instead, I would perfect his evil to its utmost and
> make an open issue, a thematic consideration of it in the play. I
> believe now, as I did not conceive then, that there are people dedi-
> cated to evil in the world; that without their perverse example
> we should not know the good. Evil is not a mistake but a fact in
> itself.[25]

Danforth and Felix both rule, bend others to their wills, and constitute
manifestations of what Miller deems wrong with the world. Yet Miller wrote
Felix nearly fifty years after he created Danforth; we must take Danforth
seriously and deal with his menace, while Felix embodies a situation that has
already moved past our control. A Danforth inspires concern and action as
we see the possibility to defeat him, but a Felix is too firmly placed and our
only option is grim humor.

Through Felix, Miller cultivates his ongoing mistrust of the operation
of government and those who govern. At a rally for Eugene McCarthy in

1968, amidst the burgeoning resistance to the Vietnam War, he demanded a departure from the craven leadership he had observed:

> The next President is going to face a revolutionary country and [a] world in revolution, and he will need a lot more than gallantry. He will need the habit of mind to perceive in the institutions he leads [that] what is dead and inhuman must be dismantled. The next President will not be able to lead by consensus, by the expert manipulation of opinion, or by calls for unity, however passionate. . . . The next President will have to weigh every action not for what it will do for our prestige or our institutions but for what it will do to people.[26]

Miller perceives the status quo as a reliance on charisma, good feelings, and expertly-managed spin, so he calls for a higher level of responsibility as well as a greater concern for human welfare.

Throughout his career, Miller has denounced censorship as a pernicious exercise of power and a special form of oppression. He interpreted his 1956 summons by the Committee as no more than his government's attempt to repress his writing.[27] In 1989, possibly looking back to his extensive experience with the repression of writers while serving as president of International P.E.N., he argued that censorship as an abuse of authority was a global problem, used "to steal power from the people and hand it over to the state."[28] *The Archbishop's Ceiling* stages his deep concern over not just censorship but active government surveillance. In the preface to the Grove edition, he wrote:

> Very recently, in the home of a star Soviet writer, I began to convey the best wishes of a mutual friend, an émigré Russian novelist living in Europe, and the star motioned to me not to continue. Once outside, I asked if he wasn't depressed by having to live in a tapped house. . . . Was he really all that unaffected by the presence of the unbidden guest? Perhaps so, but even if he had come to accept or at least abide it fatalistically, the bug's presence had changed him nonetheless. In my view it had perhaps dulled some resistance in him to Power's fingers ransacking his pockets every now and then. One learns to *include the bug* in the baggage of one's mind, in the calculus of one's plans and expectations, and this is not without effect. . . . What, for instance, becomes of the idea of sincerity, the unmitigated expression of one's feelings and views, when one knows that Power's ear is most probably overhead? Is sincerity shaken by the sheer fact that one has so much as *taken the bug into consideration*?[29]

The bug becomes the government, becomes authority, becomes the invasive presence of power that threatens to destroy the individual's mind; Miller sees how the insinuation of official control into private life cannot help but suffocate. Through *The Archbishop's Ceiling*, Miller questioned the integrity not of a specific government but of the very idea of government; the embattled writers in the play regard government as an adversary with no face and virtually limitless authority. One observes, "The government makes it very clear that you must snuggle up to power or you will never be happy."[30]

By 1995, Miller's cynicism over the operation of government had deepened to the point of offering an ironic recommendation that the nation privatize the United States Congress, that businesses and interest groups hire representatives and senators who would openly advocate on their behalf:

> The compelling reasons for privatizing Congress are perfectly evident. Everybody hates it, only slightly less than they hate the president. Everybody, that is, who talks on the radio, plus millions of the silent who only listen and hate in private.
>
> Congress has brought on this hatred, mainly by hypocrisy.[31]

He went on to argue that privatization would simply recognize the existence of the corporate state, and he suggested that the transformation extend to the Supreme Court and the Department of Justice so that criminal and civil proceedings could openly consist of striking bargains.

Yet force and tyranny are only the first layers in *Resurrection Blues'* structure of power relations; Miller then turns to the media. He once wrote, "The sin of power is to not only distort reality but to convince people that the false is true, and that what is happening is only an invention of enemies."[32] Felix understands that consolidating power involves managing what people know so that actuality becomes less significant than belief. Skip and Emily can sell virtually anything; they translate experience into the brief, intensely focused moments that they can show on television, and Skip proudly introduces Emily as the director who "has given the world some of its most uplifting commercial images" (*RB*, 29). Felix might, in his public appearances, pay lip service to his duty to his people, but Skip and Emily bear no explicit public responsibility and so can exploit their material more openly; indeed, it is their business to keep their distance from local concerns and especially to make free use of whatever they find. They create propaganda in order to serve the commercial interests that hire them, giving little thought for honesty or accuracy, and insofar as the very nature of a television commercial presupposes that the customer requires persuasion, the relationship between the producer and the customer is inherently antagonistic and the discourse is partisan. Yet their propaganda engages politics at one remove, dealing more directly with the financial influences that support and enable a government like Felix's. Miller is tracing the distance from the 1950s, when the Committee denounced propaganda as the tool of subversives, to the present moment, when propaganda serves the interests of the power elite; surely government fifty years ago used propaganda, but now it does so without shame.

Skip and Emily have become so involved in simulation that they are able to grasp certain realities only through strenuous effort. Emily at first assumes that the execution is part of a feature film that someone else is shooting; only when she sees a team of soldiers digging a hole and bolting together the cross members to construct a genuine crucifix does she realize that they expect her to film an actual crucifixion with actual nails and an actual death. She is incredulous: "Nobody dies in a commercial! Have you all gone crazy?" (RB, 33) Skip, in turn, has difficulty remembering that "Ralph" is not precisely Jesus Christ, and he keeps coming back to questions of how his American customers would react to his treatment of this supposed new Messiah. Crucifixion is actually a standard practice in Felix's country, and when the general cheerfully informs Skip that the typical victim first guzzles a couple of bottles of tequila and might have to be carried to the cross, the advertising man is convinced that many in the United States—specifically born-again Christian viewers "in like dry states . . . Kansas or whatever"— would consider such a debacle to be blasphemous (RB, 44). He is also concerned over the possibility that the condemned man might scream:

> But I should think if he is confident that he is about to . . . like meet his father in heaven, you could put it to him as a test of his faith that he not scream on camera. The camera, you see, tends to magnify everything and screaming on camera could easily seem in questionable taste. . . . I am simply saying that even though he was nailed—the Original, I mean—he is always shown hanging up there in perfect peace.
>
> [RB, 48–49]

To Skip, experience is something he arranges, designs, films, and packages; in other words, it is subject to his conscious control with specific goals in mind. Reality is what he devises rather than what happens to him. He and Emily are in the business of managing what people learn and how they interpret it, and the truth of the moment engages them much less than the effect they hope to produce, so they treat actuality as raw material.

As with Felix, Miller stages the media professionals in private rather than in public, showing not the result of the advertising agency's labors but how they operate behind the scenes, and because the potential event is so shattering, even Emily and Skip pause to contemplate their own strategies and how their work affects them. She reminds him that she makes commercials: "My genius is to make everything comfortably fake, Skip. No agency wants real. You want a fake-looking crucifixion?—call me." She shrinks from the prospect before her, assuring him, "I'm totally lost. All I know is that somebody actually dying in my lens would melt my eyeball" (*RB*, 37). When she asks whether or not the project disgusts him, in a moment of candid self-awareness, he replies, "but realistically, who am I to be disgusted?" (*RB*, 36). Skip is seduced by the advantages of the exclusive, so he retreats into cliché Hollywood justifications for the shoot by way of persuading Emily to stick with it:

> It's clear, isn't it, that you are not responsible for it happening, right?
> [SUDDEN NEW IDEA]
> In fact, showing it on the world screen could help put an end to it forever!
> [WARMING]
> Yes! That's it! If I were moralistic I'd even say you have a *duty* to shoot this! Really, I mean that. . . . In fact, it could end up a worldwide blow against capital punishment, which I know you are against as I passionately am.
>
> [*RB*, 36]

When he appears to have convictions, they are completely and conveniently focused on getting the job done; he scorns Emily's suggestion that someone provide a physician to tend to the man they will nail on the cross:

> In all the thousands of paintings and the written accounts of the crucifixion scene I defy anyone to produce a single one that shows a doctor present! I'm sorry but we can't be twisting the historical record!
> [GREAT NEW IDEA]
> . . . And furthermore, I will not superimpose American mores on a dignified foreign people. The custom here is to crucify criminals, period! I am not about to condescend to these people with a foreign colonialist mentality!
>
> [*RB*, 43]

Through these comic struggles, Miller engages with the patterns and jeopardies of rationalization and justification. In this presumptive media crisis, the issues have less to do with what people think and do and more to do with what the participants declare and how others read their messages. The politicians have given place to television producers, and the exceptional status of the artist—the standing that supported Miller's 1956 contention for the free-dom of the poet—has dissolved in the intersection of art with commerce.

To Felix, Skip, and Emily, appearance is prior to substance; the real is a matter of what they can present through image and rhetoric. They have little interest in truth or genuine experience; they are much more invested in coverage and exposure, in the quality of presentation rather than content, and in the competition over who gets there first and takes the profits. They commodify everything; Felix—who deals not in the reality of his nation but in what he can persuade others to believe about it—speaks of his coun-try in terms of its potential worth, citing coverage in both *Vanity Fair* and *National Geographic* to validate the beauty (and, by implication, the com-mercial promise) of the views near Santa Felice, while Skip and Emily value the landscape only in terms of what it can help them sell. Emily marvels at the scenery: "Look at that snow. That sun. That light. What a blue. What an orange! What mountains!" (*RB*, 27). She and Skip remember their travels only in terms of the products their agency was hired to advertise, so Nepal, Kenya, the Caucasus, Colombia, the Himalayas, and Chile are no more than locations where they shot commercials for Ivory Soap, Chevy Malibu, Vidal Shampoo, Jeep, Alka Seltzer, and Efferdent. Skip tells Emily that "what you do is make real things look fake, and that makes them emotionally real," and when she considers "Ralph," she treats him like one more public figure in need of packaging, remarking, "I assume it's important to this man what kind of public impression he makes, right?" (*RB*, 37, 48). Henri, always the intellectual voice of the piece, tries to theorize their strategies, suggesting to Skip that because ancient Egyptian art shows very little about the Jewish cap-tivity in spite of the destruction of the pharoah's army described in Exodus, the entire episode might have been no more than a work of fiction designed to present a culture's vision of itself. He draws a more recent analogy (and refers to Miller's own activist past) when he points out that the United States justified its military intervention in Vietnam by citing the Gulf of Tonkin incident even though later revelations suggested that the alleged attack on American warships never took place and that President Johnson's government exaggerated and distorted the fragmentary information in order to promote the course of action they desired.

The revolutionaries and the junta have struggled for control of the nation, but Felix and his accomplices are winning not only because they wield greater force but also because they work more closely with foreign business interests, whose financial support is crucial. Miller has traced elsewhere his growing perception that the political and financial sectors are coterminous. After serving as a delegate to the 1968 Democratic National Convention, he wrote that professional politicians regarded the process as a game and the issues as mere tokens for their use.[33] A few years later, he asserted that:

> we've become a corporate state. It has become the function of the state to make it possible for immense corporations to carry on their activities, and everything else is incidental. There are always conflicts between the corporations and between the Government and the corporations, but fundamentally what we have is a socialism of the individual corporations.[34]

Money and power come together to serve and reinforce each other; money becomes the means of power, and power facilitates profit. It was, perhaps, this vision of the corporate state that led Miller, during the elder Bush's first year in office, to declare the "moral bankruptcy" of politics.[35]

In the end, Felix, Skip, and Emily regard price as the measure of value, no matter whether they are discussing a product, a nation, or a person. When Skip's agency offers $25 million for exclusive rights, everything in Felix's framework changes. The crucifixion now has a certain financial and political worth, and the potential return drives all of the ensuing decisions. The execution of "Ralph" will be about not suffering or commitment, or even punishing a criminal, but rather coverage and profit. The $25 million expands the circle of complicity because the commercial promise of the crucifixion involves even the meanest peasant, who hopes to benefit from tourism. Many of the rural residents hope that their villages will be chosen for the crucifixion, not only for the honor, but also for the effect on property values. One of "Ralph's" followers explains:

> Well, face it, once it's televised they'll be jamming in from the whole entire world to see where it happened. Tour buses bumper to bumper across the Andes to get to see his bloody shorts? Buy a souvenir fingernail or one of his eyeballs in plastic? It's a whole tax base thing, Jeanine, y'know? Like maybe a new school, roads, swimming pool, maybe even a casino and theme park—all that shit. I don't have to tell you, baby, these people have *nothing*.
>
> [RB, 121]

This vision goes beyond the trite notion that everything has a price; here, everything carries a price tag, a label that not only fixes its ostensible value but also immures it into a paradigm where nothing has intrinsic value or meaning. The peasants might enjoy the benefit of roads and a new school, but they'll have to hawk phony fingernails and mop floors for Disney. Money takes priority over goods and services, so the point of commerce is the transaction itself, and everything, from "Ralph" to the souvenirs, is cheapened.

The Collapse of Revolution

Standing against Felix's commercial politics is a failed revolution. Miller has set up a situation that meets two criteria he once articulated: that a revolution constitutes a response to intolerable conditions and that a "classic" revolution would involve "a transfer of power between classes."[36] On Miller's terms, this country is ripe for revolution, but we enter the story after the powerful have prevailed. Henri has given up on the struggle and now wrings his hands helplessly, while Jeanine, who took command of the rebels, surrendered to despair and stepped out of an upper-story window in an attempt to end her life. Felix shakes his head over what he regards as her emotionalism, assuring Henri that "she has to know all that is finished, revolution is out" (RB, 7). He regards revolution not as a matter of passion, commitment, or historical crisis, but merely as a political strategy, even a social fashion. Even in the aftermath, Henri cannot take it so lightly:

> HENRI: A faith in the revolution is what I gave her . . . and then walked away from it myself.
>
> FELIX: I hope I'm not hearing your old Marxism again, Henri.
>
> HENRI: Oh, shit, Felix!—I haven't been a Marxist for twenty-five years!
>
> FELIX: Because that is finished, they're almost all in narcotics now, thanks be to God; but the Americans are here now and they'll clean out the whole lot of them by New Years [sic]! Your guerrillas are done!
>
> HENRI: Those are not my guerrillas, my guerrillas were foolish, idealistic people, but the hope of the world! These people now are cynical and stupid enough to deal narcotics!
>
> [RB, 11]

Savran has traced Miller's evolution from Popular Front Communist to Cold War liberal, and Henri's weary defensiveness might echo the playwright's look back to earlier days.[37] Jeanine describes the revolution as "a comedian wearing a black veil—you don't know whether to laugh or run for your life," while Henri mourns that "the comical end of everything has come and gone" (RB, 65, 26). Both comments clarify Miller's strategy in Resurrection Blues; the loss of commitment is so crushing that we must laugh it off in order to survive. Events have moved beyond serious consideration and submit only to ironic treatment.

"Ralph" is the paradox of the play in that Miller both offers and under-mines the correlation with Jesus. If he is divine, then the play veers towards spirituality, as when Henri tries to explain how seeing the man made him feel:

> But then, as they were pushing him into the van—it happened quite accidentally—his gaze rose up to my window and for an instant our eyes met.—His composure, Felix—deep inside his pain you could see something almost tranquil; his poise was . . . chilling; as though he knew all this had to happen. He seemed to transcend everything.
>
> [RB, 21]

"Ralph" compels the others—the general, the advertising executive, the television director, the corporate owner, and even the disaffected revolution-ary—to deal with what he implies. There seems to be no place for faith in the social structure they have all accepted, so each must find a strategy for coping with him. Felix dismisses him as nothing more than a renegade terrorist, a man whom the government must execute as an example in order to subjugate the rest of the nation. Yet because the peasants light candles before his image, Henri argues that a crucifixion will confirm his divinity and bring the simple people down out of the mountains in rebellion. Even Felix can't ignore the prisoner's dazzling luminescence, although he predictably refuses to attach any significance to it:

> All right, I don't understand it! Do you understand a computer chip? Can you tell me what electricity is? And how about a gene? I mean what is a fucking gene? So he lights up; it's one more *thing*, that's all. But look at him, you ever seen such total vacancy in a man's face? . . . That idiot is mental and he's making us all crazy!
>
> [RB, 23]

Despite his intentions to the contrary, Felix promotes the notion of "Ralph's" divinity by presenting him as ineffable. By positioning "Ralph" as Jeanine's savior, Miller suggests that faith can rescue a decadent and failing revolution; she tells Henri that "Ralph" came to her in the hospital "to quiet my soul," and by the last scene of the play, he has somehow caused the regeneration of her crushed spine, so she is able to limp with the aid of a cane (RB, 67). Yet "Ralph" has no answers and can't even guide himself, much less those who look to him for help. He can't make up his mind whether or not he's the son of God and so destined to die on the cross, and even though Felix blames his gunmen for a series of shootings, "Ralph" himself is virtually paralyzed, responding to news of yet another massacre with uncontrollable tears. Jeanine tells Henri that "the wind has more plans than he does," and the bluntly ruthless Felix assesses his status: "He's finished" (*RB*, 67, 14).

Henri realizes that if "Ralph" is actually divine, he represents a profound threat. He argues that while the principal purpose of most human activity is "to deliver us into the realm of the imagination," "Ralph" truly feels everything and so must be hunted down and crucified:

> Imagine, Mr. Cheeseboro, if that kind of reverence for life should spread! Governments would collapse, armies disband, marriages disintegrate! Wherever we turned, our dead unfeeling shallowness would stare us in the face until we shriveled up with shame!
>
> [*RB*, 91]

He argues that "Ralph" is calling their various bluffs, that if they truly believe in any of the principles they purport to endorse, they would have to relent. The simplicity and purity of faith, as "Ralph" represents it, seems to argue against actual engagement. Moreover, the status quo of Felix's junta and their offshore business partners relies on treating life with not reverence but contempt; if they respected people, they would no longer be able to operate and a bloodless revolution would take place overnight.

The connection between "Ralph" and Jeanine introduces a contest between faith, in the spiritual sense, and conviction, in the political sense, which leads to a consideration of the material circumstances that Jeanine has sought to change and which the consolation of "Ralph" might mitigate. The advent of "Ralph" clarifies that Jeanine is just as absorbed with the material potential of her country as the others; the difference is that she works toward giving the people the benefit of the nation's resources and of their own labor. "Ralph," however, has more to do with wonder, and if the revolution must turn to such a messiah, then it has, perhaps, lost its way.

Miller has referred to faith as "a belief, one might call it, in man as a creature transcending his appetites," and the erstwhile revolutionaries of *Resurrection Blues* have faltered amidst a crisis of faith, not in "Ralph" so much as in belief itself.[38] In "Ralph," Miller presents faith less as a spiritual matter and more as a metaphor for the kind of commitment that revolutionaries like Jeanine need in order to mount the resistance necessary to defeat the junta. They have no money, little materiel, and no allies; they are alone with only their determination to support them, but their resolve has proved inadequate. Among "Ralph's" followers is Stanley, an anachronism from the late Sixties with "sneakers, unkempt pony tail, blue denim shirt, backpack" who is also a drug addict, burned-out, and untrustworthy (*RB*, 71). He tells Felix, "I've ruined my life believing in things. I spent two and a half years in

India in an ashram; I've been into everything from dope to alcohol to alfalfa therapy to Rolfing to Buddhism to total vegetarianism which I'm into now" (*RB*, 74). Jeanine begs Felix, "Don't ask me to *believe* anything! There are too many young people buried in our earth for anyone to forgive you. It will take five hundred years of snow and rain to wash the memory away" (*RB*, 113). Henri declares simply that "there is no politics any more" and affirms that "the world will never again be changed by heroes" (*RB*, 107). The millennium has turned, and belief has given way to nihilism. Yet the activists have not forgotten what drove them, so they feel the pain of loss. Jeanine asks Henri, "Can't you remember not being afraid of death, Papa? In the mountains? If you died you died for the people, so you would never die. Have you really forgotten how real that was—how pure?" (*RB*, 106). Their skepticism and sense of loss serve to clarify how far Miller has traveled since he wrote characters whose adamant convictions drive such plays as *All My Sons* and *The Crucible*, and since he called upon his fellow Americans to take their future into their own hands and become their own masters. In this regard, *Resurrection Blues* represents the extension of the uncertainty he explores in *After the Fall* and the alienation that characterizes *The Archbishop's Ceiling*.

Because he cannot fully defeat the revolution, Felix seeks to subvert it. Feeling regenerated after a tryst with Emily, he no longer wants to crucify "Ralph" but instead hopes to offer the man a place in his government—rather than destroy his adversary, he will co-opt his influence and connections. To that end, he does his best to suborn Stanley, who denies the ability to know his own mind and reduces "Ralph's" message to "just don't do bad things" (*RB*, 79). Felix hopes, in a sense, that Stanley will name names—will cooperate with the authorities to bring "Ralph" under their control—but to do so presupposes that certain answers are available. Stanley's casual, dazed attitude and haphazard syntax reduce even Felix's determination and "Ralph's" status to a virtually trivial level: "I think he just can't make up his mind, that's all—whether he really wants to—like die. I mean it's understandable, right? . . . with this great kind of weather we're having?" (*RB*, 83). Stanley can't help Felix because he can't perceive the situation in the same terms.

Miller has, of course, more than once established his position on the issue of selling out, most notably in *The Crucible*, when a man is called upon to falsely betray others in order to save his life; in *A View from the Bridge* (1956), where a community ostracizes a man who betrays another to the authorities; in *After the Fall*, which explores loyalty, honesty, and the personal cost of turning informer; and in his own refusal to name names before the Committee in 1956. To someone with Miller's personal experience, naming names constituted an act of revelation involving a complex and conflicted mixture of betrayal, penitence, cooperation, and telling the truth while under oath. Miller's response to the Committee's crucial question has become famous:

I am not protecting the Communists or the Communist Party. . . . I
will protect my sense of myself. I could not use the name of another
person and bring trouble on him. These were writers, poets, as far
as I could see, and the life of a writer, despite what it sometimes
seems, is pretty tough. I wouldn't make it any tougher for anybody. I ask you not to ask me that question. . . . I will be perfectly
frank with you in anything relating to my activities. I take the
responsibility for everything I have ever done, but I cannot take
responsibility for another human being.

["TAM," 4686]

In spite of the nuances of Miller's testimony during the two-and-a-half hour
interrogation, the salient memory of the hearing is that in declining to name
names, he refused to cooperate, to betray others, and to submit to the power
of oppressive authority. To refuse to name names remains Miller's signature
gesture of resistance.

Like Miller, Jeanine stands in opposition to unjust authority. She has
little patience for Emily's naïveté, tersely explaining that the junta has killed
over one hundred thousand people to sustain their power, that "they've been
crucifying this country for two centuries," and that Emily herself backed their
cause simply by paying American taxes, an assertion that urges a complex
perception of complicity that Emily finds inconvenient and troubling (RB,
63). Emily tries to explain that Henri feels guilty about his failure to live up
to the convictions that drive Jeanine:

> EMILY: He's really full of remorse for deserting your people
>   up in the mountains. But he *was* partly right, wasn't
>   he—the revolution had lost the people? And only
>   more pointless killing was left?
>
> JEANINE: Partly right? The secret that eats holes in the heart—
>   is that in the end, whichever side one fought on is
>   partly right no matter how completely wrong it was.
>   Just go down below the Mason-Dixon line and see
>   what I mean.—But all that matters now is that our
>   people are scattered and are still being murdered by
>   some very bad types.
>
> [RB, 68]

Emily articulates the ambiguity that might have led to Jeanine's sense of inevitable defeat; if both sides are partly right, then there is no possibility of wholehearted commitment. At bottom, Miller's political concern is with the integrity

of one's convictions. In his Committee testimony, he followed the example of his own John Proctor as he tried to protect his sense of himself against the interrogators' attempts to seduce his cooperation and compromise his perception of the truth. Jeanine struggles with both Emily and Henri, insisting on a vision of unmediated history and of principles without negotiation.

The penultimate scene stages Jeanine's resistance to giving up not just "Ralph" but the integrity and humanity that she wishes he could represent. Felix, always looking for an advantage, insists that "Ralph" make the first concession by ordering his followers to disarm, and Jeanine, the last, desperate believer, is distraught when Stanley explains that "Ralph" is weighing the problem of allowing his own crucifixion because he is assessing others' expectations. When Stanley asks, "What's wrong with that?" Jeanine is hurt and outraged: "What's wrong is that it changes him into one more shitty politician! Whatever he does he'll do because it's right, not to get people's approval!" (*RB*, 118). Stanley begs Jeanine to intercede, to persuade "Ralph" to stop his crucifixion, and Henri joins him:

JEANINE: I'm to ask him not to be god.

HENRI: Darling, if he's god he's god, you can't change that; but he doesn't have to die to prove it and bring on a bloodbath.

JEANINE: Which, incidentally, would wreck the value of your company's shares and the farms too . . .

HENRI: All right, yes—I won't deny that. But more blood now is pointless!

JEANINE: We must beg him to live and make things safe for shopping malls!—and justice can go to hell!

HENRI: Very well, yes! Better a shopping mall than a bloodbath! Better hot and cold running water than . . .

JEANINE: . . . And the TV idiocy and the car . . .

HENRI: Very well, yes the car too, yes, the car . . . !

JEANINE: And the Jacuzzi . . . !

HENRI: All right, the Jacuzzi too, yes! There is no escape anymore, Jeanine, we must have *things*!

JEANINE: . . . And the emptiness.

[HOWLING]

   The e-m-p-t-i-nessssss!

                                                            [*RB*, 123–24]

Jeanine's agony grows out of her realization that even "Ralph," perhaps, will reconstruct himself in order to serve the commercial and political interests that surround them. To name names seems to involve betraying others, but it really means, as Miller knew in 1956, betraying one's self. Jeanine realizes that Henri wants her to ask "Ralph" to name himself what he is not, to deny himself, to become both Christ and Judas. The others are asking her to give up on activism, but "Ralph" has already done so. The result of his abdication and the others' materialism will be the emptiness that tears at Jeanine, but that emptiness is where the play concludes.

The Ironic Transfiguration

In the final scene, a bright light shines above them, and they realize that "Ralph"—who just the previous night decided to call himself "Charles," producing the inevitable nickname of "Charley"—is transfiguring. Jeanine encourages him to go, and Emily would rather not film him "hanging from two sticks" (RB, 130). Skip insists that he respect the contract that the agency has signed with the government, Henri recommends that he depart because his crucifixion "might well bring down a crashing chaos that could kill the economy for endless years to come," and Stanley warns that his return might "light the match that'll explode the whole place again" (RB, 131, 132). Felix, who was willing to drop the charges, now realizes that if he loses the television contract, he'll have to return the money: "Listen Charley, get on TV, on that cross and it means ten thousand jobs. I'm talking hotels, I'm talking new construction, I'm talking investment. You care about people? Here's where you belong!" (RB, 132). The scene disintegrates as they all shout at each other, quarreling, and then come together in a single upward appeal: "PLEASE GO AWAY, CHARLEE!!" (RB, 135). With that, the light fades, and he is gone.

So the play ends not with commitment but with trendy rhetoric, and instead of ideals, Miller gives us commercial interests and emptiness. He has set up the targets quite clearly: the flagrant exploitation of a nation by its military dictator, the capitalist greed that drives the advertising interests, the pointless compassion of the intellectual, the cynical paralysis of the revolutionary, and the general deceit and hypocrisy that suffuse it all. Yet in the end, every tortured soul rejects salvation, and the putative Messiah is, after all, probably some sort of hoax in spite of his impressive special effects. In other words, Miller brings the action to a crisis that seems to demand resolution, but in the last moment, he deflates the situation. The play therefore represents a significant move away from the sacrificial affirmations we find in certain of his earlier works, particularly Joe Keller's decision to take his own life to atone for his selfishness and John Proctor's choice to die for his integrity. The resolution of Resurrection Blues is, in its own way, more shattering than either of those calamities, barely tolerable only because of the wry, comic tone that guides the play.

The through-line in Miller's work is his liberalism, his tendency to perceive action in terms of individual initiative and choice. In 1989, for a new edition of two of his early plays, Miller wrote:

these plays are somewhat surprising testimony to me that I had not lost the belief in the centrality of the individual and the importance of what he thought and did. . . . I believed it decisive what an individual thinks and does about his life, regardless of overwhelming social forces. . . . Indeed, if these plays are to be credited, there is no force so powerful, politically as well as personally, as a man's self-conceptions.[39]

Indeed, Miller often resolves the action through the will of the individual: thus Chris and Joe Keller, John Proctor, Von Berg in *Incident at Vichy*, and Marcus and Sigmund in *The Archbishop's Ceiling*. Savran has located Miller's work in "the tradition of American liberalism, flattening out class conflicts and prizing individual initiative far more than collective action," and sees in his plays "the liberal humanist subject—that allegedly seamless individual, conceived as author and origin of meaning and action—[who] attempts to construct a linear, unified history."[40] Yet in *Resurrection Blues*, Miller brings the action to the moment when the individual might turn events away from disaster and bring about a moment of thundering closure, but each person retreats. Felix, Skip, Emily, Henri, and Jeanine are, more than their counterparts in Miller's earlier plays, more embodiments of social roles than they are agents of independent action. Miller's liberal humanist subject has failed.

In the end, irony is the essential mode in Miller's work. The theatre of irony is the theatre of denial, staging the refusal to embrace an idea or a position, moving always towards skepticism and detachment, and so leading to stalemate. Miller reaches toward a politics, but in spite of the compassion that suffuses his earlier plays, in *Resurrection Blues*, he hesitates. We can negotiate or contend with those who beset us, as Miller did with the Committee, or we can recognize that we are the problem and that there is no point to action. The *sine qua non* of activism is not just conviction, but faith in one's convictions and in the potential for action to realize them. Miller's detailed vision of his characters' weaknesses leaves him too cynical to find a resolution to the problems they create. The Messiah rises once again, but he rises from life rather than death, departing rather than returning, and all because no one on Earth will listen to him.

NOTES

1. Arthur Miller, interview by Russell Baker, *Broken Glass*, Exxon Mobil Masterpiece Theatre, 20 October 1996.

2. Arthur Miller, *On Politics and the Art of Acting* (New York: Penguin, 2001), 62. First delivered as the 30th Jefferson Lecture in the Humanities for the National Endowment for the Humanities on 26 March 2001.

3. The world premiere of *Resurrection Blues* opened at the Guthrie Theater on Friday, 7 August 2002. Companies planning subsequent productions include The Wilma

Theater, Philadelphia (opening 17 September 2003) and The Old Globe, San Diego (opening 20 March 2004).

4. Arthur Miller, *Resurrection Blues* (Minneapolis: Guthrie Theater, 2002), 135. Further quotations are cited in the text and flagged with the abbreviation RB.

5. Miller has said that the play is "about the threat of a return of a messiah. Gradually they all get absolutely terrified that it might be Him. . . . It's about American commercialism . . ." ("'Sometimes it takes a hundred years, and then you get it right,'" in Mel Gussow, *Conversations with Miller* [New York: Applause, 2002], 190).

6. Arthur Miller, "Should Ezra Pound Be Shot?" *New Masses* 57 #13 (25 December 1945): 5–6; Miller, "The Age of Abdication," *New York Times*, 23 December 1967; Henry Raymont, "Miller Refuses Greek Book Plan," *New York Times*, 3 July 1969; Robert Anderson, "Repression in Brazil," *New York Times*, 24 April 1971. Miller's thoughts on American relations with Russia and China are most readily available in his *In Russia* (New York: Viking, 1969) and *Salesman in Beijing* (New York: Viking, 1984).

7. See especially Miller's "The Face in the Mirror: Anti-Semitism Then and Now," *The New York Times Book Review*, 14 October 1984: 3. Later published in his *Echoes Down the Corridor: Collected Essays, 1944–2000*, ed. Steven R. Centola (New York: Penguin, 2000), 205–8.

8. Miller's published essays on these topics include "Arthur Miller on Rushdie and Global Censorship," *Author's Guild Bulletin* (Summer 1989): 5–6; "In the Ayes of the Beholder: With Congress Debating Obscenity in Federally Funded Art, What Will Happen to Free Expression?" *Omni* 13 (February 1991): 10; "To Newt on Art," *The Nation* 261 (31 July–7 August 1995): 118; "A Modest Proposal for the Pacification of the Public Temper," *The Nation* 179 (3 July 1954): 5–8; "The Limited Hang-Out: The Dialogues of Richard Nixon as a Drama of the Antihero," *Harper's* 249 (September 1974): 13–20; "On True Identity," *The New York Times Magazine* (13 April 1975): 111.

9. David Savran, *Communists, Cowboys, and Queers: The Politics of Masculinity in the Work of Arthur Miller and Tennessee Williams* (Minneapolis: University of Minnesota Press, 1992), 21.

10. The ostensible reason for summoning Miller was the Committee's ongoing investigation into violations of passport law. In March 1954, Miller sought to renew his passport in order to travel to Belgium to attend a production of *The Crucible*; the State Department turned him down, citing regulations that restricted anyone believed to support Communist activities and whose travel abroad would therefore not be in the nation's interest. (See "Playwright Arthur Miller Refused Visa to Visit Brussels to See His Play," *New York Times*, 31 March 1954.) For a discussion of the Committee's activities, especially in relation to the arts and the entertainment industry, see the first two chapters of Brenda Murphy's *Congressional Theatre: Dramatizing McCarthyism on Stage, Film, and Television* (Cambridge: Cambridge University Press, 1999).

11. Gerhart Eisler (1897–1968) was an Austrian journalist who worked for the Communist Party in several nations; through his brother, Hanns (1898–1962), a composer, he had ties to the film industry. See Eric Bentley, ed., *Thirty Years of Treason: Excerpts from Hearings before the House Committee on Un-American Activities, 1938–1968* (New York: Viking, 1971), 55–109.

12. House Committee on Un-American Activities, *Guide to Subversive Organizations and Publications*, 82nd Cong., 1st sess., 1951, 109, 33.

13. House Committee on Un-American Activities, "Testimony of Arthur Miller, Accompanied by Counsel, Joseph L. Rauh, Jr.," *Investigation of the Unauthorized Use of*

United States Passports, 84th Cong., 2nd sess., 1956, 4663. Further quotations are cited in the text and flagged with the abbreviation "TAM."

14. In the record, *War and Peace* is set in lower-case roman type.

15. Years later, Miller recalled, "When I confirmed that I did think a poet could legally write such a subversive poem, Mr. Scherer actually threw up his hands and turned to the other members as though to say, 'What more do we have to ask?'" (Arthur Miller, *Timebends: A Life* [New York: Grove, 1987], 409). Scherer (1906–88) was a Republican from Ohio, once the assistant prosecuting attorney for Hamilton County, Ohio (1933–41), and the junior member present.

16. More properly known as The Alien Registration Act of 1940, the law specifies penalties for anyone engaged in the following activities with the intent of overthrowing the government: "advocates, abets, advises, or teaches . . . prints, publishes, edits, issues, circulates, sells, distributes, or publicly displays any written or printed matter advocating, advising, or teaching . . . organizes or helps or attempts to organize any society, group, or assembly of persons who teach, advocate, or encourage . . . becomes or is a member of, or affiliates with, any such society, group, or assembly of persons, knowing the purposes thereof" (*U.S. Code*, title 18, sec. 2385; available on the web site of Cornell Law School's Legal Information Institute [http://www4.law.cornell.edu/uscode/18/2385.html]). Congress has amended the law, most recently in 1994, and the language I quote above is from the current version in the United States Code.

17. See Walter's foreword to House Committee on Un-American Activities, *Soviet Total War: "Historic Mission of Violence and Deceit,"* 84th Cong., 1st sess., 1956, v–ix. Walter (1894–1963) was a Democrat from Pennsylvania who served on the Committee from 1949 to his death. He acted as co-sponsor to the 1952 McCarran-Walter Immigration and Nationality Act, which empowered the government to deport any immigrant or naturalized citizen engaging or intending to engage in activities "prejudicial to the public interest" or "subversive to national security."

18. Arthur Miller, "On the Shooting of Robert Kennedy," *New York Times*, 8 June 1968.

19. Blood fluke, or *Schistosoma mansoni*, is a water-borne trematode flatworm that can live parasitically on human blood.

20. The metaphorical potential of the "faraway country" did not escape journalists who reviewed the premiere. Rohan Preston wrote, "it is a play about America. It is about how values can be corrupted by a military-political-electronic-media axis. It is about religious succor and the power of the imagination and art in a time when rampant materialism crushes all things illusory" ("Arthur Miller Lightens Up a Bit in 'Resurrection Blues,'" [Minneapolis-St. Paul] *Star Tribune*, 11 August 2002 [http://www.startribune.com/stories/458/3155518.html]), and Michael Billington described the play as "a funny, pertinent and sharp-toothed satire aimed at the materialist maladies of modern America" ("The Crucifixion Will Be Televised," *The Guardian*, 21 August 2002 [http://www.guardian.co.uk/arts/critic/feature/0,1169,778207,00.html]).

21. Olga Carlisle and Rose Styron, "Arthur Miller: An Interview," in *The Theater Essays of Arthur Miller*, ed. Robert A. Martin and Steven R. Centola (1978; rev. ed. New York: Da Capo, 1996), 289. First published as "The Art of the Theatre II: Arthur Miller, an Interview," *Paris Review* 10 (Summer 1966): 61–98. Miller was referring obliquely to the scenic design of the 1966 Franco Zeffirelli production of *After the Fall*.

22. Arthur Miller, *After the Fall*, in *Arthur Miller's Collected Plays*, volume 2 (New York: Viking, 1981), 127.

23. Carlisle and Styron, 292.

24. Miller has offered some of his thoughts on the public persona of the typical government leader in *On Politics and the Art of Acting*.

25. Arthur Miller, "Introduction," *Arthur Miller's Collected Plays* (New York: Viking, 1957), 43–44.

26. Arthur Miller, "The New Insurgency," *The Nation* 206 (3 June 1968): 717. Speech delivered at Madison Square Garden on 19 May 1968.

27. Arthur Miller, "Writers in Prison," *Encounter* 30 (June 1968): 60.

28. Miller, "Rushdie and Global Censorship," 5.

29. Arthur Miller, "Conditions of Freedom: Two Plays of the Seventies—*The Archbishop's Ceiling* and *The American Clock*," in *Theater Essays*, 474, 475.

30. Arthur Miller, *The Archbishop's Ceiling* (New York: Dramatists Play Service, 1984, 1985), 11.

31. Arthur Miller, "Let's Privatize Congress," in *Echoes Down the Corridor*, 252. First published in *New York Times*, 10 January 1995.

32. Arthur Miller, "The Sin of Power," in *Echoes Down the Corridor*, 172. First published in *Index on Censorship* 7 (May/June 1978): 3–6.

33. Arthur Miller, "The Battle of Chicago: From the Delegates' Side," in *Echoes Down the Corridor*, 76–77. First published in *The New York Times Magazine* (15 September 1968): 29–31, 122–28.

34. Josh Greenfield, "Writing Plays is Absolutely Senseless, Arthur Miller Says, 'But I Love It. I Just Love It,'" in *Conversations with Arthur Miller*, ed. Matthew C. Roudané (Jackson and London: University Press of Mississippi, 1987), 246. First published in *The New York Times Magazine* (13 February 1972): 16–17, 34–39.

35. Janet Balakian, "An Interview with Arthur Miller," *Studies in American Drama, 1945–Present* 6 (1991): 41. Interview took place on 10 July 1989.

36. Steven R. Centola, "'Just Looking for a Home': A Conversation with Arthur Miller," *American Drama* 1 (Fall 1991): 93 (interview took place on 2 August 1990); "Miracles," in *Echoes Down the Corridor*, 127 (first published in *Esquire* 80 [September 1973]: 112–15, 202–4).

37. Savran, 22–26.

38. Arthur Miller, "Arthur Miller on *The Crucible*," in *Theater Essays*, 367. First published in *Audience* (July/August 1972): 46–47.

39. Arthur Miller, "Introduction," *The Golden Years* and *The Man Who Had All The Luck* (London: Methuen, 1989), 8. The first was completed in 1940 and the second was produced in 1944.

40. Savran, 22, 29.

KEVIN KERRANE

Arthur Miller vs. Columbia Pictures: The Strange Case of Career of a Salesman

In 1951, just as Columbia Pictures was about to release the film *Death of a Salesman*, Arthur Miller threatened to sue the studio. He hated the movie, but the real target of his wrath was a short subject, *Career of a Salesman*, that Columbia had commissioned to be shown before every screening of the feature film. Its purpose was to reassure the public that Willy Loman did not represent the "modern" salesman and, by implication, that the story was not anti-American.

Miller prevailed. Columbia agreed to withdraw *Career of a Salesman*, and this ten-minute prologue has lain neglected in archives for over fifty years. When I finally tracked it down in the Stock Footage Library of Archive Films in New York, I found that the script had never been copyrighted and may no longer exist. Consequently, I made a transcript—appended here—that includes framing comments by producer Stanley Kramer and short clips from the feature film, with classroom analyses by two "experts": Jack S. Schiff, a professor in the Business Center at City College of New York, and Robert A. Whitney, president of National Sales Executives.

Today, this odd artifact looks like a parody, and Miller characterized it as such at the time. To him, the speakers in the film "all sounded like Willy Loman with a diploma, fat with their success." Confronting the Columbia executives, Miller asked, "Why the hell did you make the picture if you're so

From *The Journal of American Culture*. © 2004.

ashamed of it? Why should anybody not get up and walk out of the theatre if *Death of a Salesman* is so outmoded and pointless?" (Miller, *Timebends* 315–16).

In fact, the short subject helps to clarify what went wrong with the feature film. *Career of a Salesman* also sheds light on the political climate of the time, and on later attempts by business people to distance themselves from Miller's story. *Death of a Salesman* is a canonical work of modern drama. *Career of a Salesman* is a mere footnote, but it is also a fascinating piece of flotsam from the 1950s showing how filmmakers tried to make Miller's work more palatable during the Cold War.

Within a few months of its opening on Broadway in February 1949, *Death of a Salesman* received its first critique from a business perspective. Writing in *Fortune* magazine, A. Howard Fuller, president of the Fuller Brush Company, praised the modern professional salesman as "the real hero of American society," and thus as a worthy candidate for tragic portrayal. But Fuller argued that Miller's protagonist lacked such stature: "Willy is essentially a self-deluded man who has lost the power to distinguish between reality and the obsessions that come to dominate his life." Fuller saw *Death of a Salesman* as a cautionary tale about "enthusiasm" without governing intelligence:

> It would appear that Willy does not concern himself with modern scientific merchandising techniques, but he does display great enthusiasm, with all the advantages and dangers which that entails . . . Enthusiasm is the driving force behind any human enterprise. No achievement is possible without it. It is like the fuel that drives the automobile. But useful and necessary as gasoline may be, it can become a force for evil unless handled with intelligence. It can destroy and kill, as well as produce useful power. (Fuller 79)

Fuller's analysis would be echoed two years later in Stanley Kramer's framing narration for *Career of a Salesman*. But when Kramer first saw *Death of a Salesman* in New York, he was most impressed by the beauty of its somber story, and by its commercial potential as a movie: "I assumed the play's widespread fame would stimulate strong interest." He bought the rights from Miller for $100,000 and a small percentage of the film's profits (Kramer 79–80).

As an independent producer from 1948 through 1950, Kramer achieved success with a string of innovative films: *So This Is New York*, *Champion*, *Home of the Brave*, *The Men*, and *Cyrano de Bergerac*. Then, in March of 1951, he was signed to a production deal at Columbia Pictures by Harry Cohn, whom he later described as "the perfect image of the crude movie mogul." *Death of a Salesman* would become Kramer's very first project at Columbia even though Cohn considered the story "a piece of junk" and too "dreary" to be commercial. Cohn was exasperated by Kramer's insistence that the picture be shot in black and white to preserve the mood of the stage play, but the young producer's contract guaranteed complete control over subject matter, treatment, and casting (Kramer 76–79).

Because Kramer needed a Hollywood star in the lead role, he bypassed Lee J. Cobb, who had played Willy Loman to great acclaim on Broadway, in favor of Frederic March. But the other Lomans would be played by performers reprising their stage roles: Mildred Dunnock as Linda, Kevin McCarthy as Biff, and Cameron Mitchell as Happy.[1] To direct, Kramer chose László Benedek, a postwar émigré from Hungary whose only Hollywood features had been a musical comedy, *The Kissing Bandit* (1948), and a stylish crime film, *Port of New York* (1949). The scriptwriter would be Stanley Roberts, best known for westerns like *Colorado Sunset* (1939) and comedies like *Penthouse Rhythm* (1945).

Miller was optimistic about a film version because he had constructed *Death of a Salesman* as a "cinematic" drama: "There are scenes constantly fading in and out of each other, and the whole play can practically be shot the way it was originally written" (Miller, "Responses" 822). But the first sign of trouble appeared when Miller read the screenplay and found it flat. Stanley Roberts "had managed to chop off almost every climax of the play as though with a lawnmower." The problem was epitomized, Miller thought, by the omission of a key scene between Linda and Biff, late in Act 1 of the play, when the mother demands that the son give Willy psychological support. Biff, determined to live his own life, explodes: "I hate this city and I'll stay here! Now what do you want?" Linda replies, "He's dying, Biff," and then provides crucial exposition about Willy's plans for suicide. When Miller questioned Roberts about the deletion of this important confrontation, the screenwriter responded, "But how can he shout at his mother like that?" (Miller, *Timebends* 314–15).

In effect, the movie was taking the sting out of the story—especially, Miller believed, in reducing Willy Loman to a lunatic. On the basis of Roberts's screenplay and Benedek's direction, Frederic March incorporated gestures and pacing that suggested a pathological case study rather than a representation of social problems.[2] Miller was a good friend of March, who acknowledged a defect in the script: "Freddy was a real actor in the best sense; he was an animal and he knew that there was something wrong with making him so crazy . . . Of course these people making the film had to make him crazy or they couldn't make the film" (Bigsby 57).

Miller meant that the studio needed to soften the story's social commentary to accommodate a new Cold War mentality. Between the premiere of his play in February 1949 and the release of the film in December 1951, the Soviets exploded their first atomic bomb, a Communist government took full control in China, the Korean War began, Alger Hiss was convicted of perjury, and Senator Joseph McCarthy launched a crusade against domestic subversion. In this political atmosphere, Columbia wanted to reassure audiences that *Death of a Salesman* was not an attack on the system that employed and then discarded Willy. "If he was a nut," Miller observed, "he could hardly stand as a comment on anything. It was as though Lear had never had real political power but merely imagined he was king" (Miller, *Timebends* 315). This reductive characterization of Willy Loman would be taken to its logical conclusion in *Career of a Salesman.*

The short subject was commissioned to avert a political threat: a warning to Columbia that movie theaters showing *Death of a Salesman* would be picketed by the American Legion and other conservative groups. One reason was Miller's reputation as a leftist. In 1947, his play *All My Sons*, which attacked industrial war profiteering, had been condemned by the commander of the Catholic War Veterans as "a Party line propaganda vehicle." In 1949, at a Conference for World Peace in New York, Miller had challenged others on the left by drawing distinctions between propaganda and art, using *All My Sons* as a case study, but he was then blasted from the right for participating at all in a conference where many participants urged a restoration of friendship with the Soviet Union (Miller, *Timebends* 238). And *Death of a Salesman* presented a particular problem, as Kramer recognized:

> *Death of a Salesman* was attacked because it implied that the American free-enterprise system was in some measure responsible for the tragedy of people like Willy Loman. It suggested that American business more often than not was more interested in profits than people, tending to throw marginal or older employees on the scrap heap. (Kramer 81)

While *Salesman* was still being filmed, Columbia asked Miller to sign an anti-Communist declaration, but he refused: "I declined to make any such statement, which, frankly, I found demeaning; what right had any organization to demand anyone's pledge of loyalty?" (Miller, *Echoes* 276). At this point, studio executives approved the budget for a prologue that might make *Death of a Salesman* less controversial. Miller later estimated the cost of the short subject at "a couple of hundred thousand dollars"—at least twice what he had been paid for the film rights to his play (Miller, *Timebends* 316). *Career of a Salesman* would be produced and directed by Harry Foster, who had worked in-house at Columbia for over a decade. Foster's resumé included dozens of short subjects in series like *Thrills of Music*, featuring such groups as the

Skitch Henderson Orchestra, and *The Columbia World of Sports*, typified by
the 1942 trailer "Tennis Rhythm with Bobby Riggs."

The inspiration for *Career of a Salesman* may have come from a 1950
article in the *New York Times*, "Trained Salesmen Still Being Sought," which
highlighted a new sales engineering program at CCNY's Midtown Business
Center. Despite earlier forecasts of an economic downturn at the beginning
of the Korean War, sales managers and marketing instructors were optimistic—none more so than Jack S. Schiff, supervisor of the center's sales unit.
With consumer demand slightly down and production the same or higher,
Schiff explained, "It's little wonder that aggressive salesmen continue to be
required." He proudly cited the success of his CCNY students, trained as
"professionals," in landing good sales jobs (Nagle 142).

Schiff became the technical director for *Career of a Salesman*, and he also
appears on screen conducting a class at the Business Center. A large poster
display surrounds him like a proscenium arch, with the heading: PRIN-
CIPLES OF PROFESSIONAL SALESMANSHIP. The term "profession"
is the key to his lesson, just as Willy Loman is the object of his scorn as "a
man with an outmoded and unrealistic philosophy." Even a film clip of Willy
being fired elicits no sympathy. It only proves, Schiff tells the class, that a
salesman "needs a lot more than personality. He needs a thorough knowledge
of his product, a real grasp of his customers' needs, and a belief that he's doing
a service—a service—in bringing his product to his buyer. Willy Loman was
being fired from a job. No one can fire you from a profession."

Like A. Howard Fuller's 1949 critique of *Death of a Salesman*, *Career
of a Salesman* contrasts Willy's manic enthusiasm with a scientific approach
to modern merchandising. Schiff introduces a guest—Robert A. Whitney,
president of National Sales Executives—to comment on another film clip:
a flashback of Willy telling his brother Ben that success in salesmanship
will be assured through "contacts" and "the smile on your face." Whitney is
dismissive: "No wonder poor Willy was such a failure! He just didn't have
it—the background, the training, the preparation. He was the product of an
era which is happily long since past."

A third film clip shows good neighbor Charley puncturing Willy's
belief that a salesman must be "well liked." Whitney seconds Charley's point
by stressing the greater importance of training and product knowledge, and
he concludes, "That's the job of the salesman of today, and the sales executive
of tomorrow." The implication is that success in sales will be rewarded with
promotion to the managerial hierarchy.

Career of a Salesman ends as it began: with Stanley Kramer talking to
the audience, obviously uneasy as he reads from cue cards off to the side.
On the one hand, he praises Frederick March's "thrilling" performance as
Willy. On the other, he repeats the claim that this character represents an

all-but-extinct breed. Then Kramer concludes with a glaring non sequitur:
"I think that Willy Loman is definitely outmoded today, but his successor is
the modern, progressive man and woman engaged in the profession of selling.
I hope you will see this film: *Death of a Salesman*."

When Columbia executives showed *Career of a Salesman* to Miller,
he was outraged: "I was being asked to concur that *Death of a Salesman*
was morally meaningless, a tale told by an idiot signifying nothing" (Miller,
Timebends 315). Because his contract with Kramer included a tiny share of
putative profits, Miller argued that *Career of a Salesman* would damage his
prospects by rendering the feature film irrelevant:

> I doubted if I could make it stick in court. But as far as I was con-
> cerned they were injuring my property rights and apparently they
> were worried about this too or they wouldn't even have consulted
> me. I convinced them that they would be laughed out of existence,
> which I doubt would have happened at the moment since nobody
> was laughing about anything. (Bigsby 58)

Conservative groups made good on their threats to protest *Death of a
Salesman*, and in some cities, Kramer recalled, "there were bigger audiences
outside, blocking the entrances, than there were inside watching the movie."
In retrospect, it seems doubtful that many picketers could ever have been
dissuaded by *Career of a Salesman*. They were there not to defend American
salesmen, but to attack prominent liberals. Their placards read: FELLOW
TRAVELERS SUPPORT COMMUNISTS. YELLOW TRAVELERS
SUPPORT FELLOW TRAVELERS. DON'T BE A YELLOW TRAV-
ELER (Kramer 83).

Miller was not the protesters' only target. Frederick March and his wife
Florence Eldridge had been active before World War II in the Hollywood
Anti-Nazi League, unfairly labeled "a Communist front" by Congressman
Martin Dies (Cogley 37).[4] After the war, March drew fire for his public
opposition to the House Un-American Activities Committee. In a 1947
statement, he had asked, "Who do you think they're really after? Who's next?
Is it your minister who will be told what he can say in his pulpit? Is it your
children's school teacher who will be told what she can say in classrooms? Is
it your children themselves? Is it you, who will have to look around nervously
before you can say what is on your minds?" (Cogley 4).

Protesters also assailed Stanley Kramer, who was described by a group
called the Wage Earners Committee as "notorious for his Red-slanted,
Red-starred films."[5] Kramer was mystified. His most "liberal" film, *Home
of the Brave*, which dealt with racial prejudice in a military setting, had provoked scattered protests in the South but achieved commercial and critical

success. It was a sensitive character study, and hardly a call to arms.[6] When the Wage Earners Committee also charged that Kramer had "taught at the Los Angeles Communist training school in 1947," he sued for libel, noting that he had merely given one nonpolitical lecture about movie making at a school called the People's Education Center (Kramer 83–84).

Kramer's libel suit stopped many of the demonstrations, but the damage had been done. Despite five Oscar nominations and some appreciative reviews, *Death of a Salesman* never broke even.[7]

The playwright John Guare remembers being taken to the movie at age fourteen by his father, who was vice commander in charge of Americanism at his American Legion post in Queens, New York. The son wondered, "So why were we going tonight to this leftie *Death of a Salesman*? Hadn't the American Legion in Boston already tried to shut down this movie as Commie propaganda? The Elmjack Post #298 had decided to let the picture open in New York without protest because why give it the attention. The Commies would like that."

After the movie, Guare's father characterized it as "the usual Commie propaganda," and yet he was sufficiently moved to share a guilty secret with his son: that he was once a salesman himself, and that "It hadn't worked out." This man, who now worked on Wall Street and hated his job, mumbled his revelation as if confessing a sin. Guare later realized that the movie, even while softening the original play, had managed "to give voice to the American shame of failure" (Kolin 602–03).

The reaction of Guare's father, simultaneously touched and threatened by the drama of Willy Loman, crystalizes the response of countless viewers. In this pattern of attraction and repulsion, we might see a modern reconfiguration of Aristotle's "pity and fear" as the definitive tragic emotions. The New York reviewers who first hailed Miller's play as a masterpiece stressed the element of pity by describing Willy Loman as an Everyman.[8] And one reason Miller was so upset by the film's portrayal of a "lunatic" Willy was that it weakened the audience's identification with him:

> They knew he wasn't crazy. They were right up there with him. See, let me not underestimate it. I was ironically stating all the things that they always take seriously. A man can get anywhere in this country on the basis of being liked. Now this is serious advice, and that audience is sitting there almost about to smile but the tears are coming out of their eyes because they know that this is what they believe. This man is obviously going down the chute and he's telling them exactly what they believe. So I don't have to make a speech that this is wrong. The irony of the whole situation is what is making it work. (Bigsby 58)

By contrast, critiques of *Death of a Salesman* from a business perspective have tended to undercut pity—as in Professor Schiff's comments on the scene of Willy being fired—and to accentuate fear, especially of Willy as a threatening stereotype. Brenda Murphy has traced the efforts of American executives "to divorce the salesman's identity from that of Willy Loman," often by blaming Willy's problems on his own incompetence. By the 1960s, she notes, executives were promoting the image of a "new salesman": serious, subtle, and even studious (Murphy 758).

In their efforts to erase a stereotype, some business leaders revived the rhetoric of *Career of a Salesman*. In 1966, when CBS announced plans for a television adaptation of *Death of a Salesman* with Lee J. Cobb as Willy, the Sales Executives Club of New York sent a letter to the sponsor, Xerox Corporation, recommending changes in the script to improve the salesman's image. The Club's executive director, Harry R. White, also suggested a prologue to the production, alerting viewers that they were about to see "the tragedy of a man who went into selling with the wrong ideas, a man who had been improperly trained by today's standards." In an eerie replay of the Columbia debacle, White even proposed an epilogue titled "The Life of the Salesman" to show "that with modern, customer-oriented selling methods, Willy Lomans are ghosts of the past" (Adams 131).

The 1951 film of *Death of a Salesman*, once a staple of TV late shows, is no longer in circulation and remains unavailable on video or DVD. It has been superseded in the public mind by a 1985 version, directed by Volker Schlöndorff, which attracted a television audience of over twenty million and then became widely available on video. This film was coproduced by Dustin Hoffman, who played Willy, and by Arthur Miller himself. As a result, it stayed close to the successful theatrical performance of the preceding year, while using a few techniques of expressionistic cinema to dramatize the jumble of reality and fantasy in Willy's mind. Within the confines of a narrow frame, the 1985 adaptation focused more directly on the Loman family, and the fumbling reconciliation between Willy and Biff (played by John Malkovich) provided a powerful emotional climax (Shewey 23).

There is no record that CBS, or the sole sponsor, Apple Corporation, received any requests from business representatives to change Miller's script or add an explanatory prologue about salesmen. On the contrary, this version of *Death of a Salesman* led to lively case study discussions at the Harvard Graduate School of Business Administration in a course entitled "The Social Psychology of Management" taught by Abraham Zaleznik. "Business schools are now going through a self-searching process," Professor Zaleznik explained. "The question is, what kinds of human beings are we producing by fostering this kind of experience?" Starting with that question, the business students were encouraged to discuss *Death of a Salesman* as an exploration of family dynamics, and of the human problems that employees bring to the workplace (Collins 1).

This more mature approach to *Death of a Salesman* seems analogous to the changing perception of Tennessee Williams's *Cat on a Hot Tin* Roof, which was controversial in the 1950s for its suggestion of a homosexual element in the relationship of Brick and Skipper. Today, Williams's handling of this motive appears cautious and contrived, and what resonates most is the inescapable fact of mortality, as we watch Big Daddy go through the classic sequence of psychological responses to his impending death.

Thus, *Career of a Salesman* now seems doubly obsolete, as a strained effort during the Cold War to defuse a political problem that no longer dominates discussion of the play. Miller, who remained unimpressed by the Theatre of the Absurd, said that *Career of a Salesman* surely belongs to that genre. "Never in show business history," he concludes, "has a studio spent so much good money to prove that its feature film was pointless" (Miller, *Echoes* 276).

Career of a Salesman

The following script is really a transcript reconstructed from the screen version of *Career of a Salesman*. The original script was never copyrighted and may no longer exist.

Title card: Columbia Pictures Corporation presents CAREER OF A SALESMAN

(Music up: violins/slightly melodramatic.)

Title card:

Script by	Joseph Johnson
Technical director	Dr. Jack S. Schiff
Photographed by	Charles Wecker
Editor	S. C. Rawson

Title card: Produced and Directed by Harry Foster

Title card: This picture was made with the cooperation of the National Sales Executives and the Sales Training Unit of C.C.N.Y. Midtown Business Center

(Close-up of gilded letters on an office door: STANLEY KRAMER*)*

(Close-up of a script being held. Columbia Prod. No. 8056

Produced by Stanley Kramer
DEATH OF A SALESMAN*)*

(The camera pulls back as Stanley Kramer turns in his chair toward us. He speaks to the camera while looking off to his right, obviously reading from cue cards.)

STANLEY KRAMER: We've just finished making *Death of a Salesman* for Columbia Pictures release. It was a very great stage play, as you know, and I hope it will be a very fine motion picture. Of one thing you may rest assured: the performance of Frederick March in the role of Willy Loman is one of the really great and thrilling experiences you will find in a motion picture theater in the coming year.

(*Kramer rises from his chair and then sits on the edge of the desk, looking even farther off-camera to read his text.*)

As a matter of fact, the entire idea of the production of *Death of a Salesman* represented a challenge to all of us. As a very great stage play, most certainly we knew we were faced with the idea of trying to duplicate and approximate the impact of the material—a play which has won every single major theatrical award with a record unmatched by any other piece of dramatic material.

(*Kramer stands and walks to a wall bookcase.*)

Yet when we went into the research on *Death of a Salesman*, we found out after many weeks of research that the Willy Lomans of this world are fast becoming extinct. For Willy belonged to the lost tribe of drummers, who used the credo of a smile and a shoeshine to be able to do business. Certainly today this is far from enough, for the National Sales Executives tell us that there are over three and one-half million people making their living at the business of selling in this country today. More than that, from one end of the country to the other . . .

(*Cut to a simple line map of the U.S.*)

. . . men and women—young men and women—are being trained by our colleges and universities in the selling profession.

(*Map close-up on the state of New York, dissolving to a campus view: an archway through which we see the spires of a Gothic building.*)

At the College of the City of New York, for example, there are more than six hundred students enrolled in courses in selling—
(*Medium shot of students exiting one of the impressive buildings.*)

—young people who are going to make more than just a job of salesmanship, youngsters who will carve out a career of service in a profession that keeps the wheels of commerce and industry turning . . .

(*Cut to a classroom, where a man in a dark suit stands at a lectern surrounded by a series of posters. Overhead in bold letters are the words TRAINING FOR BUSINESS.*)

. . . in our great American economic machine. They'll have a lot more than a smile and a shoeshine.

(*Cut to students in the class, all neatly dressed and attentive. The camera pans across the room, showing about twenty serious faces, including at least six young women.*)

Today they receive a background of psychology, advertising, merchandising, market research, and industrial production. Today the axiom holds: "Salesmen are made, not born."

(*Cut back to man at lectern.*)

Here we are in a class on Applied Salesmanship, conducted by Dr. J. S. Schiff.

(*Medium shot of the professor. We can now see that the big poster behind him is headed:* PRINCIPLES OF PROFESSIONAL SALESMANSHIP. *The lecturer now speaks.*)

PROFESSOR SCHIFF: To learn the principles of a profession as up-to-date as selling must be, the instructor cannot shut himself up in an academic ivory tower. He must keep up with the outside world if he expects the students to do so. One way is through the use of a motion picture.

And so today we're going to do a sort of clinical job on the film *Death of a Salesman.* I know of nothing that might better impress upon you the new concepts of the career that you have chosen for a life work than by showing you scenes from the story of Willy Loman, a man with an outmoded and unrealistic philosophy.

In the first scene that we're going to see, Willy is about to lose his job.

(*Cut to movie scene, beginning with a close up of Frederick March as Willy. Sitting next to the desk of his young boss, Howard, Willy looks haggard, but is full of nervous energy. He is obviously replying to Howard's reminder that "Business is business. "*)

WILLY: Sure. Definitely business. But I didn't become a salesman just for the money. (*Rises and walks to front of Howard's desk, pointing.*) And I had bigger opportunities. Years ago my brother Ben asked me to go to Alaska and look after his timberlands for him. I'd almost decided to go when I—when I ran on to a salesman at the Parker House. His name was Dave Singleman. Eighty-four years old and he drummed merchandise in 31 states! Old Dave—used to go up to his room, you understand, put on his green velvet slippers, I'll never forget, pick up the phone, call the buyers and without ever leaving his room, at the age of 84, he made his living.

(Howard, bored, looks at his watch and drums his fingers. Oblivious, Willy continues.)

Even when he died, he died the death of a salesman. In his green velvet slippers, in the smoker of the New York-New Haven-Hartford going into Boston. Oh, hundreds and salesmen and buyers attended his funeral. Things were sad on a lot of trains for months after that. *(Willy sits again, subdued.)*

See, in those days there was personality in it, Howard. There was respect, and comradeship—and gratitude! Today it's all cut and dried. No chance for bringing friendship to bear—or personality.

(Dissolve back to Professor Schiff at the lectern.)

SCHIFF: *There* is an object-lesson in selling, if I ever saw one. Poor Willy lived in a dream world, admiring a man who worked in green velvet slippers and made a living just calling buyers on the phone without even leaving his hotel room.

Willy says he had bigger opportunities. No young person today has a bigger opportunity than that offered by the profession of salesmanship, but he can't get by any better than Willy did without hard work.

Then that pathetic excuse that Willy gives: "No chance for bringing friendship or personality to bear." I want to assure you that no salesman ever made a living selling to his friends. And he needs a lot more than personality. He needs a thorough knowledge of his product, a real grasp of his customers' needs, and a belief that he's doing a service—a service—in bringing his product to his buyer. Willy Loman was being fired from a job. No one can fire you from a profession.

In the next scene, Willy is trying to convince his brother that he is building a future with his company.

(Cut to close up of Ben's face and Willy's as they walk. Willy's manner is manic.)

WILLY: It isn't something you can feel in your fingers like timber, Ben, but it's there! I know it is. You take Biff, for instance. Eighteen years old and not a penny to his name, and three great universities are begging for him. And from there, the sky's the limit! Because it's not what you do, Ben, but who you know, the smile on your face.

It's contacts, Ben, contacts. The whole wealth of Alaska passes over the lunch table at the Commodore Hotel, and that's the wonder of this country—that a man can end with diamonds on the basis of being well liked!

(Cut back to Professor Schiff at the lectern.)

SCHIFF: To comment on this scene, I should like to present to you the president of National Sales Executives, Mr. Robert A. Whitney. Mr. Whitney—

(*Cut to a new speaker at the lectern.*)

ROBERT A. WHITNEY: To me this is a deeply moving scene. It portrays so graphically that which I've warned so many students, salesmen, and saleswomen against. "It's not what you do, but who you know," Willy says. What a tragic misconception! Does a doctor get by on who he knows? It's what a doctor knows—what a lawyer, what a teacher knows—that makes for success, and it's the same in the profession of selling. That's why you young people are studying the art and science of selling. That's why companies, businesses, will find it worthwhile to hire you, to welcome you as valuable additions to their staff.

"A man can end with diamonds on the basis of being well liked." No wonder poor Willy was such a failure! He just didn't have it—the background, the training, the preparation. He was the product of an era which happily is long since past. His friend Charley had a better grasp of reality, a more intelligent approach to the meaning of success, about which poor Willy could only dream, without knowing the meaning of that dream.

(*Cut to close-up of Charley's face as he speaks to Willy.*)

CHARLEY: The only thing you've got in this world is what you can sell. The funny thing is, you're a salesman, and you don't even know that.

WILLY (*standing and holding his hat*): I've always tried to think otherwise, I guess. I always felt that if a man was impressive, well liked, that nothing . . .

CHARLEY: Why must everybody like you? Why must you always be impressive? I know a man with a lot of money, a millionaire. In a Turkish bath he looks like a butcher. But with his pockets on, he's very well liked.

(*Cut back to Robert A. Whitney, still at the lectern.*)

WHITNEY: Being well liked and having a fine appearance is important in selling today, but there's a greater opportunity for each of you if you will continue your training, re-training, and gain a better knowledge of your products and your customers in the days ahead. That's the job for the salesman of today, and the sales executive of tomorrow.

(*Cut to medium shot from back of the class, as the students applaud. Professor Schiff shakes hands with Whitney and returns to the podium. Cut to close-up of Schiff.*)

SCHIFF: Thank you, Mr. Whitney. Charley was getting closer to the things you are learning than Willy in a lifetime of selling ever got. In the film *Death of a Salesman*, the star and the producer dramatize the very things that we are trying to teach you here at City College about salesmanship—that success in this field depends upon the new values of knowledge, of service, of forwarding not only oneself but also contributing to the growth of the nation's economy; that selling is a professional field of endeavor; that nothing—nothing—happens in this great country of ours until something is sold.

(*Quick cut, without student reaction, back to Stanley Kramer standing in front of the wall bookcase, script in hand. He speaks while looking off to his right.*)

KRAMER: *Death of a Salesman* is a drama, a great human drama, applicable not only to Willy Loman but to any man—doctor, lawyer, merchant, chief. I think that Willy Loman is definitely outmoded today, but his successor is the modern, progressive man and woman engaged in the business of selling. I hope you will see this film: *Death of a Salesman*.

(*Music up. Fade to . . .*)

Title Card: THE END

A Columbia Short Subject Presentation

[Total running time: 10 minutes, 40 seconds.]

NOTES

1. Mildred Dunnock and Cameron Mitchell had been part of the Broadway cast, which included Arthur Kennedy as Biff. Kevin McCarthy had played Biff in the London stage production.

2. The director, László Benedek, claimed that March was capturing the "universality" of the role: "the playing of Willy Loman had to have the quality of representing, through the tragedy of this one man, everybody in the vast audience of motion pictures everywhere." See his essay. "Transferring 'Death of a Salesman' to Film," *New York Times*, December 9, 1951, 131.

3. "I was spared having to reply to such accusations," Miller wrote, "when a Senate committee exposed the Wright Aeronautical Corporation of Ohio, which had exchanged the 'Condemned' tags on defective engines for 'Passed' and in cahoots with bribed army inspectors had shipped many hundreds of these failed machines to the armed forces" (Miller, *Timebends* 238).

4. Almost all members of the Hollywood Anti-Nazi League were non-Communists, like the Marches, who embraced a range of liberal and antifascist causes, from supporting the Spanish Loyalists to lobbying for an antilynching bill. Congressman Dies was widely criticized for his blanket accusations. See Cogley 36–37.

5. The Wage Earners Committee was supposedly a grassroots movement of ordinary working people "opposed to regimentation, communization, or dictatorship in any form." The National Labor Relations Board later found that the Wage Earners Committee was largely financed by an industrialist who hoped to break the power of labor unions. See Cogley 113.

6. *Home of the Brave* began as a stage play by Arthur Laurents and dealt with anti-Semitism rather than antiblack prejudice. It won the New York Drama Critics Circle Award in 1946 as the best play of the season. See Kramer 33–44.

7. See Kramer 81. Oscar nominations, but no awards, went to Frederick March for best actor, Mildred Dunnock for best supporting actress, Kevin McCarthy for best supporting actor, Franz Planer for best cinematography, and Alex North for best music scoring. Although *New York Times* film critic Bosley Crowther described *Death of a Salesman* as "dismally depressing," he chose it as one of the ten best pictures of 1951, largely on the strength of Frederick March's performance. See his discussion of "The Year's Best," December 30, 1951, X1.

8. See especially Robert Garland, "Audience Spellbound by Prize Play of 1949," *New York Journal-American*, February 11, 1949, 24.

Works Cited

Adams, Val. "Willy Loman Irks Fellow Salesmen." *New York Times* 27 Mar. 1966: 131.

Bigsby, Christopher, ed. *Arthur Miller and Company*. London: Methuen, 1990.

Cogley, John. *Report on Blacklisting, I: The Movies*. New York: Fund for the Republic, 1956.

Collins, Glen. "Future M.B.A.s Learn Value of a Home Life." *New York Times* 16 Oct. 1985: C1.

Fuller, Howard A. "A Salesman Is Everybody." *Fortune* May 1949: 79–80.

Kolin, Philip C. "*Death of a Salesman*: A Playwrights' Forum." *Michigan Quarterly Review* XXXVII.4 (1998): 591–623.

Kramer, Stanley, with Thomas M. Coffey. *A Mad, Mad, Mad, Mad World: A Life in Hollywood*. New York: Harcourt, 1997.

Miller, Arthur. *Timebends: A Life*, New York: Grove, 1987.

____. "Responses to an Audience Question and Answer Session." *Michigan Quarterly Review* XXXVII.4 (1998): 817–27.

____. *Echoes Down the Corridor: Collected Essays, 1944–2000*. New York: Viking, 2000.

Murphy, Brenda. "Willy Loman: Icon of Business Culture." *Michigan Quarterly Review* XXXVII.4 (Fall 1998): 755–66.

Nagle, James J. "Trained Salesman Still Being Sought." *New York Times* 1 Oct. 1950: 142.

Shewey, Don. "TV's Custom-Tailored 'Salesman." *New York Times* 15 Sept. 1985: H1+.

LAURENCE GOLDSTEIN

Finishing the Picture:
Arthur Miller, 1915–2005

When I became the editor of *Michigan Quarterly Review* in the spring of 1977, one of my first acts was to contact Arthur Miller and ask if he would sign on as a Contributing Editor of the journal. Arguably the most distinguished alumnus of the University of Michigan, Miller had steered interviews with him to *MQR* during the previous fifteen years, and I hoped to formalize and extend the working relationship. After he agreed to serve in this new position he sent me an occasional memoir or one-act play or piece of reportage. His Hopwood Lecture titled "The American Writer: The American Theatre" appeared in the Winter 1982 issue. I was always grateful for his contributions, which helped to make the journal visible not only to Miller's worldwide legion of admirers but to two generations of readers who had been exposed to one or more of the major plays and to decades of publicity about his political, marital, and artistic activities. A few months before his death he sent me "The Flight to Newark," which follows this essay. Miller was a stern moralist, but he was also a humorist, and the comic exasperation triggered by airport protocol in this anti-travel essay clearly arose from more than the two Kafkaesque experiences he documents here.

After 1977 he directed more interviews to *MQR* as well. Few writers of the twentieth century more cheerfully agreed to sit for interviews than Miller; he enjoyed expressing his opinions and retouching his life story,

From *Michigan Quarterly Review.* © 2005.

which fascinated him with an intensity that fully occupied his imagination and glows through all his writing. *Timebends*, his autobiography, is the official self-portrait, but he depicts himself compulsively and meticulously in the variety of genres he undertook in his professional career: not only stage plays but radio plays, screenplays, television drama, journalism, short fiction, the novel, essays on the theater and society, even poetry. A man with a robust, ever-changing ego, Miller constantly discovered new materials in his own experience worth exfoliating for the page in dramatic or discursive form. "We are all becoming," he told an interviewer in the Spring 1977 issue of *MQR* who asked him to rank his fellow playwrights. He did not like terminal or absolute judgments; he was an artist of the provisional and the conditional, like most authors devoted to narrative.

He did complain in a general way about what he called in *Timebends* "the bullshit of capitalism." That complaint informs and nourishes his signature play *Death of a Salesman*, which put the postwar world on alert that commerce and commodification, the idols of the tribe, threatened fundamental human values. Attempts by hostile critics to read the play as nothing more than another 1930s proletarian drama about working-class heroes and victims fell short of the truth. The play was full of bitterness about the failure of this nation to resist the triumphant postwar social and economic machine grinding the human spirit into piles of cash. Miller spelled out the lesson in an interview in the Fall 1998 special issue of *MQR* celebrating the fiftieth anniversary of his seminal play: "The politics of America is implicit in the whole of Salesman. The Salesman is close to being the universal occupation of contemporary society—not only in America, but everywhere. Everybody is selling and everything is for sale." Did that sweeping statement include Arthur Miller? Of course. He insisted on his inescapable guilt as he documented the tradeoffs and compensations involved in his own scaling the heights of Broadway, becoming rich and famous, marrying the most glamorous woman in the world, fighting off the invidious stereotypes that dogged him and pigeonholed him down through the years.

Miller told me in 1991, on the occasion of a ceremonial tribute to *MQR* in New York, that he felt full of energy and had abundant plans for future projects. And certainly the list of his writings for the period 1990–2005 is truly astonishing, beginning with *The Ride Down Mount Morgan* in 1991 and his novella *Homely Girl* in 1992 and culminating in his final produced play, *Finishing the Picture*, in 2004. Like many people who journeyed to Chicago to see *Finishing the Picture*, I speculated that this might be his last full-length work, not from any knowledge of his physical failings—in fact, he had seemed vigorous for a man of eighty-eight when he visited the University of Michigan in April of last year, undergoing a public interview on the stage of the Lydia Mendelssohn Theater and the customary round of social engagements, capped by a student performance of scenes from his plays. But from first reports the play sounded like a valedictory, a last extended exercise of self-regard, which circled back to the film he scripted for Marilyn Monroe in 1961, *The Misfits*. One of the play's characters, Paul, another self-portrait of Miller, is the unhappy consort of the wretched superstar Kitty (all the other characters have last names), who spends the play in a drug-induced depression while her coworkers and counselors fret about the stalled and possibly doomed movie they are counting on to revitalize their careers.

In an essay on *The Misfits* I contributed to Arthur Miller's *America* (University of Michigan Press, 2005), edited by Enoch Brater, I argue that the movie can profitably be seen not only as a document of the cultural malaise of the 1950s anatomized in such books as *The Lonely Crowd* and *The Organization Man*, but as an autobiographical statement about the impasse in Miller's career and marriage. Clark Gable told Miller that he had wanted to play Willy Loman, but in this film he enacts a fantasized if flawed suitor to Marilyn Monroe, who convincingly portrays a strip dancer with a long list of unsatisfactory men in her past. Gable's character, an aging cowboy, likes to imagine himself as a free soul but in fact he has a job trapping and killing wild mustangs in modern-day Nevada; he sells the meat to industrial producers of canned dogfood. No less than Willy Loman, he is caught inside a predatory economic system, until redeemed by earth mother Monroe. At the upbeat conclusion of the film he frees the mustangs and the two lovers drive off in a pickup truck into the darkness (it was the last film for both Gable and Monroe), following a star.

During filming, the scenario of *The Misfits* kept bleeding into the melodrama on the other side of the cameras. With reporters and photographers from around the world on the Nevada set and fifteen news reports filed every day of the shooting, the failing marriage of Miller and Monroe got plenty of publicity, and by the time the film came out it looked and sounded like an elegy more than the affirmation of romantic love it intended. The picture had been finished against tremendous odds, but it struck most viewers and reviewers as, in Stanley Kaufmann's words, "unsuccessful both in its treatment of its subject and as a use of the film form." Though it graduated to cult status, it seemed like a prime candidate for the kind of cultural amnesia that overtakes even the best authors' second-level creations. It was a film that would never be remade and it had a backstory, everyone assumed, that its writer would certainly make every effort to forget.

And yet, forty-four years later, Miller returned to finish the picture by tearing aside the veil of fictiveness and recasting the film's more authentic drama for the stage. Rarely have I longed so intensely to see a forthcoming play. (*Marat/Sade*, back in the 1960s, is the only comparable example.) At the Goodman Theatre the audience was giddy with pleasure at the privilege of being part of the first-week experience of a new play by the greatest living playwright, with a cast that included Stacy Keach, Frances Fisher, Heather Prete, Harris Yulin, Linda Lavin, Scott Glenn, Matthew Modine, and Stephen Lang. I'm guessing that most of the theatergoers had taken the trouble to watch a videotape of *The Misfits*, savoring it for once as an "unfinished" work on the verge of being completed and installed in the canon as an American classic. Writers have the last word, especially on their earlier writings. Miller had often revised the myth of the making of *The Misfits*—in his autobiography, in interviews, in his offhand remarks to James Goode for the unauthorized on-site book, *The Making of The Misfits*. The play was obviously going to soulsearch beyond the mere settling of scores, and with other patrons my wife and I awaited the opening lines with the keen attention of heirs waiting for the reading of the last will and testament.

The play is set entirely in the Reno hotel penthouse of the producer, whose anxiety about the fate of the distressed film is tempered by his compassion for the leading lady, who bursts naked into his residence in the opening scene and takes over his bedroom for the entire course of the play, lying in a fetal haze and unable to speak coherently much less perform before the cameras. Her husband-screenwriter, director, cameraman, and secretary gather to schmooze about their predicament and trade accusations as to who is most responsible for her psychological collapse. They wait and wait and wait for her to revive, reminding the spectator of plays with similar structure, Clifford Odets's *Waiting for Lefty* and Samuel Beckett's *Waiting for Godot*. As the situation becomes more hopeless two witch doctors arrive to practice their mumbo jumbo over the recumbent body. Jerome and Flora Fassinger are venomous portraits of Miller's longtime antagonists Lee and Paula Strasberg, whom he blamed for imposing a soul-destroying regimen of method acting and method thinking on his vulnerable wife. The play quickens to extraordinary life when these two prima donnas begin their hilarious and orphie routines of self-justification. Miller has probably erased forever the magisterial dignity of Lee Strasberg by dressing his parody double in cowboy chaps and flame-red boots and having him strut around his hotel room with the manic narcissism of a frontier Dr. Strangelove.

"This play is about power," Miller remarked in an interview for the *Chicago Tribune*. The power all belongs to the frail, arrested figure of Kitty, who lacks even the power of speech. But we are made aware, in retrospect, of how much power Miller wields as the playwright who can turn his vindictive wrath upon the Strasbergs and his hardly less vindictive pity upon his former wife. Finishing the Picture, among other things, closes the books on the 1950s even more emphatically than did *After the Fall*, his Walpurgisnacht of a play that summoned the ghost of Marilyn Monroe in 1964, as well as that of the faithless Elia Kazan, for retributive poetic justice. It is not that Miller exonerates himself in either play at the expense of his antagonists—far from it, he heaps guilt on himself in the characters of Quentin and Paul with a talmudic zeal beyond the merely Jewish. The dominant image of Miller's self-portrait had always been that of a man compromised by the effects of his self-knowing moral conscience. As Miller acquired more power, more cultural capital and more worldwide influence, he suffered more and more from the corrosive bitterness he felt over mankind's brutalities, for which he, a representative man, took a share of responsibility. Miller was the only important American playwright to gaze at the Medusa head of the Holocaust and the other horrors of World War II, and to measure the nastiest implications of the Cold War. He believed fervently in the power of art as a counterforce to history, including personal history. In *Timebends* he wrote, "I could not imagine a theater worthy of my time that did not want to change the world."

And then there is the fire. Throughout the play a rosy glow is reflected in the windows of the hotel room; it comes from a forest fire raging near the filming site, threatening the future of the picture. The phone rings occasionally and the producer gets updates on the progress of the fire. Watching the play I regretted this ham-handed Symbol, of a kind that Miller learned from Ibsen and Chekhov and O'Neill (the wild duck, the sea gull, the fog) in his drama courses at the University of Michigan. The Forest Fire seemed a contrived metaphor for the destructive angers and thwarted desires of the assembled chorus in that Reno penthouse. But afterward, and now after Miller's death, I think back on that fire as a potent figure for the ultimate power in the universe, the force that lays waste every generation and threatens every artwork invented, and reinvented, to fend off its all-consuming effect. Willy Loman shouts "The woods are burning! . . . There's a big blaze going on all around" in the throes of his despair, and he succumbs to the fire's terrible advance. In *Finishing the Picture* however, the fire retreats, and the chance to finish the picture revives. We know that the picture-within-a-play is *The Misfits*, though it is never named. This latter-day Misfits also achieves an upbeat closure, having satisfied an eager audience with its stylish humor and its wisdom about the human condition.

"The past reaches into the present, usually destructively, but leaving some illumination behind," Miller says in an interview from the Spring 1990 *MQR*. In the same issue he contributed a short story, or fable, or memoir, titled "Bees," in which the narrator finds the walls of his home infested with bees and tries to exterminate them by one method or another. Finally he locates the right poison and they die by the thousands, leaving a corpse pile easily imaginable as a recollection of Auschwitz. And yet, years after he sells his house he encounters the new owner, who tells him that the house had become infested with . . . what else, bees. The last line of the story is this: "The house . . . definitely had to go because it belonged, obviously, to the bees." The cycle of ruthless life, the inextinguishable tenacity of it, the deep ironies of its repetitive patterns—these motifs are summoned in his brief allegory. In the ensuing interview he speaks about how "time becomes an obsessive thing. It has become more mysterious with me over the years, possibly because I'm getting older, and . . . echoes of the past are loud in the present so that the idea of time as a circular motion becomes more and more realistic." But time must have a stop, as the Bard remarked, and for this play-wright, the Shakespeare of his era in the view of many, like me, who lived concurrently with his writings, that time came on February 10 of this year. But who can doubt that those writings, like bees in the walls of our cultural domain, will survive to delight and trouble us with their irresistible murmurs and their persistent stings?

WENDY SMITH

Miller's Tale: The playwright drew a line between reaching out and selling out

Broadway theaters dimmed their marquees at curtain time the evening after Arthur Miller died. I like to think that somewhere in Times Square at that moment Miller's raspy chuckle could be heard floating sardonically through Manhattan's sooty air. He would have been amused by this traditional tribute from the American commercial theater, which for 60 years viewed him with an ambivalence he fully reciprocated. Only *All My Sons* and *Death of a Salesman* were unequivocal hits in their initial Broadway productions, way back in the late 1940s. During the last three decades of his life, exactly two of his plays premiered on the Great White Way, 14 years apart, and both flopped.

Miller, who died February 10 at the age of 89, professed never to have expected anything other than "the celebratory embraces soon followed by rejection or contempt" that he defined in his autobiography *Timebends* as the lot of every serious American playwright operating in the New York marketplace. He claimed to be content to see his later plays produced in the saner environs of England's subsidized national theaters or America's regional, nonprofit companies. "I was not raised to be surprised when a marriage between commerce and art collapsed," he explained, referring obliquely to his parents' troubled union as well as to his native country's perennial suspicion of high-falutin writers who aimed to do more than entertain.

From the *American Scholar*. © 2005.

Yet the breakup of art's marriage to commerce was still bothering him in 1987, when *Timebends* was published. His description of the Broadway that welcomed *Death of a Salesman* was notably conflicted. "I thought the theater a temple being rotted out with commercialized junk, where mostly by accident an occasional good piece of work appeared," he wrote. But, he continued, "it was also a time when the audience was basically the same for musicals and light entertainment as for the ambitious stuff. . . . Serious writers could reasonably assume they were addressing the whole American mix, and so their plays, whether successfully or not, stretched toward a wholeness of experience that would not require specialists or a coterie to be understood."

Miller never stopped regretting the loss of that relatively diverse audience and the resulting diminishment of American theater's reach. "When my plays were first produced, there was a still-extant tradition that the theater was a public matter," he once told me. "The theater was the ultimate tribunal in which we were to test all our beliefs." His most open testament to that tradition wasn't exactly warmly welcomed on Broadway in 1953, when nervous reviewers criticized *The Crucible* as a tiresome message drama without daring to explain what the message was: that communist-hunting and witch-hunting were equally insane. But it was on Broadway for six months, and it even won a Tony Award. Spectators ran the gamut from politically conservative theatergoers who, according to Miller, froze when they realized what the play was driving at, to the audience on June 19 that stood in silence as John Proctor was taken away to be hanged, knowing that Julius and Ethel Rosenberg were being executed at Sing Sing that same day.

It's difficult to imagine an American playwright today having that kind of broad cultural impact. Miller himself, though he wrote fine dramas into the 1990s, never again quite so successfully probed our social, personal, and political anxieties as he had during his first few years as a professional playwright. (He touched a nerve one more time in 1964 with *After the Fall*, which portrayed his marriage to Marilyn Monroe with an admittedly one-sided honesty that was brutally at odds with the media's sanctimonious breast-beating when she died in 1962.) His often crotchety pronouncements as an elder statesman averred that the commercial theater simply had no room anymore for "big, world-challenging plays." Theater critics and a good many higher-browed intellectuals, however, suggested that time had simply passed Miller by. They might honor his political activism, including defiance of the House Un-American Activities Committee in 1956 and defense of persecuted writers worldwide during his 1965–1969 tenure as president of International PEN, but Miller's artistic populism led them to dismiss him as a middlebrow: an old-fashioned realist and moralist adhering to an outmoded tradition of social protest, stubbornly resisting both the stylistic innovations and the radical existential angst of Beckett

& Co. That was definitely the undercurrent in many of the respectful but faintly lugubrious obituaries.

Reservations about Miller, whether expressed by a critic patronizing his lack of avant-garde aspirations or a Broadway producer unwilling to finance anything but yet another revival of *Salesman*, seem to me to reflect a deeper unease with his notion of what theater is. For more than half a century, everything he wrote and said glowed with the belief that theater is a public art with a mission to bring people together in a public place to speak to them about matters of common concern. That is an old-fashioned idea, and not just because commercial theater is now so ridiculously expensive that its increasingly grayhaired and well-heeled patrons are wary of anything except guaranteed entertainment. It's more fundamental than that. We live in an age when public libraries and public schools, for example, are too often regarded as institutions of last resort for those who can't afford anything better, and when many people can't walk down a street or through a park without isolating themselves in a private space via their cell phone conversations. Theater is a beleaguered outpost of collective life, an activity that cannot take place in your living room, online, or over a headset. That is why Miller's old-fashioned idea is eternally relevant and spiritually indispensable.

As I was reading the obituaries, wondering why they annoyed me so much and trying to figure out why Arthur Miller mattered so much to me, an odd assortment of memories bounced off each other. Surprisingly, they weren't of his work, but of younger artists and more recent shows. I thought of the riveting performance of Tony Kushner's musical play *Caroline*, which I saw in the final week of its too-short run at the Eugene O'Neill Theatre, where the actors soared on a current of energy flowing between them and the audience. I thought of last year's blistering revival of the 1991 musical *Assassins*, playing to packed houses at Studio 54 when it abruptly closed in June, prompting rumors that the producers had been pressured to shutter Stephen Sondheim's sardonic ode to presidential killers before the Republican National Convention hit town. I thought of Caryl Churchill's meditation on cloning, *A Number*, staged this winter at the New York Theatre Workshop with stadium-style seating encircling the couch that served as the battleground for actors Dallas Roberts and Sam Shepard. The setting recalled both an ancient Greek amphitheater and a 19th-century surgical theater, inviting spectators to observe each other as well as the players while the cast explored Churchill's thoughts on the complexities of human identity, guilt, and responsibility.

None of these three 2004 productions had much stylistic connection to the plays that made Miller famous. All took advantage of the liberation from literal realism that blew into the theater in *Waiting for Godot*'s absurdist wake: the washing machine sang in *Caroline*; a carnival barker brought on the attackers in *Assassins*; oblique conversations, roiled by menacing emotional undercurrents, in *A Number* recalled the work of Harold Pinter (or Sam Shepard, for that matter). Only Kushner, blunt and direct even when wildly imaginative, has a clear temperamental affinity with Miller; Sondheim's cynicism and Churchill's ease with indirect dialogue and narrative are both equally outside Miller's range. What all three share with Miller, the quality that made their recent plays spring to mind after his death, is a wholehearted faith in the essential nature of theater. Each of the productions breathed with charged interactions between the performers and the audience and among the audience members. Swept up though I was in the performances, I was always aware of the people watching them with me: the scattered walkouts at *Assassins*, still shocking 13 years after it was created; *Caroline*'s enthusiastic, sometimes vocal crowd, considerably younger and blacker than the Broadway norm; the intent faces, clearly visible in the spill of light from the playing area they flanked so closely, of the hushed spectators at *A Number*.

We were experiencing these works together, creating with the performers an event that would never be repeated. We were responding to a single vision, expressed through many voices. (No good dramatist—and that includes *Assassins*' book writer, John Weidman—makes every character onstage parrot an authorial point of view.) "What a welcome change from the torrent of raw information that bombards us beyond the stage door, some of it from sources we can't even identify, which leaves us with the daunting task of ordering these fragments into some kind of meaningful understanding. Theater offers us unity. It's no accident, though it certainly reflects my personal preferences, that these three plays, like Miller's, couple strong social and political content with explorations of individual longings, fears, and neuroses. Theater at its most exciting and engaging embraces the wholeness of life; it sees how alone we are, yet how entangled we are with others. Today, we frantically connect via the Internet or our cell phones, but it seems harder and harder just to occupy a particular physical space and to live "in the moment"—a state of being, significantly, that actors are always striving to attain onstage. When I go to the theater, no matter how harrowing (or trivial) the show is, I am always happy simply to be in a room with a substantial number of people participating in the same adventure. In our digital, virtual age, I think we crave that human contact more than ever.

What does this have to do with Arthur Miller's fraught relationship with Broadway? Bear with me a little longer. Another theatrical experience that came to mind when considering Miller's legacy took place in November, when I watched Eve Ensler, long a mainstay of the downtown scene. She zestfully took advantage of the Booth Theatre's resources to trot out a bunch of fancy audiovisual toys to amuse her midtown audience at *The Good Body*, a one woman show that scathingly and hilariously connected her obsession with her stomach to the larger subject of a global culture that encourages women to be at once narcissistic and self-hating. "It's amazing to have brought me to Broadway!" she exclaimed afterward with unabashed egocentricity. "I felt it would be really great if we could move things that concern women to a bigger venue and make them more substantial in the culture."

Although I said it's difficult to imagine an American playwright today having the impact that Miller once did, I could easily make the contrary point with Ensler's previous play, *The Vagina Monologues*. It shattered taboos, was translated into dozens of languages, and ran in theaters around the world. The author used her newfound status to launch V-Day, an annual event that has raised millions of dollars for organizations working to stop violence against women. And her brand of populism inspires just as much unease as Miller's, though for different reasons: the same sorts of cultural authorities who disdained him as on old fuddyduddy knock Ensler as a creature of the modern publicity system, regrettably willing to work the media and to enlist pop celebrities to promote her causes. Is *The Vagina Monologues* a masterpiece? No, but *Caroline* is, and Tony Kushner was so determined to move it uptown from its limited run at the Public Theatre that he personally appealed to potential investors and producers, putting himself into the commercial fray in a way that would have had Eugene O'Neill reaching for the whisky bottle. Strange as it seems, Broadway still matters—or, more accurately, the audience it can deliver does.

Why? Because the confinement of theater to a coterie, be it subscribers or tourists, is a condition that goads every truly ambitious artist. Sondheim, a generation older than Ensler and Kushner, has made it clear in interviews how painful he finds the loss of the Broadway audience that in the 1950s embraced sophisticated musicals like *Gypsy* (for which he wrote the lyrics) and was willing through the '70s to take a look at the more challenging, confrontational shows he created with Hal Prince, from *Company* to *Sweeney Todd*. He may have had to accept smaller theaters and limited runs, but no one can make him like them.

Younger playwrights and composers have learned to live with the new order, and so have theatergoers looking for something more than an evening's anesthesia. Serious plays and musicals are developed in workshops and performed to tiny audiences of the artists' friends and potential backers. Then they move on to the regional theaters or to New York's nonprofits, which are limited by union contracts to auditoriums seating no more than 499 people—and often many fewer. I subscribe to some of these theaters, and I'm grateful that they exist. But it's a fairly homogeneous group of intellectuals and bohemians that fills these small spaces, while *The Lion King* grabs the out-of-towners and the families. The cozy interchange among a few hundred folks will never match the electricity generated when a thousand or more peo-

ple metamorphose into an enthralled Broadway audience. *Lion King* director
Julie Taymor and Pulitzer Prize-winner Suzan-Lori Parks (who's writing a
musical for Disney) are among the avant-garde artists who've decided they
might be able to work in the commercial theater without merely dispensing
pabulum to the masses. Venerable non-profit organizations like the Roundabout and Manhattan Theatre Club have moved to Times Square, while
plays that make a hit in limited engagements (like John Patrick Shanley's
Doubt this season) transfer to Broadway houses. The process has changed,
but the goals are still the same: to keep theater in the mainstream American
cultural landscape, to attract as many people as possible to a medium like no
other.

Theater, by its nature, assumes that we can communicate with each
other directly and in person. That kind of communication is frighteningly
endangered in contemporary life, and any art form that sustains it is too
important to be abandoned to the happy few. I doubt that Arthur Miller,
born in 1915, thought in those terms, but he felt theater's necessity in the
context of the time that shaped him. No one was ever more contemptuous of
Broadway's crassness than Miller, but he worked there as much as he could
because he believed that the popular theater—and in this country that's
always been the commercial theater—was the arena in which he could convey
his ideas to the widest cross section of his fellow citizens. That belief continues to impel his successors in the American theater.

Those dimmed marquees on Broadway might have been a fitting tribute to Miller after all. They reminded us of a commercial theater that was
once genuinely inclusive, presenting fluff and food for thought to a broad
audience. Broadway today is not so immediately welcoming to serious playwrights as it was to the young Arthur Miller, but new generations have found
new means to bring us together in new places—and to move on to Broadway
when they can. In many ways, the American theater is more democratic and
broader based than it ever was, even if for every regional nonprofit nurtur-
ing new work there's a 3,000-seat barn of a venue presenting a touring,
brand-name musical so over-amplified and dependent on special effects that
you might as well be watching a movie. The theater's special qualities are
still being defended and extended by artists who struggle to draw the line
between reaching out and selling out. Miller's vision of theater's vital place in
our public life endures. As it must, if theater is to endure.

STEVEN R. CENTOLA

Arthur Miller and the
Art of the Possible

While commenting on the difference between playwriting and screenwriting in his Preface to *Everybody Wins*, Arthur Miller used the following illustration to illuminate his point about the subtextual dimension of the theater:

> If a telephone is photographed, isolated on a table, and the camera is left running, it becomes more and more what it is—a telephone in all its details . . . Things go differently on a stage. Set a phone on a table under a light and raise the curtain, and in complete silence, after a few minutes, something will accrete around it. Questions and anticipations will begin to emanate from it, we will begin to imagine meanings in its isolation—in a word, the phone becomes an incipient metaphor. Possible because we cannot see its detail as sharply as on film or because it is surrounded by much greater space, it begins to animate, to take on suggestive possiblities, very nearly a kind of self-consciousness. Something of the same is true of words as opposed to images. The word is not and can't be any more than suggestive of an idea or sensation; it is nothing in itself.
>
> ("On Screenwriting and Language" vi)

From *American Drama*. © 2005.

Indeed, in itself a word is nothing. If we believe the structuralists, a word is a symbol, a signifier or sign, a marker of meaning that points to something, some referent or vast reservoir of negotiable meanings beyond itself. The diacritical nature of language inevitably means that even small differences in sound and sense will produce tremendous variance in the determination and reception of meaning. Even more significantly, and perhaps more problematically, if we take a post-structuralist approach to language, a word points to an endless chain of linked signifiers, and given the arbitrary nature of the signifier and the system of which it is a part, this endless linked series of associations inevitably multiplies the potential meanings of every word and every word and every sequence of words forming sentences in written texts. The nuance that every word takes on and generates in the reader's mind is affected by the nuances all these words have in combination with each other, and all of this is then complicated by unanticipated associations which generate a host of linked associations and impressions, which collectively form unexpected meanings as they stimulate the reader's imagination and even tap into the unconscious. Perhaps for this reason, then, Miller, almost sounding a little like a deconstructive theorist, characterizes the word as nothing, but for Miller in its very nothingness lie the richness, density, and infinite possibilities of the word. After all, Miller tells us, "a description in words tends to inflate, expand, and inflame the imagination, so that in the end the thing or person described is amplified into a larger-than-life figment" ("On Screenwriting and Language" v). And that is the crucial part of the equation for the playwright: how to generate, shape, and string together words; how to invent and hone theater language in such a way that what is created constructs metaphorically an impression of reality that is powerful and suggestive enough to stimulate an imaginative response within the audience. As Miller recognizes, the possibilities inherent within the whole dramatic event are limitless, for the fundamental indeterminacy of meaning—an indeterminacy that Roland Barthes says inevitably results from the plural nature of the play text as a discourse that can be experienced only in the art of production—poses no nihilistic threat in Miller's world. Such indeterminacy instead opens up the possibility for rich speculative and imaginative discovery and generates endless opportunities for creative and diverse interpretations—possibly, even, a reinscription of oppositions, both with his own work and in the life and condition of humanity he depicts in his art. Miller's comments on the limitless and constantly mutating accretions accumulating around the words spoken and objects presented on the stage not only call attention to the subtextual dimension of the theater, but also show why this very important feature of dramatic art makes the theater what Miller described in 1999 as "the art of the possible" (*Echoes* 312).

Although in his commentary on the difference between the cinema and the theater Miller does not give enough credit to good film directors who can skillfully use the camera's eye to capture, isolate, and present certain aspects of individual objects or scenes on the screen in such a way that endows these scenic images with tremendous symbolic significance, he does make an important point about the special nature of theatrical presentation that causes words and objects on the stage to gather accretions around them and take on a subtextual dimension that knows no bounds. Whether it is the word or the scenic image, lighting or sound, gesture or action, the language of the theater resonates with extraordinary suggestiveness at almost any moment in a good play. And that suggestiveness resonates with a stream of endless associations and impressions that change not only from performance to performance but also for every new audience. Christopher Bigsby effectively describes the magical transformation that occurs during a theatrical performance:

> Theatre is a form of alchemy and if the end-product is not always gold at least certain transformations have been effected. Frederick March, Lee J. Cobb, Dustin Hoffman, and Warren Mitchell have all played the part of Willy Loman in *Death of a Salesman*. They spoke the same lines to the same characters but they spoke them differently to different audiences, in different sets, in front of different people, in different theatres, at different times on different continents . . . Whenever any of us open our mouths we speak the past. The words we use have passed through other mouths. They've been shaped, over time, by pleasures not our own. They're like our own, but they're not our own. They've shed and accumulated meanings. Perhaps that's the reason we're drawn to the theatre. It enacts our own central dilemma as actors inhabit someone else's words and struggle to make them their own, just as we try to imprint ourselves on the given.
>
> ("British View" 19–20)

As Bigsby points out, the theater is a place of transformation. The theater is a place where nature is transmuted into art, where reality meets and fuses with illusion, where text and subtext, character and action, word and gesture become one, where opposites are held in balanced suspension, and that, of course, is why the theater is the realm of the possible.

The theater, unlike everything else—the cinema, the novel, and the poem—is a living spectacle. That is why Clive Bloom says that the

> visceral, three-dimensionality of theatrical space, at once muscular presence and fragile voice, is the sinful nature of raw knowledge.

Unlike film and television, even and especially unlike commercial radio, the theater offers an authenticity which is shocking and peculiarly distressing . . . a type of primary authenticity which unravels or questions the inauthenticity of popular consumer culture and the values of the American system."

(Introduction to *American Drama* 2–3)

"The sinful nature of raw knowledge," the peculiar "authenticity" of the theatrical event, as Bloom puts it, derives mainly from the fact that it is a live performance and therefore its success depends on the performance, and oftentimes the interpretation, of the performer who responds to cues within the script and directorial decisions, and helps to turn word into speech and action, which transmutes art into life and makes a text a living presence on the stage for a live audience. The theater is not limited to or constrained by the script. That is certainly the play's beginning, but that is most definitely not its end. Undeniably, because it is a collaborative art form, the play, even more so than the novel, the cinema, or the poem, transcends the author's intentions and understanding and essentially takes on a life of its own in each performance. The world of the play can never be entirely circumscribed by the playwright's intentions any more than an author writing in any other genre of literature can completely know or predict the implication, association, or interpretation of every single word for each individual reading, and reacting to, a particular work. To borrow a phrase from John Barth, who used it in a different context, focusing more on the art of narrative composition than on the act of reading or responding to literary works, we can accurately characterize the genre of drama as "a literature of replenishment" (The Friday Book 206). Text and subtext, word and gesture, speech and action—all of these are fused into a remarkably coherent orchestration of sound and silence, light and darkness, time and space, past and present, reality and illusion. Opposites maintain a steady equilibrium in a carefully balanced and beautifully suspended presentation that momentarily, almost magically, transports us not only to an imagined world inhabited by invented people, but that also mysteriously invades our deepest consciousness and somehow suspends our individual ego while facilitating a group consciousness that affects us not only in the theater but also long after we experience the magic of the theatrical event. "What the performance of a play gives an audience," says Robert A. Martin, "is less a set of ideas, propositions, or abstractions about life and how to live it than what Arthur Miller has called a 'felt experience,' the imaginative sharing and participation in the lives and action of imaginary characters" ("The Nature of Tragedy" 97). "The performance is mythic; our sensibilities are enlivened by imaginary characters and we become engaged in their conflicts . . . [and by vicariously living through the characters' conflicts in the theater] we also see how their lives illuminate, by association, our own lives as individuals and as members of a larger society" (98). For all of these reasons, Arthur Miller is right in calling theater "the art of the possible" (*Echoes* 312).

What about Miller's own theater—a theater that has addressed the problems of war-profiteering crimes, anti-Semitism, the Holocaust, the Salem Witch Trials of 1692, the Great Depression, the inherent flaws in the American Dream of material success, mental illness, memory loss, infidelity, bigamy, incestuous desire, corruption in the American criminal justice system, censorship and the invasion of privacy in totalitarian countries, and other problems threatening to diminish the value of human life in the modern age? His theater emphasizes the tragic conditions of human existence, a theater that oftentimes depicts frustration, anguish, and failure as the prevailing condition of people trapped by circumstances and the crush of overwhelming forces in their society or within their own psyche. Can we justifiably call Miller's theater the art of the possible too? I believe that we can, and my purpose in this essay is to attempt to explain why I believe that his humanist values and postmodernist perspective provide audiences worldwide with a vision of humanity that is uplifting and life-affirming. His plays offer hope and solace for a world desperately seeking to find a glimmer of hope in a world of darkness. In spite of his tragic vision and brutally honest confrontation with the dark forces of human depravity, Miller's plays show the possibility for redemption, transcendence, even triumph in the face of seemingly overpowering odds and adversity most inimical to human enterprise and achievement. Miller's theater is not escapist in nature, but neither is it fatalistic, pessimistic, or nihilistic. It is a drama of hope not despair, transcendence not reduction, and, above all else, the limitless potentialities and possibilities of the human spirit.

When I interviewed Arthur Miller in August 2001, he spoke of one of his more recent creations: *Mr. Peters' Connections*, which was produced at the Signature Theater in 1998. The play is set in a dilapidated nightclub, which Mr. Peters has entered to meet his wife. On one level, it seems as if they may be interested in purchasing and renovating the establishment for future use, but during the course of his conversations with other characters, it becomes clear that Mr. Peters seems uncertain of why he's even in this particular setting. On another level, though, it is easy to view the set as completely symbolic, representing the interior consciousness of Mr. Harry Peters, an elderly man on the verge of death, trapped somewhere between life and death, between consciousness and unconscious reverie. As the play progresses and Mr. Peters engages in spirited, but sometimes puzzling and even depressing, conversations with both real and imagined characters, some alive and in the present and some dead and resurrected from memories and images of the past, it becomes evident to the audience that Mr. Peters is primarily concerned with finding some thread to his life experience that ties everything together into a neat package, an orderly and meaningful whole that has purpose, design, definition, and clarity. His obsessive interest in finding the unseen inherent order is blatantly shown through his repetitive questioning of both himself and the others about the "subject" he searches for in their conversation. Early in the play, Mr. Peters, on the verge of understanding his dilemma but never completely coming to full conscious awareness of his insight, says: "I just cannot find the subject! Like I'll be strolling down the street, and suddenly I'm weeping, everything welling up.—What is the subject? Know what I mean? Simply cannot grasp the subject" (8). Clarifying the significance of this repeated insistence by Mr. Peters on finding and understanding "the subject," Miller, in his Preface to the play, tells us that Mr. Peters is searching for "the secret, the pulsing center of energy, what he calls the subject—that will make his life cohere" (viii). By the play's end, Mr. Peters is no more certain of what the subject is than he was at its beginning, and this lack of resolution—this failure to reach a definitive position about the subject—was not received well by Miller's critics, and is perhaps even primarily responsible for the play being greeted with what Robert Brustein has characterized as "the worst reviews of Miller's career" ("Still Searching for Theater" 29–30).

Undoubtedly, one of the negative reviews Brustein refers to is his own. Writing for the *New Republic* in 1998, Brustein describes *Mr. Peters' Connections* as "windy, tiresome, self-conscious, and full of moony maundering." Associating what he views as the play's structural flaws with the playwright's inability to articulate his vision coherently, Brustein assumes that Miller unintentionally creates a formless play that lacks resolution. Brustein writes:

> Miller is so eager to get things off his chest that he hasn't bothered to provide his new play with a plot, a form, or even much effort at characterization . . . *Mr. Peters' Connections* is like a long confession to a friend which has yet to be proofed or edited. . . . He [Mr. Peters] is looking for some continuity with his history in "the hope of finding a subject." It is like watching Arthur Miller at his typewriter wrestling with the same elusive goal. ("Still Searching for Theater" 29–30)

Brustein is not alone in identifying Harry Peters' struggle for certitude with Miller's own personal frustrations, both as a writer seeking to find the perfect form for his vision and as an alienated artist who has sadly witnessed the terrible transformation of the world surrounding him. Writing for the *Village Voice*, Michael Feingold argues that Harry Peters is nothing more than a mouthpiece for Arthur Miller. Feingold writes: "Like his hero, the

82-year-old Miller barely seems to be connecting to the outside world these days. His connections are to his memories, to his puzzlement over the countless ways life has changed in this half-century, and to whatever method he uses now to get words on paper" ("The Old Miller Stream" 147). Making the same assumption, Nina Raine and Frances Stonor Saunders, reviewing the play for the *New Statesman* during its production in London during the fall 2000 season, also identify the playwright with his character: "thoughts of a dry brain in an off-Broadway season. As Mr. Peters (or, rather, Miller) repeatedly exclaims: 'There is no subject any more'" ("Miller's Tale" 30). This brief sampling of the critical response to the New York and London productions of *Mr. Peters' Connections* reveals two trends in the reviewers' response to the play: one, the tendency to identify the author with his character and, two, the conclusion that Miller, and his play, present the audience with a grim, maybe even pessimistic, view of the human condition, a view in their minds undoubtedly invited by the play's unsettling approach to its central thematic interest, which echoes jarringly in the phrase "There is no subject any more." While many have taken *Mr. Peters' Connections* to be a radical departure from Miller's other works and have read the play as a depressing conclusion to a long and distinguished career, the play's thematic center can actually be seen as perfectly consonant with the playwright's vision throughout his career and, in fact, offers its audiences a vision of hope and human possibility, not despair.

In our discussion in August 2001 Miller confirmed that there is a subject in *Mr. Peters' Connections*; the playwright identifies it for us in his play. Humanity, as Miller put it in our conversation, the human mind, is the subject. Miller does not find it disturbing or depressing that there is no inherent order or purpose to life and human existence. The greatness of humanity lies in its ability to forge meaning out of chaos. The human mind, Miller believes, shapes, defines, clarifies, orders, and gives purpose and meaning to life and human existence. In its unmediated state, life is chaos. Entropy is more than just a theory; it is the fundamental condition of the expanding universe, within which we struggle to resist the forces of chaos and destruction and to elevate and ennoble the human condition. The human mind alone brings light into a world of darkness, and because of its power of transcendence and capacity for reason and logical discourse, the human mind is worthy of celebration. "What is the subject?" asks Mr. Peters. Miller answers: we are—and his play implicitly provides this answer by showing us Mr. Peters' thoughtful attempt to wrest some meaning out of his life's experiences. In essence, his quest parallels that of Oedipus and other great tragic figures who seek to understand the conditions of life and their own unique role in shaping their personal destiny. Mr. Peters is no tragic figure, but his efforts are noble and commendable and comment positively on the potential of humanity for honest self-exploration. *Mr. Peters' Connections*, like so much of Miller's work, is ultimately a tribute to the art of the possible.

Earlier in his career, Miller wrote plays that more forcefully explored this subject in the tragic mode and seemed, even more so than *Mr. Peters' Connections*, to have little to do with human possibility. In *All My Sons* and *Death of a Salesman*, for example, we are presented with characters who clearly seem to be and even controlled by environmental forces that severely diminish their capacity for free choice. However, nothing is that simple in Miller's world. There always remains a strong interplay between freedom and fate, a paradoxical balance between deterministic forces at play in the lives of individuals and the exercise and expression of one's own free will that invariably triggers some catastrophic event.

All My Sons tells the story of a successful Mid-Western manufacturer of airplane parts who knowingly allows defective engines to be shipped to the United States Army during the Second World War. As a result of his war profiteering crimes, twenty-one American pilots die when the cracked cylinder heads cause their planes to malfunction and crash. Exonerated by the courts for his role in the catastrophe, Joe Keller, the play's central character, triumphantly returns to his community and futilely attempts to return to a life of normalcy, pretending the crime never occurred. The semblance of family harmony is maintained until his son, Chris, himself under pressure as his fiancee's brother forces him to acknowledge his own acquiescence, questions Joe about his role in the sordid business transaction. Chris, who fought bravely in combat during the war and had seen many of his troops perish under his command, has a different outlook from his father on the question of an individual's social responsibility. After several powerful scenes of intense debate over the individual's relation to society, Chris finally discloses his father's guilt and challenges him to accept responsibility for his actions. Until his son forces him to acknowledge his wrongdoing, Joe Keller steadfastly maintains his innocence and justifies his anti-social behavior by proclaiming his right to do anything necessary to keep the business from collapsing and ensure his family's survival. Ultimately, as a suicide letter discloses that his older brother preferred death over the ignominy that issued from his father's war crime, Chris convinces his father that he has an obligation to others in society as well. Tortured by his guilt and unable to deal with the shame in his son's eyes, Keller tries to escape from his intolerable situation by putting a bullet in his head. The play ends with Chris facing with horror his own complicity in his father's death. With Joe Keller's suicide, the play forcefully repudiates anti-social behavior that derives from the myth of privatism in American society.

So why should we see this play as exemplifying what Miller calls "the art of the possible"? Where is the hope and possibility in a man's suicide following his realization of the enormity of his anti-social behavior? In an interview with Henry Brandon in 1960, Miller made a statement that seems to point toward an understanding of the process of indirection that enables his drama to leave us with hope, while presenting his audiences with portraits and chronicles of despair. Miller said: "a playwright provides answers by the questions he chooses to ask, by the exact conflicts in which he places his people" (quoted in *Theater Essays* 227). In *All My Sons*, as in the rest of his drama, Miller conveys a sense of possibility for humanity by showing his audience the opportunity for choice; for the selection of a different course of action in his characters' lives. Like Willy Loman in *Death of a Salesman*, Eddie Carbone in *A View from the Bridge*, and Maggie in *After the Fall*, Joe Keller chooses to see himself as a victim of others, and of circumstances imposed on businessmen like himself during the Second World War. He adopts a counterfeit innocence and embraces the illusion that he is a victim of society, of the competitive business world, of the culture that makes it imperative for a man in American society to feel driven by the need to prosper, provide for the family, and succeed in attaining the forever elusive, unquestionably mythic American Dream. Keller denies his personal culpability so that he can preserve his false image of himself and maintain the illusion that he has regained his rightful place in society. He blinds himself from the impulses that make him a danger to himself and others in his society. Keller cannot face what Miller calls "the murder in him, the sly and everlasting complicity with the forces of destruction" (quoted in *Theater Essays* 256). Keller chooses his behavior; it isn't chosen for him or forced on him. His betrayal of trust and refusal to accept responsibility for others sets in motion the chain of events that lead to his self-destruction. Through showing us what happens when a man nullifies the value of the social contract through the performance and justification of indefensible anti-social acts, Miller emphasizes the importance of socially responsible behavior and makes clear why crimes against society must be censured. The sense of possibility in *All My Sons* derives from one simple fact: Joe Keller chose his fate and could have chosen differently. Among other things, *All My Sons* shows that the impulse to betray others and deny responsibility for the welfare of society, when left ungoverned, can run rampant and wreak havoc on the individual, his family, and his society—even, perhaps, civilization as a whole. The Kellers, and many of those around them, choose to blame everyone else for their dilemma, but the play actually shows its audiences that they are the authors of their destiny and failure to accept the tremendous burden of their freedom and responsibility is itself the cause of their personal tragedy.

In an essay published in 1964, Richard Loughlin offers an interesting perspective on the way *All My Sons* leaves its audiences with a sense of hope for the future. Discussing the play as a tragedy in Aristotelian terms, Loughlin argues that

The spectacle of the crimes and sufferings of another stimulates our sympathy; it reminds us of the perils and uncertainties of the human condition and of the golden thread of strength of character that ties us all together. Such meditation on life's challenges and values may prompt us to rededicate our lives to those ideas of the good, the true, and the beautiful that any work of art enshrines. What ideals are apparent or implied in *All My Sons?* Honesty, brotherhood, patriotism, and true love, to mention the most obvious ones.

("Tradition and Tragedy in '*All My Sons*'" 27)

More recently, Hersh Zeifman discussed the play's extraordinary fusion of form and vision as deriving from the playwright's "rage for order, for an anodyne to [our] 'helplessness before the chaos of existence'" ("*All My Sons. After the Fall*: Arthur Miller and the Rage for Order" 107). In its "relentless Ibsenite . . . linearity, chronology, causality . . . the quest for order is dramatized in the play . . . not only formally but thematically: the conflict between Chris Keller and his father is precisely the struggle between order and chaos" (108). In their life-and-death struggle of ethics and values, the Kellers present audiences with an important lesson about "relatedness" and the necessity for "a connection with the larger family of humanity" (108). The conflict they experience speaks directly to every member of the audience, for as Robert A. Martin points out,

Miller's great achievement as a playwright allows us to see and understand particular characters or groups of characters as possessing universal, human traits, even as we also see how their lives illuminate, by association, our own lives as individuals and as members of our larger society. In recognizing these larger concerns, we recognize as well that Miller's plays are not exclusively about individuals, but more precisely, are about humanity and human societies with all their contradictions and complications.

("The Nature of Tragedy" 98)

Nowhere is this aspect of Miller's drama more evident than in his masterpiece, *Death of a Salesman*, for in its searing portrait of a family in conflict, Miller achieves a near-perfect synthesis of the social, moral, psychological, personal, and metaphysical levels of experience, and shows how the death of a single individual touches everyone in his family and audiences that witness his tragic collapse.

Much like *All My Sons*, *Death of a Salesman* presents us with an individual, and a family, that have lost their ability to separate fact from fiction, truth from lies, reality from illusion. The Lomans are so deeply entrenched in the life-lie they have embraced that they find it nearly impossible to communicate with each other without resorting to the cliched rhetoric they have imbibed from the prevailing success myths in their capitalistic society. *Death of a Salesman* is possibly Arthur Miller's greatest play. It has been called the quintessentially American play, and perhaps it has generated more critical and scholarly discussion over the efficacy of the popular concept of the American Dream than any other work of literature dealing with American society. Studies of this play invariably discuss Willy Loman's self-delusion and moral confusion in relation to Miller's indictment of the competitive, capitalistic society that is responsible for dehumanizing the individual and transforming the once promising agrarian American dream into an urban nightmare. But whether it is approached as a tragedy of the common man, a social drama indicting capitalism and American business ethics, a sociological consideration of work alienation and its impact on identity, a cultural critique of the American family and stereotypical gender roles in American society, a modern morality play about today's Everyman, or a complex psychological study of guilt, repression, and psychosis, *Death of a Salesman* is a compelling drama that makes for an intensely moving and hauntingly memorable theatrical experience. Despite its overwhelming sense of tragic inevitability, the play gains most of its power from Miller's ability to turn the self-destructive journey of Willy Loman into a tribute to the worth and nobility of the human spirit. Even in the very process of showing the devastating consequences that result when the individual succumbs to the lure of denial and self-delusion, *Death of a Salesman* somehow manages to affirm the value of human life and the potential for every individual to strive to achieve the impossible dream of human perfectibility.

Miller's masterpiece tells the story of the irrepressible sixty-three-year-old traveling salesman, Willy Loman, who strives to retrieve his lost dignity and his family's love on the last day of his life. This icon of the American theater represents every person, both in American society and throughout the world, who has ever felt displaced from his rightful position in his society and longed to attain a sense of peace and belonging in a world that suddenly seems foreign and even hostile to his pretensions. Using a highly suggestive multiple set to emphasize the subjective nature of the play, Miller collapses past and present and takes us inside the mind of Willy Loman to show us how an individual nurtured on success-formula platitudes and get-rich-quick schemes buys fully into the notion of the American Dream without ever really evaluating or understanding how false and incomplete are the values he embraces in his venal American society. Desperate to make sense of his life and to avoid seeing himself as a failure, both as salesman and father, Willy Loman tries to escape the burden of responsibility for the choices he has made and, instead, seeks facile solutions to complex personal and economic problems. Willy's painful struggle "to evaluate himself justly" ("Tragedy," *Theater Essays* 4) is what grips audiences around the world, for everyone, not just people who are culturally or ideologically predisposed to embrace the American Dream, can understand the anguish that derives from "being torn away from our chosen image of what and who we are in this world" ("Tragedy," *Theater Essays* 5).

During this last day in his life, Willy drifts back and forth between the past and the present, groping for answers to his problematic relationship with his son Biff, and futilely trying to ease his conscience about past indiscretions and missed opportunities that he fears have cost him the love, respect, and honor that society has trained him to expect as customary entitlements for male heads of household in the American family. As he sets up and then destroys opportunities for disclosures that would reveal his role in creating the destiny he seeks to avoid, Willy repeatedly attempts to deny his role in any wrongdoing in the past that would demand his acknowledgment and acceptance of responsibility for his own, and his sons', failures. He tries to preserve an inflated image of himself as both salesman and father and convince others that the identity he has manufactured is real. As a result of submerging himself so thoroughly in his life-lie, Willy experiences a complete disengagement from reality and virtually drives himself mad. His psychological disorientation is strongly evoked in the play's setting, lighting, music, and dramatic structure, particularly in director Robert Falls' postmodernist set design for the play in 1999, which vividly conveys and externalizes the fragmentation rending Willy apart and driving him inevitably to his tragic suicide.

Again, one has to wonder how a play that depicts the unmitigated frustration and failure of delusional and desperate characters can succeed in conveying any sense of hope and possibility for its audiences. According to Zygmunt Adamczewski, Willy's tragic suicide "gives poignancy to existence in protest" as an individual who senses "the loss of his self," the fact that "he is not what he is" (*Tragic Protest* 190, 191). In other words, Willy's tragic protest comments on the paradoxical condition that defines human existence: the constant struggle within the individual between self and society, right and wrong, love and hate, joy and sorrow, consciousness and unconsciousness, work and play, success and failure, past and present, life and death. Life is flux, and human life is frequently characterized by internal conflict. If the value of a human life may ultimately be determined by the extent to which an individual struggles against contradictory and entropic impulses in an effort to give existence purpose and meaning, then it is easy to see why *Death of a Salesman* is so popular and successful and moves audiences around the world with its searing presentation of the Loman tragedy. Willy Loman's battle is everyone's battle, for despite his particular failings and annoying eccentricities, Willy's futile attempt to resist reduction and atomization, and his constant flight from his alienated condition, reflect a universal need for personal triumph over the forces that deny individuality and threaten to diminish our humanity. Life is change: conflict, tension, a war of wills and desires, an everlasting struggle to bring order to chaos and impose meaning on a fundamentally absurd world. It is the entropic condition that Willy Loman resists, and because of Willy's fierce determination to fight an impossible battle against the inherent conditions of human existence, Miller tells us that "There is a nobility . . . in Willy's struggle" (*Beijing* 27). Willy, explains Miller, "is trying to lift up a belief in immense redeeming human possibilities" (*Beijing* 29). That is the attraction and glory of Willy Loman: his limitless hope in the face of hopelessness and refusal to accept defeat even when thoroughly defeated. Willy's persistent struggle to resist the force of entropy in his life is ultimately what defines the tragic spirit of Miller's vision in *Death of a Salesman*.

Miller's play gives us an unblinking look at the terrifying darkness that lies coiled within existence. Attendant to this dark vision is the discovery that the light enkindled by human kindness and love can give human life a brilliance and luster that will never be extinguished. Willy dies, but death does not defeat Willy Loman; as the Requiem demonstrates, Willy will continue to live on in the memories and lives of others. Through his remarkable fusion of opposites that express both the form and the vision of the play, Miller reveals the condition of tension that is life and human existence. Because of its perfect integration of form, character, and action, *Death of a Salesman* is a modern masterpiece that celebrates, as Chris Bigsby eloquently states, "the miracle of human life, in all its bewilderments, its betrayals, its denials, but, finally, and most significantly, its transcendent worth" ("Poet" 723).

The Crucible," writes Miller, "is, internally, *Salesman*'s blood brother. It is examining the questions I was absorbed with before—the conflict between a man's raw deeds and his conception of himself; the question of whether conscience is in fact an organic part of the human being, and what happens when it is handed over not merely to the state or the mores of the time but to one's friend or wife" ("Brewed in *The Crucible*," *Theater Essays* 172–173). The powerful manner in which *The Crucible* explores these questions explains why it is also regarded as a masterpiece of the modern stage. *The Crucible* is Arthur Miller's most frequently produced play and speaks to people all over the world of the need to resist tyranny and oppression. Miller's play transcends cultural and geographical boundaries with its inspired depiction of one man's heroic struggle to preserve his honor when threatened by a corrupt state authority. With its intense dramatic action and its absorbing look at the debilitating effects of guilt, fear, repression, personal betrayal, mass hysteria, and public confession, *The Crucible* shows how an individual can rise above the conditions surrounding him and transform guilt into responsibility and thereby defeat the deterministic forces, both within and outside him, that threaten to destroy his identity as well as his humanity.

The Crucible dramatizes one of the darkest episodes in American history: the Salem Witch Trials of 1692. Making just a few alterations to the historical record in the interest of intensifying the play's dramatic action and clarifying and revealing the characters' hidden motivation, Miller shows what happens when girls in the repressive Puritan community of Salem Village in 1692 make unfounded accusations of witchcraft against their neighbors. Hundreds are arrested and convicted of witchcraft and nineteen innocent people are hanged. Among those incarcerated is John Proctor, a citizen of the community, a successful farmer and landowner who has committed adultery with Abigail Williams, one of the principal accusers and witnesses for the state. Proctor's guilt over his infidelity and conviction that he is a sinner, and therefore not like the falsely accused, temporarily causes him to sign a phony confession of witchcraft in an effort to save his life and protect his family. But when he realizes that his confession must be made public and therefore will be used to damage the credibility of his friends and neighbors and justify their persecution, Proctor fiercely denounces the court and tears up his confession. In a powerful dramatic scene, Proctor insists that his name not be used to damage the reputation of others, and even though his inspiring act of courage and nobility leads directly to his execution, it simultaneously becomes the basis for his own personal redemption.

Ironically, because of Proctor's defiant act of heroism and decision to die a noble death rather than live ignobly, it is easier to see how *The Crucible* demonstrates the possibility for human transcendence than is at first evident in both *All My Sons* and *Death of a Salesman*. Yet the conditions for such individualistic behavior are certainly far less favorable in the Puritan community of 1692 that Miller dramatizes in *The Crucible* than in the American society of the 1940s he depicts in *All My Sons* and *Death of a Salesman*. Because Salem Village was a theocracy, every facet of an individual's life in that community could arguably be seen as demonstrating the inevitable intersection of the societal and personal dimensions of a person's experience. In essence, everything a person said or did in Salem Village in 1692 could have been construed as having a direct bearing on society and, therefore, would unquestionably receive the close scrutiny of the larger community. Yet, in spite of the strong limitations and constraints placed on an individual's personal liberties and freedoms in that society, John Proctor is able to rise above the deterministic conditions surrounding him and find the courage and strength needed to denounce the court's inane proceedings. Through the crucible of his personal suffering, Proctor embraces values that are life-affirming, and with his acceptance of his personal responsibility for the welfare of others, Proctor defeats death and wins a victory for humankind.

Perhaps the situation that was most inimical to the potentialities of the human spirit in the twentieth century was the Holocaust. Yet, even in this most disturbing spectacle of human depravity and unspeakable atrocity, Miller finds hope for the triumph of the human spirit. As Edward Isser rightly asserts, "Arthur Miller is perhaps the foremost spokesman for a universalist and humanistic interpretation of the Holocaust" ("Arthur Miller and the Holocaust" 155). This horrible testament to human depravity and the capacity for evil and despicable acts of human aggression looms large in three plays, a novel, a screenplay, and even an autobiography by Miller.

Miller first tackles this subject in his novel *Focus* (1945), which establishes strong parallels between the Nazi movement in Europe and the Anti-Semitism promoted in America by the Christian Front and other hate groups who persecuted Jews during the Second World War. Only after experiencing the unjust persecution that results from being mistakenly identified as a Jew does the novel's central character find the courage to stand up to the fascists persecuting Jews in his neighborhood, and counter their barbaric behavior with socially responsible action. In *After the Fall*, Miller creates even greater discomfort for his audiences by asking them to find within themselves the locus of evil that gives rise to such movements as nazism and the terrible hate crimes associated with the Holocaust. To concretize this direct association between private and public acts of aggression, the silhouette of a concentration camp tower is illuminated periodically in *After the Fall*, as the play's central character, Quentin, struggles to understand why his own personal acts of betrayal and cruelty are linked in his mind with the horrors that occurred at Auschwitz and other concentration camps. Quentin ultimately accepts his culpability in the horrors he detests because he realizes that no one is innocent after the fall. In *Incident at Vichy*, detainees awaiting interrogation by their Nazi captors are fearful that, if discovered to be Jews, they will be sent in locked boxcars to concentration camps in Poland for extermination. Each prisoner adopts what ultimately amounts to an ineffective strategy for explaining his captivity and dealing with the absurd impending interrogation. One by one, they are treated inhumanely by their captors, checked for circumcision, and then sent to certain death in the camps. Only one prisoner, the psychiatrist Leduc, is able to elude this horrible destiny as a result of the heroic and noble sacrifice of an Austrian Prince, who hands over his pass to freedom and courageously proves that it is possible to resist tyranny and oppression by transforming guilt into responsibility.

The advent of the Holocaust is the subject of *Broken Glass*. The play's central character, Sylvia Gellburg, suffers severe hysterical paralysis as she learns that old Jews and young children are being abused and ridiculed in

Germany during *Kristallnacht*. Her anxiety over their condition and unconscious association of the Nazis' cruelty with her husband's abusive treatment
of her and condescension toward Jews triggers the emotional disorder that
leaves her physically incapacitated until her husband's unexpected death. Perhaps, though, Miller's most disturbing and direct treatment of the Holocaust
occurs in his television screenplay adaptation of Fania Fenelon's memoirs:
Playing for Time. This brutally frank depiction of the anguish and heroism
of a woman captive in a concentration camp during the Second World War
celebrates the courage and nobility of spirit exhibited by an individual who
refuses to relinquish her dignity and act in a way that degrades the human
species. In spite of the unspeakable horrors and ordeals she faces and the
severe constraints imposed on her by her captors, her environment, and her
impossible situation, Fania Fenelon, says Miller, shows that "it was possible to
exercise free will even in a concentration camp" (quoted in Atlas 32).

Among other things, says Miller, his Holocaust drama teaches us an
important lesson about ourselves:

> that we should see the bestiality in our own hearts, so that we
> should know how we are brothers not only to these victims but to
> the Nazis, so that the ultimate tenor of our lives should be faced—
> namely our own sadism, our own fear of standing firm on humane
> principles against the obscene power of mass organization.
> ("The Shadow of the Gods," *Theater Essays* 187)

The lessons do not end there. In his Holocaust drama, as in all of his other
plays, the twin pillars on which his characters' personal morality rests are
freedom and responsibility. As a character struggles not only to survive but
also to do so with honor and integrity, Fania Fenelon demonstrates that it is
imperative that the individual accept the possibility for free, and responsible,
choices and behavior. In *Playing for Time*, Fania Fenelon counters the evil
darkness of the Nazis with her commitment to a morality that fosters and
promotes compassion, understanding, tolerance, honesty, and self-discipline.
She selects and upholds values that ennoble the human species and affirm
the value and importance of every individual life. In the most abhorrent
conditions that are most inimical to the exercise of free will, a concentration
camp prisoner finds it possible to prove that human beings are capable of the
most courageous moral action even when faced with the threat of imminent
death.

By writing so powerfully about the Holocaust, Miller may be suggesting that though art cannot guarantee the survival of humanity, it can help to
justify and validate the worth of human existence. Miller clearly creates art
for life's sake. He once said that the Great Depression made him "impatient

with anything, including art, which pretends that it can exist for its own sake and still be of prophetic importance" ("The Shadows of the Gods," *Theater Essays* 179). For Miller, literature, and particularly the theater, must "speak to the present condition of man's life and thus would implicitly have to stand against injustice as the destroyer of life" (*Timebends* 596). Nowhere is this commitment made more evident than in his harrowing screenplay of humanity's darkest hour and greatest triumph. In the midst of a hellish landscape of human suffering and depravity, one woman faced the ultimate challenge to her dignity and proved that nothing, not even the threat of a horrible death, could force the individual to act ignobly or relinquish her sense of personal responsibility. Fania Fenelon's triumph is ultimately a triumph of the human spirit—one that Miller presents dramatically to confirm the possibility of giving meaning and dignity to human existence.

Regardless of the conditions and limitations on the individual in Miller's plays, his characters have the ability to choose the course of action that determines their values and behavior. The moral truth that speaks so loudly in Miller's plays derives from a single premise: we are free to create our destinies. His characters have the ability to face and accept what is real and thereby to discover the truth about their lives and identities. Although characters like Joe Keller, Willy Loman, Eddie Carbone, and Lyman Felt do not exercise their freedom to choose honestly and responsibly, that fact does not mitigate the possibility for such expression of their free will to occur.

Bigsby has long maintained that for Arthur Miller the theater has always been "a realm of possibility" (*American Drama* 248). By creating plays that show the human will as inexhaustible and irrepressible, Miller expresses a vision of humanity that shows that transcendence is coexistent with consciousness, and this special attribute of human existence both curses and blesses humanity because it invariably sets us off on a life-long journey to attain the impossible dream—a more-than-American dream for perfection. Struggle endows our lives with meaning; the theater of Arthur Miller offers the following message to his audience: as long as we continue to wrestle with our givens, resist the forces of chaos and entropy, and struggle to impose order on the natural world and our mental landscape, we will have an opportunity, a possibility, for a meaningful life. No easy task, admits the playwright, but entirely within the realm of the possible.

Works Cited

Adamczewski, Zygmunt. The *Tragic Protest*, The Hague: Martinus Nijoff, 1963.
Atlas, James. "The Creative Journey of Arthur Miller Leads Back to Broadway and TV," *New York Times* 28 September 1980, Sec. 2:1+.
Barth, John. "The Literature of Replenishment: Postmodernist Fiction," *The Friday Book*. Baltimore: Johns Hopkins UP, 1984. 193–206.

Bigsby, Christopher. *"A British View of an American Playwright."* *The Achievement of Arthur Miller: New Essays.* Ed. Steven R. Centola. Dallas: Contemporary Research, 1995. 15–29.

___. "Arthur Miller: Poet." *Michigan Quarterly Review* 37 (Fall 1998): 713–25.

___. "Arthur Miller: The Moral Imperative," *Modern American Drama, 1945–1990.* Cambridge: Cambridge UP, 1992. 72–125.

Bloom, Clive, Ed. Introduction. *American Drama,* New York: St. Martin's, 1995. 6–20.

Brustein, Robert. "Still Searching for Theater," *New Republic* 3 August 1998: 29–30.

Feingoid, Michael. "The Old Miller Stream." *Village Voice* 26 May 1998: 147.

Isser, Edward R. "Arthur Miller and the Holocaust." *Essays in Theatre* 10.2 (May 1992): 155–64.

Loughlin, Richard L. "Tradition and Tragedy in *All My Sons.*" *English Record* 14 (February 1964): 23–27.

Martin, Robert A. "The Nature of Tragedy." *South Atlantic Review* 61 (1996): 97–106.

Miller, Arthur. "Brewed in *The Crucible.*" *The Theater Essays of Arthur Miller.* Edited by Robert A. Martin and Steven R. Centola. New York: DaCapo, 1996. 172–74.

___. *Echoes Down the Corridor.* New York. Viking, 2000.

___. "Forward to *After the Fall.*" *The Theater Essays of Arthur Miller.* 255–57.

___. Interview with Steve Centola. Roxbury, Connecticut, 9 August 2001.

___. *Mr. Peters' Connections.* New York: Penguin, 1999.

___. *Salesman in Beijing.* New York: Viking, 1984.

___. "On Screenwriting and Language." *Everybody Wins.* New York: Grove Press, 1990. v–xiv.

___. "The Shadows of the Gods." *The Theater Essays of Arthur Miller:* 174–94.

___. "The State of the Theater." Interview with Henry Brandon. *The Theater Essays of Arthur Miller.* 223–36.

___. *Timebends: A Life.* New York: Grove, 1987.

___. "Tragedy and the Common Man." *The Theater Essays of Arthur Miller.* 3–7.

Raine, Nina and Frances Stonor Saunders. "Miller's Tale." *New Statesman* 14 August 2000. 30–32.

Zeifman, Hersh. "All My Sons After the Fall: Arthur Miller and the Rage for Order." *The Theatrical Gamut. Notes for a Post-Brechtian Stage.* Ed. Enoch Brater. Ann Arbor: University of Michigan Press, 1995. 107–20.

Chronology

1915   Arthur Miller is born on 17 October into a Jewish immigrant family from Poland. His father owns a prosperous coat and suit factory.

1938   Graduates from University of Michigan with A. B. and joins the Federal Theatre Project.

1940   Marries Mary Grace Slattery.

1944   *The Man Who Had All the Luck*, his first play produced on Broadway.

1947   *All My Sons* is produced on Broadway. Runs 328 performances. Wins New York Drama Critics Circle Award for best play. Elia Kazan purchases movie rights, initiating a long personal and professional relationship.

1948   *The Death of a Salesman* opens on Broadway for a run of 742 performances. It wins a Tony Award, National Book Critics Award, and Pulitzer Prize.

1953   *The Crucible* opens on Broadway. It wins a Tony Award. The play closed after 197 performances, but it runs for 800 performances in its 1958 revival.

1954   Miller is denied a passport when he attempts to travel to Brussels for the opening there of *The Crucible* because he is suspected of Communist activities.

1956   Miller divorces Slattery and marries Marilyn Monroe. He is called to testify before the House Committee on Un-American Activities when she refuses to be photographed shaking hands with the HCUA chairman. Refusing to testify, Miller is charged and convicted of contempt of Congress.

1958   Miller's conviction is overturned by the U.S. Court of Appeals.

1959   Miller is presented American Academy of Arts and Letters gold medal.

1961   Miller and Monroe are divorced, a year before her death by suicide.

1962   Miller marries Ingeborg Morath.

1965   Miller is elected president of PEN International; serves until 1969.

1984   Miller is presented John F. Kennedy Award for Lifetime Achievement.

1999   Miller is presented Tony Lifetime Achievement Award.

2001   Miller is awarded National Book Medal for Distinguished Contribution to American Letters.

2002   *Resurrection Blues*, the last of Miller's twenty plays, opens in Minneapolis.

2005   Miller dies of heart failure on February 10.

Contributors

HAROLD BLOOM is Sterling Professor of the Humanities at Yale University. He is the author of thirty books, including *Shelley's Mythmaking* (1959), *The Visionary Company* (1961), *Blake's Apocalypse* (1963), *Yeats* (1970), *A Map of Misreading* (1975), *Kabbalah and Criticism* (1975), *Agon: Toward a Theory of Revisionism* (1982), *The American Religion* (1992), *The Western Canon* (1994), and *Omens of Millennium: The Gnosis of Angels, Dreams, and Resurrection* (1996). *The Anxiety of Influence* (1973) sets forth Professor Bloom's provocative theory of the literary relationships between the great writers and their predecessors. His most recent books include *Shakespeare: The Invention of the Human* (1998), a 1998 National Book Award finalist, *How to Read and Why* (2000), *Genius: A Mosaic of One Hundred Exemplary Creative Minds* (2002), *Hamlet: Poem Unlimited* (2003), *Where Shall Wisdom Be Found?* (2004), and *Jesus and Yahweh: The Names Divine* (2005). In 1999, Professor Bloom received the prestigious American Academy of Arts and Letters Gold Medal for Criticism. He has also received the International Prize of Catalonia, the Alfonso Reyes Prize of Mexico, and the Hans Christian Andersen Bicentennial Prize of Denmark.

EDMUND S. MORGAN is Sterling Professor emeritus of History at Yale University. He has authored dozens of books on Puritan and early colonial history, including the award winning *Inventing the People: The Rise of Popular Sovereignty in England and America* (1988), *American Slavery, American Freedom* (1975), *Birth of the Republic*, (1956) and *The Puritan Dilemma* (1958).

His other works include biographies of Ezra Stiles and Roger Williams, and a book on George Washington.

DAVID SAVRAN is the Vera Mowry Roberts Professor of American theatre at City College of New York Graduate Center. He earned a Ph.D. in theatre arts from Cornell. He was professor of English, modern culture, and media; and theatre, speech, and dance at Brown. He is the author of seven books about New York experimental theatre and American playwrights. He is the editor of the *Journal of American Drama and Theatre*, associate editor of *Theatre Journal*, and vice president of the American Society for Theatre Research.

JAMES A. ROBINSON was professor of English at the University of Maryland.

VALERIE LOWE received her Ph.D. in linguistics from Lancaster University, U.K. She is currently a professor in the School of Education and Humanities at East Lancashire Institute of Higher Education of Blackburn College.

JOHN S. SHOCKLEY is associate professor of political science at Augsburg College. He is currently researching the role of money in American politics.

SUSAN C. W. ABBOTTSON has taught English for over fifteen years, both at the high school and university levels. She is currently a lecturer in English at Rhode Island College. She is author of *Critical Companion to Arthur Miller* (Facts On File, 2007) and co-author of *Understanding Death of a Salesman* (Greenwood, 1999).

BRENDA MURPHY is a Board of Trustees Distinguished Professor of English at the University of Connecticut. She has published more than thirty articles and essays on twentieth-century American literature and modern drama. She is also a prominent lecturer on this subject throughout the United States.

JEFFREY MEYERS grew up in New York City, graduated from the University of Michigan and received his doctorate from Berkeley. He is the recipient of a Fulbright Fellowship and a grant from the Guggenheim Foundation. He is the author of forty-three books, among them biographies of Katherine Mansfield, Joseph Conrad and F. Scott Fitzgerald. Meyers lives with his wife in Berkeley, California.

JULIUS NOVICK received his B.A. from Harvard and his D.F.A. from the Yale School of Drama. He has been a Fulbright Scholar, a Woodrow Wilson

Fellow, a Ford Foundation grantee, and a Guggenheim Fellow. He has taught in various capacities at New York University, the Juilliard School, Columbia University, and the O'Neill Critics Institute. He is Emeritus Professor of Drama Studies at Purchase College of the State University of New York. He was a theatre critic at the *Village Voice* for thirty years, and many other major publications throughout the years. He is the author of *Beyond Broadway: The Quest for Permanent Theaters*, a pioneering study of the resident theatre movement. He has served twice on the Pulitzer Prize Drama Jury, once as chairman.

JEFFREY D. MASON is Professor of Theatre at California State University, Bakersfield since 1984. He's directed nearly fifty theatrical productions and acted in almost thirty more, and he is the author of *Melodrama and the Myth of America* and co-editor, with J. Ellen Gainor of Cornell University, of *Performing America: Cultural Nationalism in American Theater* (Michigan, 1999).

KEVIN KERRANE is professor of English at the University of Delaware. He has edited several anthologies of drama and has co-edited (with Ben Yagoda) *The Art of Fact: A Historical Anthology of Literary Journalism.* He is the author of *Dollar Sign on the Muscle: The World of Baseball Scouting*, recently cited by *Sports Illustrated* as one of the "100 Best Sports Books of All Time."

LAURENCE GOLDSTEIN is professor of English at the University of Michigan and editor of the *Michigan Quarterly Review.* He is also the author of the critically acclaimed *The American Poet at the Movies: A Critical History.*

WENDY SMITH, a free-lance journalist, is author of *Real Life Drama: The Group Theatre and America 1931–1940.* She earned her Ph.D. in Documentary Film Studies from University of Paris X, Nanterre, France. She has authored and published over twenty articles and literary pieces in English and French in academic, business, and literary journals.

STEVEN R. CENTOLA is professor of English at Millersville University. The founding president of the Arthur Miller Society, he has edited four books, including two that he collaborated on with Arthur Miller. He has also published three interviews with Arthur Miller, as well as numerous articles on the playwright in various books and scholarly journals.

Bibliography

Abbottson, Susan C. W., *Critical Companion to Arthur Miller*. New York: Facts On File, 2007.

Abbotson, Susan C. W., and Murphy, Brenda, *Understanding Death of a Salesman*. Westport, CT: Greenwood Press, 1999.

Altena, I., and Aylwin, A. M., *Notes on Arthur Miller's Death of a Salesman*. London: Eyre Methuen, 1976.

Bhatia, Santosh K., *Arthur Miller: Social Drama as Tragedy*. New York: Humanities Press, 1985.

Bigsby, Christopher W. E., *A Critical Introduction to Twentieth-Century American Drama*, volume 2: *Tennessee Williams, Arthur Miller, Edward Albee*. Cambridge: Cambridge University Press, 1984.

———. *File on Miller*. London: Methuen, 1988.

———. ed., *Arthur Miller and Company: Arthur Miller Talks about His Work in the Company of Actors, Designers, Directors, Reviewers, and Writers*. London: Methuen, 1990.

———. ed., *Modern American Drama, 1945–1990*. Cambridge & New York: Cambridge University Press, 1992.

———. ed., *The Cambridge Companion to Arthur Miller*. Cambridge & New York: Cambridge University Press, 1997.

———. ed., *Remembering Arthur Miller*. London: Methuen, 2005.

Bloom, Harold, ed., *Arthur Miller*. New York: Chelsea House, 1987.

———. ed., *Modern Critical Views: Arthur Miller.* New York: Chelsea House, 1987.

———. ed., *Arthur Miller: Death of a Salesman.* New York: Chelsea House, 1988.

———. ed., *Arthur Miller's All My Sons.* New York: Chelsea House, 1988.

———. ed., *Willy Loman.* New York: Chelsea House, 1991.

———. ed., *The Crucible: Modern Critical Interpretations.* New York: Chelsea House, 1999.

Brater, Enoch, *Arthur Miller: A Playwright's Life and Works.* London: Thames and Hudson, 2005.

———. ed., *Arthur Miller's America: Theater & Culture in a Time of Change.* Ann Arbor: University of Michigan Press, 2005.

Carson, Neil, *Arthur Miller.* New York: St. Martin's Press, 1982.

Centola, Steven R., *Arthur Miller in Conversation.* Dallas: Northouse & Northouse, 1993.

———. ed., *The Achievement of Arthur Miller: New Essays.* Dallas: Contemporary Research, 1995.

Corrigan, Robert, ed., *Arthur Miller: A Collection of Critical Essays.* Englewood Cliffs, NJ: Prentice-Hall, 1969.

Evans, Richard I., *Psychology and Arthur Miller.* New York: Dutton, 1969.

Ferres, John H., ed., *Twentieth Century Interpretations of The Crucible.* Englewood Cliffs, NJ: Prentice-Hall, 1972.

———. *Arthur Miller: A Reference Guide.* Boston: G. K. Hall, 1979.

Gelb, Philip, "*Death of a Salesman*: A Symposium," *Tulane Drama Review,* 2 (1958).

Gottfried, Martin, *Arthur Miller: His Life and Work.* Cambridge, MA: Da Capo, 2003.

Griffin, Alice, *Understanding Arthur Miller.* Columbia: University of South Carolina Press, 1996.

Harshburger, Karl, *The Burning Jungle: An Analysis of Arthur Miller's Death of a Salesman.* Washington, DC: University Press of America, 1979.

Hayashi, Tetsumaro, *An Index to Arthur Miller Criticism,* second edition. Metuchen, NJ: Scarecrow Press, 1976.

———. *Arthur Miller and Tennessee Williams, Research Opportunities and Dissertation Abstracts.* Jefferson, NC & London: McFarland, 1983.

Jensen, George H., *Arthur Miller: A Bibliographical Checklist.* Columbia, SC: Faust, 1976.

Koon, Helen Wickam, ed., *Twentieth Century Interpretations of Death of a Salesman: A Collection of Critical Essays*. Englewood Cliffs, NJ: Prentice-Hall, 1983.

Koorey, Stefani, *Arthur Miller's Life and Literature: An Annotated and Comprehensive Guide*. Lanham, MD.: Scarecrow Press, 2000.

Marino, Stephen, ed., *"The Salesman Has a Birthday": Essays Celebrating the Fiftieth Anniversary of Arthur Miller's Death of a Salesman*. Lanham, MD: University of America Press, 2000.

Martin, Robert A., ed., *Arthur Miller: New Perspectives*. Englewood Cliffs, NJ: Prentice-Hall, 1982.

Martine, James J., *The Crucible: Politics, Property, and Pretense*. New York: Twayne, 1993.

———. ed., *Critical Essays on Arthur Miller*. Boston: G. K. Hall, 1979.

Meserve, Walter J., ed., *The Merrill Studies in Death of a Salesman: A Collection of Critical Essays*. Columbus, OH: Merrill, 1972.

Moss, Leonard, *Arthur Miller*, second edition. New York: Twayne, 1980.

Murphy, Brenda, *Miller: Death of a Salesman*. Cambridge: Cambridge University Press, 1995.

Otten, Terry, *The Temptation of Innocence in the Dramas of Arthur Miller*. Columbia: University of Missouri Press, 2002.

Panikkar, N. Bhaskara, *Individual Morality and Social Happiness in Arthur Miller*. Atlantic Highlands, NJ: Humanities Press, 1982.

Roudané, Matthew C., ed., *Conversations with Arthur Miller*. Jackson: University Press of Mississippi, 1987.

———. ed., *Approaches to Teaching Miller's Death of a Salesman*. New York: Modern Language Association, 1995.

Savran, David, *Communists, Cowboys, and Queers: The Politics of Masculinity in the Work of Arthur Miller and Tennessee Williams*. Minneapolis: University of Minnesota Press, 1992.

Weales, Gerald, ed., *Arthur Miller, Death of a Salesman: Text and Criticism*. New York: Viking, 1967.

———. ed., *The Crucible: Text and Criticism*. New York: Viking, 1971.

Welland, Dennis, *Miller: The Playwright*, second edition. New York: Methuen, 1983.

White, Sidney H., *Guide to Arthur Miller*. Columbus, OH: Merrill, 1970.

Acknowledgments

"Arthur Miller's *The Crucible* and the Salem Witch Trials: A Historian's View" by Edmund S. Morgan. From *The Golden and Brazen World: Papers in Literature and History, 1650–1800*, edited by John M. Wallace: pp. 171–186. © 1985 The Regents of the University of California. Published by the University of California Press. Used with permission of the publisher.

"The Wooster Group, Arthur Miller and *The Crucible*" by David Savran. *The Drama Review*, Volume 29:2 (Summer 1985), pp. 99–109. © 1985 New York University and the Massachusetts Institute of Technology. Reprinted with permission.

"*All My Sons* and Paternal Authority" by James A. Robinson. *Journal of American Drama and Theatre*, Volume 2:1 (Winter 1990), pp. 38–54. © 1990 *Journal of American Drama and Theatre*. Reprinted with permission.

"'Unsafe convictions': 'unhappy' confessions in *The Crucible*" by Valerie Lowe. *Languages and Literature*, 3:3 (1994), pp. 175–195. © 1994 Lancaster University, U.K. Reprinted with permission.

"*Death of a Salesman* and American Leadership: Life Imitates Art" by John S. Shockley. *Journal of American Culture*, Volume 17:2 (June 1994), pp. 49–56. © 1994 *Journal of American Culture*. Reprinted with permission.

"Issues of Identity in *Broken Glass:* A Humanist Response to a Postmodern World" by Susan C. W. Abbotson. *Journal of American Drama and Theatre,* Volume 11:1 (Winter 1999), pp. 67–80. © 1999 *Journal of American Drama and Theatre.* Reprinted with permission.

"'Personality Wins the Day': *Death of a Salesman* and Popular Sales Advice Literature" by Brenda Murphy. *South Atlantic Review,* Volume 64:1 (Winter 1999), pp. 1–10. © 1999 *South Atlantic Review.* Reprinted with permission.

"A Portrait of Arthur Miller" by Jeffrey Meyers. *The Virginia Quarterly Review,* Volume 76:3 (Summer 2000), p. 416. © 2000. Reprinted with permission of the author.

"*Death of a Salesman:* Deracination and Its Discontents" by Julius Novick. *American Jewish History,* Volume 91:1 (March 2003), pp. 97–107. © 2003 American Jewish Historical Society. Reprinted with permission of the Johns Hopkins University Press.

"Arthur Miller's Ironic Resurrection" by Jeffrey D. Mason. *Theatre Journal,* Volume 55:4 (December 2003), pp. 657–677. © 2003 The John Hopkins University Press. Reprinted with permission.

"Arthur Miller vs. Columbia Pictures: The Strange Case of *Career of a Salesman*" by Kevin Kerrane. *The Journal of American Culture,* Volume 27:3 (Summer 2003), pp. 280–289. © 2004 *The Journal of American Culture.* Reprinted with permission.

"Finishing the Picture: Arthur Miller, 1915–2005" by Laurence Goldstein. *Michigan Quarterly Review,* Volume 44:2 (Spring 2005), pp. 209–215. © 2005 *Michigan Quarterly Review.* Reprinted with permission.

"Miller's Tale: The playwright drew a line between reaching out and selling out" by Wendy Smith. *American Scholar,* Volume 74:2 (Spring 2005), pp. 121–125. © 2005 *American Scholar.* Reprinted with permission from the author.

"Arthur Miller and the Art of the Possible" by Steven R. Centola. *American Drama,* Volume 14:1 (Winter 2005), pp. 36–86. © 2005 *American Drama.* Reprinted with permission.

Every effort has been made to contact the owners of copyrighted material and secure copyright permission. Articles appearing in this volume generally appear much as they did in their original publication with few or no editorial changes. Those interested in locating the original source will find bibliographic information in the bibliography and acknowledgments sections of this volume.

Index